S0-BUF-946

Understanding the Child with a Chronic Illness in the Classroom

Understanding the Child with a Chronic Illness in the Classroom

Edited by Janet Fithian

The rare Arabian Oryx is believed to have inspired the myth of the unicorn. This desert antelope became virtually extinct in the early 1960s. At that time several groups of international conservationists arranged to have 9 animals sent to the Phoenix Zoo to be the nucleus of a captive breeding herd. Today the Oryx population is over 400 and herds have been returned to reserves in Israel, Jordan, and Oman.

2214 North Central
Phoenix, AZ 85004-1483

Published simultaneously in Canada

Printed and Bound in the United States of America

Library of Congress Cataloging in Publication Data
Main entry under title:

Understanding the child with a chronic illness in the classroom.

Includes bibliographical references and index.
1. Chronically ill children—Education—United States—Addresses, essays, lectures. 2. Physically handicapped children—Education—United States—Addresses, essays, lectures. 3. Mainstreaming in education—United States—Addresses, essays, lectures. I. Fithian, Janet.
LC4561.U53 1984 371.9′046 83-43250
ISBN 0-89774-083-1

To Louis and Harriet Gant—
Who have helped in so many ways

Contents

Preface

Advances in medical care for children with serious chronic illnesses, though not always providing a cure, have resulted in such effective treatment that attending school and preparing for the future is as appropriate for these children as for their more healthy counterparts. The increasing number of medically handicapped children at school can cause stress among school personnel, whether these be nurses, teachers, guidance counselors, or teacher's aides. The information in this book is intended to foster a more comfortable and productive interaction between school staff and students who have a chronic illness. Each chapter covers a specific disease; is written by a physician, nurse-specialist, and/or social worker; and offers practical and comprehensive information that can be related to how the child can be expected to function in the classroom and what problems may or—sometimes more important—may not arise at school. Because the book has been developed as a resource for nonmedical as well as medical professionals, terms have been defined within each chapter. References to medical information known to all in the field have not been given, but sources for statistics and specific studies are referenced at the end of each chapter.

I am deeply appreciative of the authors of the chapters, many of whom contribute frequently to the medical literature and all of whom have numerous professional obligations, for giving their time and knowledge to this project. They unhesitatingly made themselves available for discussions of their manuscripts and displayed an enthusiasm for and a commitment to this project. I am also very indebted to Dr. Toshio Asakura and Dr. Reed W. Hoyt for perceptive and expert editorial advice and patient support of the practical aspects of this project. Also appreciated is the helpful reading of my introduction by Judith Ross, as well as her other valuable suggestions. I am grateful to Dr. Elias Schwartz for providing me with many opportunities for professional growth and to Dr. Marie O. Russell, whom I admire as a pediatrician and human being, for her many kindnesses and friendship.

Rose Seabo, a school staff member with a great love for children, offered valuable practical suggestions and much encouragement. I thank Karen Peterson, who persevered through high school and college despite her chronic illness to take her place as a working adult. Her experiences provided the impetus for this book. Finally, but not least, I am appreciative of Carol Hunter and Susan Slesinger for their guidance through the publication of this manuscript.

Janet Fithian
March 1984

Contributors

Balu H. Athreya, M.D. is Associate Professor of Pediatrics at the University of Pennsylvania School of Medicine and Director of the Rheumatology Clinic of Children's Seashore House and The Children's Hospital of Philadelphia. Children's Seashore House, which has facilities in both The Children's Hospital of Philadelphia and in Atlantic City, NJ, is a specialized hospital for the treatment of chronically ill children.

David Beele, M.S.W., A.C.S.W. is the social worker for the Cystic Fibrosis Center at The Children's Hospital of Philadelphia; on-site social work educator for the Philadelphia Pediatric Pulmonary Center; Field Instructor for the University of Pennsylvania School of Social Work; and a part-time social work consultant for the Pennsylvania Department of Health, Division of Rehabilitation.

Marilyn Boos, R.N., M.S. is Patient Care Coordinator at the Alfred I. duPont Institute in Wilmington, DE. Her duties include the development of home care programs for children with orthopedic problems and the preparation of patient and professional education materials.

Inez Burg, R.N., C.P.N.P. is a certified pediatric nurse-practitioner in the Division of Allergy-Immunology-Pulmonology at The Children's Hospital of Philadelphia and is a member of the Pediatric Pulmonary Committee of the Philadelphia Chapter of the American Lung Association.

Barbara R. Burroughs, R.N., M.S.N. was Pediatric Nurse Education Coordinator, Philadelphia Regional Pediatric Pulmonary Disease Program, at The Children's Hospital of Philadelphia, from 1980 until 1983. As a clinical pulmonary nurse specialist, she was deeply involved in the care of children with cystic fibrosis at the Cystic Fibrosis Center at The Children's Hospital. She is an Adjunct Clinical Lecturer at the University of Pennsylvania School of Nursing.

Regina B. Butler, R.N. is the Nurse-Coordinator of the Hemophilia Program at The Children's Hospital of Philadelphia and Chairperson of the National Hemophilia Foundation's Nursing Committee. She is a member of the National Hemophilia Foundation's Medical and Scientific Advisory Council, the Patient Education Committee, and the Educational Resources Project.

Claire M. Chee, R.N. is a neurology nurse at The Children's Hospital of Philadelphia, a member of the Neurosurgical Nurses Association, and Coordinator of the hospital's Muscular Dystrophy Clinic.

Robert R. Clancy, M.D. is an Assistant Professor of Neurology and Pediatrics at the University of Pennsylvania School of Medicine and is an attending physician at The Children's Hospital of Philadelphia and the Hospital of the University of Pennsylvania.

Janet Fithian is Coordinator of the Education Program in the Division of Hematology at The Children's Hospital of Philadelphia. She is also a medical writer/editor for the Division of Hematology.

Roslyn M. Garlonsky, R.N., C., M.S.N. is a clinical nurse specialist at the Alfred I. duPont Institute in Wilmington, DE. As a spinal dysfunction clinical specialist, she assesses, plans, teaches, and coordinates the care of children, mainly those with myelomeningocele, in a family setting.

Grace Gaston, M.S.W. is Assistant Director of the Social Work Department at The Children's Hospital of Philadelphia. Prior to assuming that position, she provided social work services for the Division of Hematology and the Sickle Cell Program at The Children's Hospital of Philadelphia. Mrs. Gaston is a graduate of Temple University School of Social Administration.

Frances M. Gill, M.D. is board-certified in pediatrics and pediatric hematology-oncology. She is Senior Physician and Associate Professor of Pediatrics at The Children's Hospital, Department of Pediatrics, University of Pennsylvania School of Medicine, and Director of the Hemophilia Center at The Children's Hospital of Philadelphia.

Carrie Goren Ingall, R.N., M.S.N. was Nurse Coordinator of the Rheumatology Program at Children's Seashore House and The Children's Hospital of Philadelphia for three years where she coordinated the care of chronically ill children.

Haewon C. Kim, M.D. is a pediatric hematologist. She is an Assistant Professor of Pediatrics at the University of Pennsylvania School of Medicine and is an attending physician in the Division of Hematology at The Children's Hospital of Philadelphia. She is also Director of the Blood Bank, Transfusion Unit, and Donor Center. Dr. Kim is active in the care of children with sickle cell anemia and has been involved in a study of stroke in children with sickle cell anemia.

Gerald Kolski, M.D., Ph.D. is Director of Allergy at The Children's Hospital of Philadelphia and Assistant Professor of Pediatrics at the University of Pennsylvania School of Medicine. He is Chairperson of the Pediatric Pulmonary Committee of the Philadelphia Chapter of the American Lung Association. He is board-certified in pediatrics and allergy-immunology and was a fellow at the National Jewish Hospital National Asthma Center.

Kenneth R. Lyen, M.A., B.M., B.Ch., M.R.C.P., D.C.H. is a Senior Lecturer and Consultant in Pediatric Endocrinology at the National University of Singapore. After graduating from Oxford University in England, he received his pediatric training at the University of London. He has had considerable experience in the care of diabetic children as a Registrar in Endocrinology at The Hospital for Sick Children, Great Ormond Street, London, and as a Juvenile Diabetes Foundation Research Fellow at The Children's Hospital of Philadelphia.

G. Dean MacEwen, M.D., C.M. is Medical Director of the Alfred I. duPont Institute in Wilmington, DE, and Clinical Professor of Orthopaedic Surgery, Thomas Jefferson University, Philadelphia, PA.

Anna T. Meadows, M.D., is Associate Professor of Pediatrics at the University of Pennsylvania School of Medicine and Senior Physician in the Division of Oncology at The Children's Hospital of Philadelphia. She is also the Associate Director for Epidemiology, Etiology, and Genetics in the Children's Cancer Research Center at The Children's Hospital. In addition to providing clinical care for children with cancer, she pursues her major research interests in childhood cancer epidemiology and the status of long-term survivors.

Roger J. Packer, M.D. is Assistant Professor of Neurology and Pediatrics at the University of Pennsylvania School of Medicine and is an attending physician at the Hospital of the University of Pennsylvania and The Children's Hospital of Philadelphia.

Judith W. Ross, M.S.W., A.C.S.W. is Coordinator of Social Services for the Children's Cancer Research Center at The Children's Hospital of Philadelphia, where she has worked with pediatric cancer patients and their families for the past 10 years. She has written extensively about psychosocial aspects of pediatric malignancy. Since 1978, she has conducted annual seminars for educators involved with young cancer patients.

Fredric Serota, M.D., is a board-certified pediatrician and pediatric hematologist-oncologist. He was Assistant Professor of Pediatrics at the University of Pennsylvania School of Medicine and staff physician for the bone marrow transplantation program at The Children's Hospital of Philadelphia. He is currently in the private practice of pediatrics in Ambler, PA.

Nina Steg, M.D. is board-certified in pediatrics and pediatric nephrology. She is Director of Pediatrics at the Alfred I. duPont Institute in Wilmington, DE, and director of its Spinal Dysfunction CLinic. She is a visiting Associate Professor of Pediatrics at the Medical College of Pennsylvania and consultant in pediatrics at the Wilmington (DE) Medical Center.

Robert Wilmott, M.D. is a full-time pediatric pulmonologist. He is Assistant Professor of Pediatrics at the University of Pennsylvania School of Medicine. At The Children's Hospital of Philadelphia, he is Clinical Director, Pulmonology Section; Director, Pediatric Pulmonary Function Laboratory; and Co-Director, Cystic Fibrosis Center. He trained in pediatrics at The Hospital for Sick Children, Great Ormond Street, London, England, and completed a research fellowship investigating the clinical significance of allergy in cystic fibrosis.

Paul K. Woolf, M.D. is Assistant Professor of Pediatrics at New York Medical College and Attending Pediatric Cardiologist at Westchester Medical Center, Valhalla, NY, and Metropolitan Hospital, New York, NY. Dr. Woolf is a graduate of Columbia University College of Physicians and Surgeons and is a Fellow of the American Academy of Pediatrics.

Understanding the Child with a Chronic Illness in the Classroom

General Overview

by Janet Fithian

One in 10 children will develop a chronic illness before the age of 15.[1] To a first grade teacher, this means that one child in the class will have a chronic illness. The high school teacher responsible for five sections may teach a dozen or more such children daily. In view of these numbers, information is needed to help teachers, school nurses, guidance personnel, and other school staff work effectively and confidently with these children.

This book provides comprehensive coverage of 13 of the most common chronic health disorders found in the school-age population. These disorders were selected on the basis of a survey of educators, pediatricians, school nurses, and others in the field. Conditions inevitably associated with retardation or physical disability so severe as to require enrollment in special classes are not covered. In most cases, such children are taught by specially trained educators with access to much helpful literature. In summary, this book is intended for school staff who are responsible for children in classes in which the majority of children are healthy and without serious retardation or learning disabilities.

UNDERSTANDING THE ILLNESS—A NEED FOR COMPREHENSIVE MEDICAL INFORMATION

Those responsible for a child with a chronic illness at school—whether classroom teachers, guidance counselors, or school nurses—should have sufficient medical knowledge to feel comfortable with the child, to anticipate and manage medical problems that may arise in the classroom, to recognize situations that warrant communication with the parents or physicians, and to make appropriate concessions to the illness or disability.

The material prepared for school personnel on many chronic illnesses is superficial, providing little more than definitions. Often the seriousness of the condition is underplayed—possibly because it is thought that a frank discussion would create such fear in school staff as to adversely affect the child's school life. Frequently only the primary manifestation is discussed, with the complicated nature of these disorders being ignored. As a result, it usually comes as a surprise to school staff that children with sickle cell anemia are at increased risk for stroke or that children with some forms of juvenile rheumatoid arthritis may develop serious vision problems. Yet early and perhaps subtle signs of these complications are often more noticeable at school than they are at home.

Several studies have indicated that more complete information is needed for school staff. Counselors and teachers in a secondary school had a median of slightly greater than 50 percent on a test about diabetes in students.[2] They were poorly informed about the need for eating regularly and for appropriate physical education. Misconceptions about epilepsy and childhood cancer were such that expectations could be inappropriately diminished for these children.[3,4] The wrong assumptions that children with hemophilia can quickly bleed to death from simple cuts or that children with sickle cell anemia die from painful episodes often lead to overprotection at school and needless anxiety among school staff. In addition to offering comprehensive information on the causes, manifestations, and treatment of a disorder, the authors have explained which signs and symptoms should cause concern and which should not.

This material should assist educators in helping the child with a chronic illness become an integral part of the class and to motivate him or her to achieve. Unpleasant or frightening signs and symptoms should not cause the child to be excluded from appropriate classroom activities or his or her academic life to be taken less seriously than that of a healthier classmate.

Education can be negatively affected by a misunderstanding of a child's illness. Physicians, nurses, and social workers are often dismayed to find that while the child's medical needs were being attended to, his or her education was being so neglected that the child would have little chance to achieve his or her potential. Not knowing what should be expected of certain chronically ill children academically or having an erroneous perception that the child might not live into adulthood may contribute to such situations. Some educators feel it is unkind to burden a child with acquiring knowledge that will never be used.

OPTIMAL CARE—A POSSIBILITY FOR EVERY CHILD WITH A CHRONIC ILLNESS?

Reading the various chapters may increase one's knowledge to the extent that questions may arise. Is a certain child receiving appropriate or optimal treatment? Are some symptoms of the illness getting enough attention? Isn't there more that could be done about the side effects of drugs? It is not out of order for caring and concerned school personnel to take an active role in the child's care and ask such questions. Yet many hesitate to question a student's treatment, feeling that a family's confidence in the physician is an important component of therapy and essential to their ability to deal with the illness. To shake such confidence may cause harm. Also, health care services in a given locality may be limited. To travel farther for medical care may put added stress on a family. These are important considerations, but a school nurse or an interested teacher may be the child's only advocate, or even the only person the family knows aside from the physician with any medical knowledge.

Sometimes a word or two to parents goes a long way. A family might harbor doubts but not feel qualified to question a physician or to suggest that more comprehensive care could be given. When a school nurse expresses a similar feeling, parents then gain the confidence to proceed on their own and seek a second opinion. Other parents may be pleased to have school personnel communicate with a child's physician, especially if they do not feel confident asking questions.

Medical centers providing comprehensive care are mentioned frequently in this book. The advantage of a specialized center is that many aspects of the child's illness are taken care of: social workers help families and children cope with the psychosocial and economic issues of the disease; nurse-specialists provide instruction on home care and education so families can cope in an organized and confident manner; and physicians have the expertise to manage the entire range of problems related to the disorder.

Many primary care physicians are aware of these advantages but do not make a referral because they feel the extra travel and expense would overburden an already harassed family. Care through a specialized center need not be expensive or time-consuming. Many treatment centers, usually established at hospitals that are associated with medical schools, have the personnel to educate, even by telephone, primary care physicians and to answer their questions regarding cases in their practices that are unusual. Frequently it is only requested that the child be seen for an initial consultation. Follow-up care can then be coordinated between the center and the child's pediatrician. There may even be financial advantages to receiving care at a designated center. Many such programs are supported by state or federal funding or funded by nonprofit charitable organizations. By using the Useful Address section at the end of each chapter, information about such centers and financial help can be obtained.

A NORMAL CHILD WITH AN ILLNESS—OR A CHILD WITH AN ILLNESS TRYING TO BE NORMAL?

Physicians and nurses will often try to comfort parents of a child newly diagnosed with diabetes by telling them that they have a "normal" child with diabetes and stressing the "normal" life that the child can live.[5] This advice, despite being well meaning, has unwanted consequences simply because it is not true and trivializes the experiences related to the disorder.

It is not normal to have diabetes, just as it is not normal to have lupus erythematosus, cystic fibrosis, or spina bifida. It is not a trivial matter to undergo time-consuming treatments, endure pain and discomfort and sometimes embarrassment, and to have one's hopes for certain goals dashed. Long-term disorders in childhood can significantly and permanently interfere with the child's physical and emotional growth and development.[6]

How children cope with their disorders and the success they have in normalizing their lives depend on many factors. These children have all the problems of other children in addition to the problem of illness. They must cope with the emotional turmoil of domestic problems as do normal children. They may feel responsible for the breakup of a marriage or that unhappy, quarreling parents stay together. A child with a hereditary disorder realizes relatively early why he or she is the only child in the family—or why a mother expecting another child is hoping for a child not like him or her. When a painful crisis in sickle cell anemia or an asthma attack wrecks family plans, the ill child frequently feels guilt as well as disappointment. A sense of not being dependable or not being able to count on things can develop. Sometimes siblings blame the child for spoiling family fun or for getting too much parental attention. Children may be aware of financial stresses caused by their illnesses. A family might communicate, albeit indirectly, that they would have or do certain things were it not for the child's condition.

These children, like all children, must master many difficult developmental tasks to become self-sufficient adults. Depending upon the age of onset and the extent of the physical manifestations, a chronic illness can thwart this mastery. Separation from family in the form of overnight trips, so easy for most children, can be complicated in children with diabetes, who must have insulin on schedule and whose meals must be monitored, or an embarrassment in a child with sickle cell anemia who suffers from enuresis, a problem in some but not all children with this disorder. Physical therapy necessary in juvenile rheumatoid arthritis or cystic fibrosis also restricts a child's time away from home. Children with seizures, asthma, or hemophilia may find that people do not want to be responsible for them unless their parents are there. Orthopedic surgery can reduce a self-sufficient individual to the dependency of an infant—a state naturally repugnant to adolescents or to younger children who are proud of having mastered tasks of personal care. Also, there may not be the physical capacity for the summer and after-school jobs that so often start a youngster on the road to financial independence. In effect, a gradual, normal separation from family is not always possible for these children. Dependence in many cases is built into the disease process.

Even when independence is possible, it may not be easily achieved for youngsters with chronic illnesses. Often, fearful parents inappropriately shelter these children. It is admirable when, during adolescence, a youngster can achieve separation while continuing with an appropriate treatment regimen.

The presence of a chronic illness can disrupt the formation and maintenance of peer relationships. The type of disorder, age of onset, and the personality of the child will determine the degree to which this takes place. Obviously, a physically disabling condition limits an important area of social life for children—sports and active play. The time and energy needed to cope with the symptoms of the disorder or treatment reduces opportunities for after-school play and participation in such activities as band and scouting.

Frequent hospitalizations or illnesses at home can disrupt established friendships. In the quickly shifting groups of early and middle childhood, a few weeks' absence may mean exclusion from the group. Children, like adults, do not like to be reminded of their own vulnerability and may shun a child who is obviously ill or who is said to have a serious disease. On the other hand, friends may feel rejected by the ill child. A child might enjoy friends when well but reject social contacts when not feeling well, which may be interpreted as moodiness.[7] In a study of cystic fibrosis patients, a majority of patients felt isolated.[8] Some made overtures, which were rejected, while others had difficulty relating to peers because of their concern about personal appearance.[9] Some long-term survivors of cancer, feeling mature beyond their years because of their experiences, feel isolated and distant from people their own age.[10]

How do these children cope? Success depends on understanding the nature of the illness and accepting limitations while compensating by finding other satisfactory physical and intellectual pursuits.[11] The appropriate expression of emotions, including sadness, anxiety, anger, and impatience when things are going badly and confidence and guarded optimism during good periods, is important, as is the judicious use of denial.[12]

Denial is misunderstood in our society. We are supposed to look the progression of illness and death straight in the eye. But denial is a useful emotion, as several chapters suggest. It helps us carry on our daily lives by tempering realities too painful to confront. For example, a child with cystic fibrosis can appropriately push back the reality of the usual outcome of the disorder while accepting the challenge of a current hospitalization. Denial is, of course, inappropriate when it is used to ignore the existence of the illness and the need for treatment and adherence to certain restrictions. Extreme fearfulness, lack of outside interests, marked dependency on family, inactivity, and risk taking are evidence of a poor adjustment.[13]

FORMULATING AN APPROPRIATE APPROACH TO THE CHILD WITH A CHRONIC ILLNESS IN THE REAL SCHOOL WORLD

The suggestions in the various chapters are based on the reality, not the ideal. In the real school world, classes are crowded; many children have a variety of problems; and support personnel are not always available. Very few, and only very young, students have "a teacher." After the first four grades, sometimes even earlier, children are taught by a number of specialists. Even so, caring teachers do come to know their students well, to treat them as individuals, and to want to meet their special needs.

Also considered is the real world of the school nurse. Cutbacks in funding have affected staffing by nurses in many school districts. Yet conscientious nurses still inform teachers of the health problems of the students, pass on suggestions as to appropriate expectations for these children, and communicate with the students' physicians and families when necessary. This book is designed so that the additional knowledge needed to do these things can be gained efficiently. Because a nurse may not always be available, it is imperative that other staff be prepared for emergencies. The section Medical Problems in the Classroom, which appears in many of the chapters, is intended for both medical and nonmedical school staff.

To deal appropriately with children who have chronic illnesses does not require expending a large amount of time to the detriment of other students. Sometimes it only requires a few second thoughts, such as allowing a child who has difficulty walking to slip out of class early or a child who must go to the lavatory frequently to leave without asking each time. It is just as easy to seat these children by the door as by the window. Allowing a child to have two sets of schoolbooks—one for school and one for home—is a major help to a student with muscle weakness or frequent, unexpected absences. Such concessions to a child's physical condition can be thought out in the first few weeks of school and will require no further action by the teacher. However, the child will benefit almost daily.

Children with many of the disorders addressed in this book will be absent more than others. It is crucial that they be provided with a mechanism for making up work. This should be decided on before an absence has occurred and activated at the first absence. If the child is too ill or it is impractical to make up all work, teachers can help the child set priorities as to what must be done.

Because absences may be expected does not mean that they should be automatically excused. When there are frequent, short absences—or long absences without a physician's note—the school nurse should contact the parents. Permission should be sought to call the child's physician and discuss the matter. School avoidance by the child or keeping the child home because of unnecessary fears on the part of parents can be a problem; the sooner these issues are addressed, the better.

A serious medical condition does not confer the wings of an angel on a child. Some children use their illnesses to get out of difficult, tedious, or uninteresting school tasks. A clear definition of what the child should and should not be excused from should be obtained from the physician or nurse-specialist. Behavior problems—whether they emanate from a child with cancer or a child with no illness at all—have the same impact on the class. Disruptive behavior should not be excused in any child. When it is excused in a child with a serious illness, the child gets the message that the condition is so hopeless that he or she is allowed to act unacceptably to make up for the unfortunate situation. This attitude creates fear and insecurity. If these children are to take their place in the adult world—and most of them will—they should not be allowed to grow up to be obnoxious, self-centered, and inconsiderate.

It is always appropriate to provide motivation to succeed at school tasks, even when the child might not be expected to reach adulthood or go on to work or to college. To some teachers, this may seem unkind; in reality it is not. As long as the child is attending school, he or she is a part of the world of his or her peers. Sometimes these children must expend great energy and courage to get to school and then more to get through the day. To have their teachers regard their presence as meaningless is insulting. Also, to convey the impression that his or her academic life is unimportant certainly, though unintentionally, excludes the child from an important aspect of childhood and from having common interests, challenges, and even problems of peers. It is analogous to taking meaningful work away from an adult with a serious illness but leaving him or her with a desk.

In the future, cures and improved treatments may be developed for many more childhood illnesses. Just a few years ago, a diagnosis of cancer meant that the child would surely die; today, more than 60 percent of such children are cured. Concessions may have to be made, as in making up tremendous amounts of schoolwork after a long absence, but goals should be set with the expectation that they will be reached. In some children it may be more appropriate to provide goals that may be achieved within weeks or months instead of years. This is stated quite eloquently in the chapter on cystic fibrosis.

THE FAMILY OF THE CHILD WITH A CHRONIC ILLNESS

The setting for this book is the school, and the main characters are the child, classmates, and school staff. Only when it is necessary to understand more fully the disease or the management of the child at school are the parents brought onstage. It is not that they are unimportant; it is just that this book centers on the child at school rather than at home. This special focus aims to help school staff play their roles most effectively in the lives of these children. Sometimes the degree of effectiveness will depend on the quality of their communication with parents. An understanding of feelings and problems common in families of children with long-term illnesses will promote satisfactory communication.

Family life is affected on many levels by the long-term illness of a child.[14] Although advances in medicine have improved survival in children with many disorders, the family's burdens have in many cases intensified.[15] Parents are expected to obtain a widening range of health services for their children as well as offer home care, some of it very demanding. The degree of family disruption depends on the illness and the frequency and severity of its manifestations, the availability of suitable medical care, financial resources available either through health insurance or other sources, and the flexibility of the parents' work situation.

Not as variable from disorder to disorder are the anxieties and behavior evoked by the child's condition. Literature on this subject reveals guilt as a common feeling among parents, no matter what condition the child has.[16–21] Parents of children with inherited disorders feel guilty for causing the child such suffering. More emotionally charged is the situation in which the disorder can be inherited through only one parent, as in hemophilia or Duchenne dystrophy. A small study of families of children with hemophilia reported five mothers who had ignored the possibility that they might be carriers even though they had relatives with hemophilia.[22] In three cases, the father offered less support than did the other fathers in the study, tended to blame the mother, and implied that responsibility for bringing up the child was hers.

Parents may feel that the child's illness was brought about by something they either did or failed to do. The feeling that more could have been done or an earlier diagnosis made can cause guilt even when parents and physicians acted correctly. Guilt also may be related to the treatment of siblings; parents may feel, in some cases correctly, that these children are not getting their share of family resources and attention or are being disciplined more strictly than the ill child.[23,24]

Anxiety and emotional stress are reported in relation to chronic illness, especially when symptoms can come on quickly, as in epilepsy or asthma, or when the disease can return after a remission, as in cancer. In a study of parents of asthmatic children, it was suggested that parents who neither understand the illness nor are capable of dealing with the exacerbations may experience more anxiety than better prepared families. Also, they fail to encourage constructive self-care attitudes and habits in their children.[25] Such a finding can be extrapolated to include other illnesses where the parent is the primary caretaker during periods of emergency.

Guilt and anxiety frequently result in overprotection and lack of discipline. Parents of children with sickle cell anemia, asthma, epilepsy, and other disorders in which symptoms may be manifested quickly hesitate to discipline for fear of provoking symptoms. Other children are not disciplined in an effort to "make up" to the child for having the illness. A study of young adults with cystic fibrosis revealed that they were frequently overprotected and infantilized.[26]

Persons working in a children's hospital can understand how such patterns of response can develop even when they are not outgrowths of guilt and anxiety. Young children with sickle cell anemia can get pneumonia as quickly as other children catch cold. A child with hemophilia who tumbles may have to go to the emergency room. Children on chemotherapy for cancer are susceptible to severe complications from ordinary diseases. Strenuous exercise can induce an asthma attack in asthmatic youngsters. Diabetic children must eat regularly and properly to avoid hypoglycemia. Young people with lupus may have an exacerbation if exposed to sunlight. Parents learn early and graphically the consequences of certain exposures, activities, or even emotional states on their children.

Sometimes the perception of cause and effect is incorrect. It is not surprising, however, that parents seek causes for a child's symptoms so that, once identified, the situation can be avoided in the future. Also, the line between sensible precautions and overprotection may be a fine one. Some parents walk the line with more skill than do others. Relatives may offer advice on precautions that differs from the physician's, and in the interest of family harmony, the child is unnecessarily restricted. Overpermissiveness may result from pressure from the extended family as well as from the parents' feelings of trying to "make up" to the child.

When a child's behavior indicates an overprotective or overpermissive family, it is appropriate for teachers to try to bring about some balance.

School nurses should get permission to speak directly with the child's medical caretakers to find out what symptoms indicate an absence from school and what physical activities are allowed. They should not hesitate to ask any questions they have. Physicians and nurses like to know when parents have misinterpreted their advice or are needlessly restrictive so they can tactfully educate families and patients. In the case of overpermissiveness, the child must be shown that undesirable behavior will not be tolerated at school regardless of what is permitted at home.

Other inappropriate parental responses, though less common, are neglect, rejection of the child, or denial of the severity of the symptoms. In such cases, there is no question that school staff must act as the child's advocate.

Once it was thought that serious illness in a child brought parents together; then it was said that it tore families apart.[27] Current thinking is somewhere in between, but increased marital tensions are reported from informal observation and from formal studies. A study of parental discord and divorce in families of 191 children with cancer revealed a divorce rate of 1.19 percent per person year, slightly lower than the 2.03 percent for parents of children in the same geographic area.[28] Since increased marital discord is shown by so many investigators, this lower divorce rate in families with sick children may reflect "sticking it out" because of the child.

Management of the child's illness frequently falls to the mother. A study of patients with cystic fibrosis observed that as mother and patient became excessively close, the father became more remote.[29] Sixty percent of fathers were perceived as distant and unsupportive. Frequently the mother carries the major responsibility for diabetic management, with the father in a peripheral and sometimes nonsupportive role.[30] In contrast, in a group of hemophiliacs, the fathers saw themselves as caretakers and protectors and participated more in child-rearing than in the nonhemophiliac families observed.[31] Mothers of children with serious ongoing illnesses are at risk for psychological distress.[32]

Fathers have not been considered as closely in the literature. Social and health scientists often equate maternal responses with paternal responses, contributing to the belief that mothers and fathers always act as a team.[33] Interviews with 10 fathers of children with various illnesses revealed that most rarely spoke with a doctor or a nurse and that medical information was usually relayed through the mother. This not only deprives the father of emotional support through health caregivers but leaves the father vulnerable to any misinterpretations the mother may have. Half reported a weakening relationship with their wives and 9 of 10 a diminished social life.

Lack of time and money can contribute to a diminished social life. Friends also become uncomfortable when a child is diagnosed as having a serious illness and they suddenly realize how vulnerable their own families are.[34] The resulting feeling of isolation can contribute to marital discord, as sharing friendship and fun can relieve the tensions that accompany family life.

A child's illness can affect the jobs of both parents. Taking time off for physician's visits or caring for the child may mean loss of pay or the chance of a promotion. Parents may hesitate to risk changing jobs or accepting transfers to other areas, which would mean leaving the child's medical caregivers. Some mothers face criticism for working when an ill child is involved, the feeling being that the mother should make herself more available to her children and should sacrifice material rewards of the extra income. Such criticism can be difficult for a family to cope with. Even when insurance is adequate, a child's illness does involve extra expense. The lack of a second income may exacerbate tensions and deprive siblings of enriching experiences and educational opportunities. Not unimportant are the personal satisfaction and social interaction that working provides a woman. Many women say that their jobs give them the normality needed to cope. Also, the sick child may benefit. In a report of adult cystic fibrosis patients who were judged competent and functioning, 70 percent had mothers who worked at outside jobs or in community activities, allowing the child daily responsibilities at home. An additional 20 percent were coping at the fair level. In contrast, 12 of 13 families where the mother stayed home performed only at the fair to poor level.[35]

In contacts with families of children with a chronic illness, it will be helpful to have some understanding of the feelings and situations that could arise. However, it must be remembered that not every family will experience all of these conflicts, emotions, and problems. What is manifested will depend on the personal resources of the parents, the extent and seriousness of the child's illness, and other conditions within the lives of the parents. Many families do quite well and must be admired for their adaptability and coping skills.

ATTITUDES OF SOCIETY TOWARD LONG-TERM ILLNESS

While society today puts much emphasis, backed by huge expenditures of money, on health and medicine, we seem to have little tolerance for or patience with the actual expression of illness. Advertising stresses the "cure" aspects of medicine; fund-raising telethons and television programing stress the drama in medicine; and the press is full of advice about the prevention of illness or disability from conception until old age.

These attitudes have a profound effect on children with chronic illnesses and their families. That there is a "cure" for almost all disease is, of course, a fallacy. However, it is a fallacy that frequently leads families with ill children to seek unorthodox treatments for their children and leads to tension between them and their medical caretakers. When a cure is not forthcoming, it seems as if someone must be to blame. Emphasis on the dramatic aspects of illness frequently leaves the public unprepared to face the daily drudgery associated with the treatment of many conditions and the fact that this must go on for years. The emphasis on prevention and early diagnosis accounts for much of the guilt felt by the parents and, in some cases, even the children.

Since the school is very often the microcosm of society, these attitudes may be expressed even unconsciously. Many of the illnesses described in this book as yet have no cure, although research is being done on all. Time does not stop for these children until cures or more effective treatments are found. School caretakers, like medical practitioners, must focus on the present while hoping for the future and do what they can for these children now. It should be pleasing to see that many of these children, approached appropriately, can have school lives satisfactory to themselves and that are a credit to the teachers, school nurses, and others who look beyond the illness to the possibilities within the child.

REFERENCES

1. K. Williams and M. Baeker, "Use of Small Group with Chronically Ill Children," *The Journal of School Health* 53 (1983): 205.
2. D. W. Guthrie and R. A. Guthrie, "Diabetes in Adolescence," *American Journal of Nursing* 75 (1975): 1,740.
3. G. Stores, "Problems of Learning and Behavior in Children with Epilepsy," in *Epilepsy and Psychiatry,* ed. E. H. Reynolds and M. R. Trimble (Edinburgh and New York: Churchill Livingstone, 1981).
4. P. K. Klopovich, T. S. Vats, G. Butterfield, N. U. Cairns, and S. B. Lansky, "School Phobia. Interventions in Childhood Cancer," *The Journal of the Kansas Medical Society* 82 (1981): 125.
5. L. Baker and K. R. Lyen, "Childhood Diabetes Mellitus," in *Diabetes Mellitus and Obesity,* ed. B. N. Brodoff and S. J. Bleicher (Baltimore, MD and London: Williams & Wilkins, 1982).
6. A. Mattson, "Long-Term Physical Illness in Childhood: A Challenge to Psychosocial Adaptation," *Pediatrics* 50 (1972): 801.
7. Guthrie and Guthrie, "Diabetes in Adolescence," p. 1, 740.
8. I. R. Boyle, P. A. di Sant'Agnese, S. Sack, F. Millican, and L. L. Kulczycki, "Emotional Adjustment of Adolescents and Young Adults with Cystic Fibrosis," *The Journal of Pediatrics* 88 (1976): 318.
9. Ibid.

10. J. W. Ross, ''The Role of the Social Worker with Long Term Survivors of Childhood Cancer and Their Families,'' *Social Work in Health Care* 74 (1982): 1.
11. Mattson, ''Long-Term Physical Illness in Childhood,'' p. 801.
12. Ibid.
13. Ibid.
14. L. Burton, *The Family Life of Sick Children* (London and Boston: Routledge and Kegan Paul, 1975).
15. N. Breslau, K. S. Staruch, and E. A. Mortimer, Jr., ''Psychological Distress in Mothers of Disabled Children,'' *American Journal of Diseases of Children* 136 (1982): 682.
16. Klopovich, Vats, Butterfield, Cairns, and Lansky, ''School Phobia. Intervention in Cancer,'' p. 125.
17. Burton, *The Family Life of Sick Children.*
18. J. W. Ross, ''Coping with Childhood Cancer: Group Intervention as an Aid to Parents in Crisis,'' *Social Work in Health Care* 4 (1979): 381.
19. I. Williams, A. N. Earles, and B. Pack, ''Psychological Considerations in Sickle Cell Disease,'' *Nursing Clinics of North America* 18 (1983): 215.
20. M. Pearse, ''The Child with Cancer: Impact on the Family,'' *The Journal of School Health* 47 (1977): 174.
21. I. Markova, K. MacDonald, and C. Forbes, ''Impact of Haemophilia on Child-Rearing Practices and Parental Co-Operation,'' *Journal of Child Psychology and Psychiatry* 21 (1980): 153.
22. Ibid.
23. M. Firth, D. Gardner-Medwin, G. Hosking, and E. Wilkinson, ''Interviews with Parents of Boys Suffering from Duchenne Muscular Dystrophy,'' *Developmental Medicine and Child Neurology* 25 (1983): 466.
24. P. T. McKeever, ''Fathering the Chronically Ill Child,'' *American Journal of Maternal and Child Nursing* 6 (1981): 124.
25. H. Staudenmayer, ''Parental Anxiety and Other Psychosocial Factors Associated with Childhood Asthma,'' *Journal of Chronic Disease* 34 (1981): 627.
26. Boyle, di Sant'Agnese, Sack, Millican, Kulczycki, ''Emotional Adjustment with Cystic Fibrosis,'' p. 318.
27. S. B. Lansky, N. U. Cairns, R. Hassanein, J. Wehr, and J. T. Lowman, ''Childhood Cancer: Parental Discord and Divorce,'' *Pediatrics* 62 (1978): 184.
28. Ibid.
29. Boyle, di Sant'Agnese, Sack, Millican, Kulczycki, ''Emotional Adjustment with Cystic Fibrosis, p. 318.
30. L. Baker and C. A. Stanley, ''Diabetes in Childhood,'' in *Endocrinology. Metabolic Basis of Clinical Practice*. ed. L. DeGroot et al. (New York: Grune and Stratton, 1978).
31. Markova, MacDonald, and Forbes, ''Impact of Hemophilia,'' p. 153.
32. Breslau, Staruch, and Mortimer, ''Psychological Distress in Mothers,'' p. 682.
33. McKeever, ''Fathering the Chronically Ill Child,'' p. 124.
34. Pearse, ''The Child with Cancer,'' p. 174.
35. Boyle, di Sant'Agnese, Sack, Millican, Kulczycki, ''Emotional Adjustment with Cystic Fibrosis,'' p. 318.

Asthma

by Robert Wilmott, M.D., Gerald Kolski, M.D., Ph.D., and Inez Burg, R.N., C.P.N.P.

OVERVIEW

Asthma is a lung disease that is characterized by reversible obstruction of the airways. The amount of air that goes in and out of the lungs depends on the sizes of the air passages as well as on the amount of effort exerted in breathing. In patients with asthma, the airways are very sensitive to various stimuli, with an "increased reactivity" that causes them to become smaller. This narrowing depends on several factors: increased production of mucus, spasm of the smooth muscle of the airways, and inflammation or swelling of the airway linings.

Asthma can demonstrate a wide spectrum of clinical severity, ranging from occasional, intermittent coughing to repeated episodes of severe airway obstruction requiring hospitalization. Patients with the latter form account for only a small proportion of asthmatic children.

Asthma is a common disease of children. Although estimates vary, 10 to 15 percent of children will have symptoms of asthma at some stage during their development. The problem is seen more commonly in boys than in girls, although the difference in frequency is quite small. Most commonly, the symptoms appear during the first five years of life, but onset may occur at any time.

The diagnosis of asthma is usually made fairly easily by a pediatrician or an allergist, and the treatment may be remarkably effective.

Cause

The exact cause of asthma is unknown. Asthma may have two components: an inherited abnormality of airway reactivity ("twitchy bronchi") and a precipitating cause or causes ("trigger factors"). Although there is no clearly defined hereditary pattern as seen in hemophilia or sickle cell anemia, asthma is seen most frequently in children of families with a history of allergic complaints, such as hay fever, eczema, or asthma. However, it is controversial whether increased airway reactivity is a primary inherited abnormality or an acquired disease. Recent research has shown that airway reactivity can increase with exposure to allergens (allergy-provoking substances).[1] Allergic adults have shown a lessening of reactivity of the airways to nonallergenic triggers such as exercise or cold air while living in special research quarters where there was a reduced exposure to allergy-provoking substances (allergens).

Allergies are important factors in triggering asthmatic symptoms. For instance, many children who are allergic to ragweed experience an increased frequency of asthma attacks during the ragweed season. Whether allergies truly cause asthma is not yet established, but they certainly can provoke asthma attacks.

It is not thought that asthma is a result of another illness. There is, however, an association between increased airway reactivity and viral infections in early life. We know that viral infections of the airways in infancy (for example, the respiratory virus that causes bronchiolitis) increase the risk of later wheezing episodes. Whether the virus always needs a genetically susceptible infant to produce this effect or whether the increased airway reactivity can persist as a residual complication of the infection alone is not known.

Clinical Manifestations

Factors that Cause Symptoms

"Trigger factors" for an airway reaction in a susceptible individual vary from patient to patient. These may be nonspecific irritants, such as cigarette smoke, paint fumes, pollutants, dust (especially chalk dust), and irritant chemicals. Some patients may be affected by specific allergens, which include pollens (grasses, trees, or weeds), molds, hay, animal danders, and insects, particularly house dust mites and cockroaches. Many children seem to be sensitive to changes in weather or air temperature and typically develop symptoms on cold days when the air is dry, probably because of airway cooling. Infections and emotional stress can also play a role. Exercise is another common trigger for an asthmatic attack and the degree of symptomatology. It also varies with the type of exercise. Some adult patients have symptoms of asthma only after exercise. Pure exercise-induced asthma is unusual in children, although many have symptoms after exercise as well as at other times.

Symptoms

A reversible obstruction of the airways, the hallmark of asthma, can present itself in many ways. In a patient with mild obstruction, coughing and a decrease in exercise tolerance may be the only symptoms, and the child's daily life will be minimally affected. The symptoms are more apparent in patients with more severe airway obstruction. These patients have difficulty in breathing and may complain of tightness of the chest. They usually have a persistent cough, which is particularly troublesome at night or after exercise. Other common symptoms are easy fatigability, sleep disturbance, and, occasionally, failure to thrive. The latter is manifested by reduced weight gain and stunted physical growth. Some of these patients have what appears to be recurrent pneumonia. There are repeated episodes of coughing, fever, and shortness of breath, with abnormal shadowing on the chest radiograph. Such attacks can be difficult to distinguish from an actual infection of the lung (pneumonia).

The increased effort of breathing in severe asthma is apparent from labored respiration with increased use of neck, shoulder, and abdominal muscles. The spaces between the ribs may become more prominent with respiration; this is called intercostal retraction. Patients with chronic asthma sometimes develop a permanent abnormality of the chest shape, with prominence of the breast bone. In the most severe cases, asthma can be associated with blueness of the lips and tongue, agitation, extreme difficulty in breathing, and lethargy.

Mechanism of an Asthma Attack

Asthma attacks vary from very mild ones that reverse themselves without treatment to those severe enough to require treatment and possibly hospitalization. To understand exactly what happens to a child during an asthma attack, some knowledge of the respiratory system is necessary. The airways are the passages that carry air between the larynx (voice box) and the alveoli (the small air sacs in the lungs where oxygen and carbon dioxide are exchanged in the blood). These passages branch and progressively decrease in size. They consist of the trachea, then the bronchi, and finally the bronchioles (Figure 1). In the larger airways, there is a layer of smooth muscle wrapped around the air passage within the wall of the tube. Smooth muscle is the type of muscle that is found in blood vessels, airways, the intestine, and the bladder. Persons with asthma have three abnormalities that cause airway narrowing. First, the bronchial smooth muscle reacts too readily to trigger factors. This abnormality is called "increased bronchial lability" or "increased bronchial reactivity." The other two associated abnormalities of the airways are swelling of the epithelial lining (mucosal edema) and excessive production of mucus by the airway mucous glands. The main airways involved are the larger bronchi. A comparison between a normal and asthmatic bronchiole can be found in Figures 2A and 2B.

Figure 1. The anatomy of the airways. The larynx is supported by the thyroid and cricoid cartilages.*

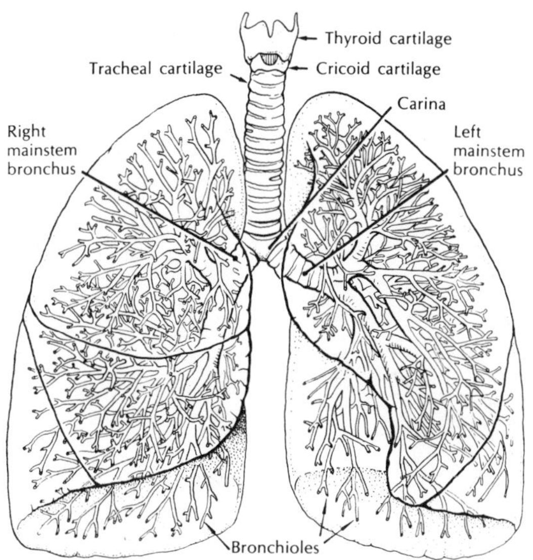

In normal breathing, the pressure within the chest increases and decreases with each breath. The size of the airways is affected by these pressure changes within the chest: the passages become larger during inspiration (breathing in) and smaller during expiration (breathing out). In airways that are already abnormally narrow, these changes in diameter result in an overall increase in resistance to airflow, which is more pronounced during expiration. This increased resistance to expiration causes an increase in the volume of gas in the lungs, which is called "gas trapping."

Gas trapping is especially seen in asthmatic children with troublesome symptoms. When gas trapping is marked, as it may be during a severe asthma attack, the increase in gas volume can contribute to increased stiffness of the lungs and reduced ventilation of the alveoli. As breathing out becomes more difficult, the child must use the muscles of the abdomen, neck, and shoulders to help force out air. This increased "work of breathing" results in greater oxygen consumption and greater production of carbon dioxide, which places even more strain on the failing respiratory

---

*The figures used in this chapter are "reproduced with permission from Des Jardins, T.R.: CLINICAL MANIFESTATIONS OF RESPIRATORY DISEASE. Copyright © 1984 by Year Book Medical Publishers, Inc., Chicago."

Figure 2A. The normal lung. ALV, alveoli; BA, bronchial artery; BG, bronchial glands; BI, bronchi; BM, basement membrane; BR, bronchioles; BV, bronchial vein; C, cartilage; EP, epithelium; GC, globlet cell; LP, lamina propria; PN, parasympathetic nerve; SM, smooth muscle; TBR, terminal bronchioles.

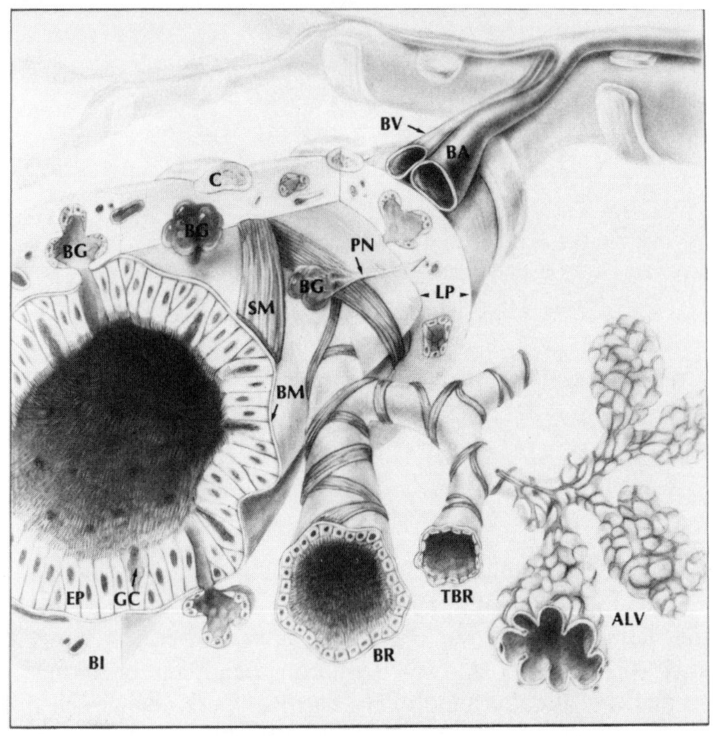

system. Beyond a certain point, the increased demand causes a build-up in the carbon dioxide level in the blood and a reduction in the blood's oxygen level. These changes increase the acid content of the blood. In an advanced state of respiratory failure due to asthma, the chemical changes described above result in agitation, headache, and cardiovascular instability, with progression to drowsiness and coma in the worst cases.

In some patients asthma attacks come on very gradually, whereas in others they may appear very quickly and rapidly become serious.

Course

A common misconception is that children will completely outgrow their symptoms of asthma. Although in many patients symptoms do become milder with age, this is not invariable, and only some children

Figure 2B. The asthmatic lung. E, eosinophil; HALV, hyperinflated alveoli; MA, mucus accumulation; SMC, smooth muscle constriction; SMH, smooth muscle hypertrophy.

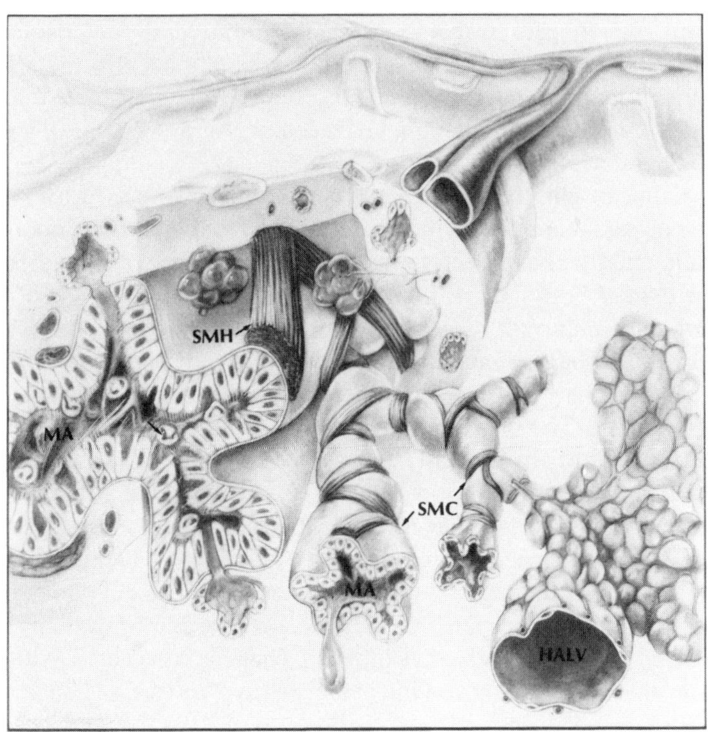

outgrow asthma completely. Lung function studies of adults with a history of childhood asthma often reveal mild abnormalities, which indicate that the underlying condition still exists and may manifest itself again.

The prognosis for asthma is difficult to evaluate. Although the short-term outlook is good, as most patients slowly improve and their symptoms become less troublesome, the long-term prognosis has not been defined by suitable follow-up studies. Some asthmatic patients with chronic obstructive abnormalities appear to develop irreversible obstructive pulmonary disease in later years; these patients may form a subgroup of adults with chronic obstructive lung disease and emphysema. Asthma is not associated with other health problems, such as cancer or heart disease, later in life. However, even asthmatics who have no symptoms should avoid cigarette smoking because of the risk of aggravating silent obstructive pulmonary disease.

Psychological Aspects

In the past, asthma has often been labeled a psychosomatic illness. This has led to inappropriate referrals for psychological evaluation and treatment and to parents being blamed for the child's symptoms. An increasing understanding of the disease has largely negated the idea that asthma is primarily a psychosomatic disorder. We believe there must first be an underlying increase in bronchial reactivity for psychological mechanisms to operate.

Asthma in children is not associated with any specific personality disorder or personality type. In detailed studies, only a small proportion of asthmatic children have been found to have psychiatric disorders, and the incidence may be no more than that in normal school children. Some children with recurrent, severe asthma appear to have behavioral and emotional disturbances, and this may account for the apparent "asthmatic personality." Many parents of children with asthma overprotect and fail to discipline them. The children may manipulate their parents by failing to comply with treatment or manifesting symptoms. Generally, the severity of the psychological problems is related to the severity of the asthma.

Emotion sometimes has been misunderstood as a precipitator of asthma attacks because children may have attacks after laughing, yelling, crying, or even coughing. It is probably not the emotional component of these activities that is responsible for the onset of asthma symptoms but the deep breathing and other physiological changes associated with these emotions that stimulate narrowing of the airways.

THERAPY

Mild cases of asthma can be managed by family practitioners or by pediatricians. Only more severe cases need the specialized care of an allergist or a pediatric pulmonologist. Every child should be evaluated with a comprehensive history and a full physical examination. The doctor should make specific enquiries regarding precipitating factors, when taking the allergy history. Special investigations such as chest and sinus radiographs, blood counts, allergy skin tests, pulmonary function tests, and antibody levels should be considered in children with severe or recurrent symptoms.

Medications

Medications are used either intermittently or continuously, depending on the severity of the disease. There are three main modes of administration of asthma medications: oral use of tablets, syrups, or granules; inhalation of powders; and inhalation of pressurized aerosols. The most common method of administration is the oral one.

Patients with more severe asthma often require continuous treatment to keep them in good health and to prevent frequent episodes of hospitalization resulting in poor school attendance. These regimens should be clearly established by the doctors and should be conveyed to the school nurse by the child's parents. Most regimens do not require more than one dose of medicine during the school day. In more severe cases, an oral medicine is sometimes combined with a pressurized inhaler, but whether such a combination is prescribed will depend on the age of the child. Patients on intermittent therapy usually require treatment with tablets or syrups only when they have symptoms or with exercise. An inhaler used before exercise is very effective in controlling exercise-induced asthma.

Instead of medicine in tablet form, older patients with mild asthma may have pressurized inhalers to be used every four to six hours when they have difficulty in breathing and tightness in the chest. These pressurized inhalers usually contain epinephrine-like drugs that have been modified to make them more selective for the β_2 receptors of the lung (see below).

Theophylline

The most frequently used medicine for asthma given to children in the United States is theophylline, which is taken orally, except in hospitalized patients who may receive intravenous theophylline. Theophylline works by relaxing the bronchial smooth muscle. Theophylline preparations are more often given continuously than intermittently, and the prescribing doctor adjusts the dose to establish a therapeutic blood level. Theophylline should be taken as prescribed and no extra doses should be taken, as this may produce an increased blood level causing side effects, such as nausea, vomiting, indigestion, and headaches. Some children have an increase in activity and appear to be stimulated by the drug. These symptoms may decrease once the patient has taken theophylline for a few days.

β_2-selective Drugs Related to Epinephrine

The body's natural hormone, epinephrine, is released at times of stress and mediates the "flight or fight" reaction. Changes in the body's function in response to the hormone include dilated airways, increased heart rate, dilated pupils, sweating, and tremors. Epinephrine stimulates several responses simultaneously through different receptors (α , β_1, β_2). The β_2

receptor is found on bronchial smooth muscle and, when stimulated, causes dilation of the airway. Epinephrine is therefore a nonspecific bronchodilator, and its use may be associated with unwanted side effects. Drugs, such as isoproterenol, which act on β_1 and β_2 receptors, are more specific but still stimulate the heart. β_2-selective drugs have been developed during the past 15 years to reduce this side effect. Such drugs include albuterol, metaproterenol, fenoterol, and terbutaline. These compounds may produce a slight muscular tremor, an increase in level of activity, and, rarely, mild palpitations (fluttering of the heart). This class of drug can be administered orally or by inhalation.

Corticosteroids

Corticosteroids are powerful anti-inflammatory drugs related to hormones released by the body's adrenal glands during stress. The occasional patient who has repeated, severe attacks may be treated with corticosteroids, which may be inhaled or taken orally. The inhaled version is not normally associated with any significant side effects. However, orally ingested corticosteroids are associated with many problems, including increased appetite, behavioral changes, weight gain, a moon-shaped face, an increase in body hair, easy bruising, stretch marks, acne, oily skin, and stunting of growth, as well as other metabolic abnormalities. The latter may only be revealed by special investigations.

Cromolyn

Cromolyn is used only as a preventive drug, and it is not usually given during an acute attack. Cromolyn's action is to block the effects of allergies on the airways by inhibiting the release of inflammatory chemicals by white cells in the lungs. It is also effective in exercise-induced asthma if taken before sports and gym. The drug is normally supplied as a powder in capsules that must be administered by inhalation with a special spinhaler device. It may also be administered by a pressurized cannister inhaler. Children who use the powder are normally instructed very carefully in the use of the spinhaler device, for if used improperly, the drug tends to deposit in the mouth and throat where it is ineffective.

SCHOOL LIFE

Since 10 to 15 percent of school children develop wheezing sometime before adulthood, it is clear that most asthmatic children can attend school and take part in normal activities without undue attention. Asthma does not usually affect a child's learning ability or academic performance unless attendance is poor because of illness. An important component of modern asthma treatment is an enlightened approach by teachers and parents. Such an approach combined with drug therapy will keep most patients in good general health.

Unfortunately, asthma in children is often not recognized and is therefore not treated. It is important to recognize symptoms that may be the result of undiagnosed asthma, as they may result in poor academic performance, bad school attendance, reduced physical activity, stunted growth, or poor self-esteem.

School Attendance

Children with mild asthma whose symptoms are well controlled by medications should miss very little school. Children with more severe asthma usually need four to five days to recover from each attack, with some of this time spent in the hospital. If a child has many episodes of school absence, it is reasonable to provide homebound tutoring, but every effort should be made to keep the child in school. With a child who frequently misses school, school personnel should investigate whether the child is receiving adequate medical supervision from a physician. If there is any change in frequency or severity of symptoms, compliance with treatment should be questioned. When absences become a problem, teachers, the school nurse, and parents should be in close and regular contact with the physician to attempt to improve attendance.

Physical Activity

Guidelines for exercise should always be established with the physician and parents. Many children will have no exercise limitations. However, performance in athletics and gymnastics can be severely affected by exercise-induced bronchospasm. In the child with decreased exercise tolerance, it is important that teachers, the school nurse, parents, and physicians work together to reduce symptoms and allow maximum participation in school activities. School personnel should inform the family when problems arise so that treatment can be arranged to minimize symptoms. A graduated program of physical activity can improve an asthmatic's tolerance if the program is carefully established. Pretreatment with inhaled β_2 drugs and a series of warm-up exercises can help reduce symptoms related to exercise. Swimming is a form of exercise that is beneficial to most asthma patients and is not usually associated with exercise-induced wheezing. There are highly competitive international athletes with asthma who have learned to manage their symptoms.

In children who have had severe attacks and need hospitalization, there may be some decrease in exercise tolerance for a short period following discharge. It should be remembered that these are temporary restrictions. The doctor should offer some guidelines to the parents and school concerning the level of activity that is appropriate for the child's condition.

Peer Relationships

Poor academic performance as a result of absenteeism and poor athletic ability can negatively affect the child's relationship with peers and can lead to further absenteeism and further alienation from both academic and social endeavors. Peer relationships can also suffer if it seems evident to classmates that the asthmatic child is getting out of unpleasant school situations because of the disease.

Environment

Teachers should be aware of any trigger factors that the child should avoid while at school. The most important factor is exercise, which has already been discussed. Other environmental factors peculiar to schools are chalk dust, chemicals from school laboratories, and fumes from materials, such as solder, used in shop courses. When a teacher notices something that consistently triggers an asthma attack, the parents and the child's doctor should be notified. For example, a teacher might observe that a child wheezes when handling classroom pets, such as hamsters or guinea pigs.

Air temperature may affect many children, but it is not possible to give clear guidelines with regard to climate or air temperature. Certain children develop symptoms after exposure to cold, dry air, and some form of pretreatment may be necessary before such exposure. If certain seasons, climate conditions, or activities are commonly associated with symptoms, pretreatment rather than avoiding activities should be the goal.

APPROACH TO THE CHILD WITH ASTHMA

The asthmatic child should be treated as a normal child, and blanket restrictions should not be imposed. It is only possible to give general guidelines, as the approach must be individualized for each child. A careful supportive attitude by the teacher and school nurse can help considerably in encouraging a confident, independent attitude, and this may help reduce the frequency of attacks.

Overprotection and undue lack of discipline are approaches by school personnel that can lead to lack of confidence, unruliness, or manipulative behavior in the child. Fearfulness of symptoms may increase the child's tension, interfere with relationships with peers, and exacerbate underlying disease. It is seldom appropriate to attempt to shield children from stressful situations, such as academic competition, debates, athletics, or musical performances. Such a negative approach can put additional strain on peer relationships. The well-stabilized child should be capable of normal activities and should not be especially vulnerable to stress.

Although we advocate an encouraging approach to the child with asthma, the child's condition should not be ignored or belittled. For instance, on field trips, paticularly if they entail overnight stops, the odds of encountering new or unusually high concentrations of asthma-provoking allergens are greater than normal. In these circumstances, it is particularly important that the student bring along medication and even bedding. Also, in some children, undertreatment by doctors or parents and lack of attention to persistent symptoms have been problems.

Although asthmatic children should be encouraged to participate in physical education and active games, some limitation on exercise is unavoidable at times. It is important for physical education teachers to accept the fact that exercise capacity can be restricted by asthma symptoms.

MEDICAL PROBLEMS THAT MAY OCCUR IN THE CLASSROOM

When children with asthma have attacks at school, they should be allowed to sit quietly, relax, and drink warm fluids. The teacher or school nurse should ascertain whether the child received his or her morning treatment. If the attack does not resolve within 5 to 10 minutes treatment should be started. Plans should already have been made with the parents and the child's physician to handle such attacks, and a medical regimen should be outlined for each child. Staff should attempt to remain calm when an asthmatic child has an attack, for any tension or anxiety will make it worse. If the child is more than seven or eight years old, inhaled bronchodilators may be used. Otherwise, most children are treated with oral medicine. Some children will not respond to these measures and will require an emergency room evaluation.

A very small proportion of asthmatic children have repeated attacks of severe asthma of sudden onset. Response to these attacks requires careful advance planning. Oxygen should be administered during the acute attack, and some form of therapy should be agreed upon in advance. Such treatment may include injections of epinephrine by the school nurse or treatment by inhalation of a bronchodilator in mist form. Contingency plans should be made for medical evaluation at the local hospital. A child who does not respond to the measures outlined is considered to be in *status asthmaticus*. Such a child needs to be transferred to a hospital.

FOSTERING CLASSMATES' UNDERSTANDING

Other children in the class should be told that the patient has a disorder that makes breathing difficult at times and that medicines are available to help him or her breathe normally again. It should be made clear that, although the child seems distressed during an attack, both the child and the staff know what to do. They should be told that these attacks occur intermittently, that they are not infectious, and that the patient will recover. The other children should be encouraged to treat the child as normally as possible. However, they should also be told that the child does occasionally need special consideration. Examples of these times are with strenuous activities, during seasons when allergies are most likely to flare up, and when the child is exposed to certain environmental substances. Children should be encouraged to respect the patient's right to use common sense in avoiding problems that could cause symptoms. An asthmatic child's avoidance of a situation that has been difficult in the past could be compared to refusal to run in front of a car or to jump from a fence that is too high.

If the child's peers, as well as teachers and parents, are successful in treating the patient as normally as possible, with a considerate and supportive attitude, asthma in childhood should be associated with very little physical disability in the majority of cases. This approach is also usually associated with very little educational, psychological, or psychosocial disability.

REFERENCE

1. D. W. Cockcroft, "Hypothesis: Mechanism of Perennial Allergic Asthma," *Lancet* 2 (1983): 253–55.

RESOURCES

Suggested Reading

Evans, Hugh E., M.D. *Lung Diseases of Children*. American Lung Association. 1740 Broadway, New York, NY 10019.

Useful Addresses

American Lung Association, 1740 Broadway, New York, NY 10019 (provides educational material on asthma).

Asthma and Allergy Foundation of America, 19 W. 44th St., New York, NY 10036 (provides useful pamphlets on asthma).

Allergies

by Gerald Kolski, M.D., Ph.D. and Inez Burg, R.N., C.P.N.P.

OVERVIEW

An allergy is an abnormal reaction to a particular substance, termed an "allergen." The reaction may take various forms, such as sneezing and excessive nasal discharge or hives and rashes, depending on the allergen and the sensitivity of the individual. Allergies are common and probably occur in as much as 20 percent of the population. This may be a relatively low estimate, with many people having an occasional allergic reaction to a particular substance.

The symptoms of allergies may be very disconcerting to the child and, if severe, adversely affect school performance. Because allergies are very common and rarely lead to major complications, children having them are often not thought of as "sick," although the symptoms may cause as much discomfort as those from what are considered actual diseases.

It is not uncommon for allergies to be manifested through several generations of a family. The reaction to a particular allergen may be a familial trait, or there may be a hereditary predisposition to the development of allergies in general. In the latter case, the tendency to develop allergies is inherited, but the type of allergy could differ among members of the family. This is called an "atopic predisposition."

Mechanism of the Allergic Reaction

An allergic reaction is complex and involves the immune system. The allergen (also termed "antigen") can either be a protein or a nonprotein. It stimulates the production of antibodies of a class called IgE. Antibodies are components of the immune system, which defend the body against invasion from foreign and potentially harmful substances, such as viruses or bacteria. IgE is an antibody particularly characteristic of the atopic or allergic person, although it can be found in everyone and, under some conditions, such as in the presence of parasites, can be formed in large amounts. In atopic persons, however, large amounts of IgE can be produced in the presence of common environmental substances, such as dust or pollen.

A property of IgE is its ability to bind to certain tissue cells, the mast cells, and to basophils, a white blood cell. Mast cells are present most commonly in the upper respiratory tract, gastrointestinal tract, and on the skin. When an allergen is absorbed through the respiratory or gastrointestinal tract or the skin and comes in contact with the IgE on mast cells, it causes these cells to release various potent chemicals. These chemicals produce effects in the area where they are released. Such effects include increased vascular permeability, smooth muscle contraction, itching, and increased mucus production.

The site where this interaction takes place will determine the nature of the reaction. Allergens coming in contact with mast cells in the nose will produce symptoms of allergic rhinitis, allergens in contact with mast cells in the lower respiratory tract will produce symptoms of asthma, and those in contact with mast cells in the gastrointestinal tract will produce symptoms of gastrointestinal allergy, which may include diarrhea and vomiting. If the allergen is absorbed into the bloodstream, generalized reactions such as hives and swelling may occur. Occasionally there may be an anaphylactic reaction, which is a reaction of the entire system to the allergen that has been absorbed. This is a very serious reaction and may lead to shock (see Anaphylactic Reactions).

Sensitization

For an allergic reaction to take place, a susceptible person must have had prior exposure to sufficient amounts of an allergen. This is called "sensitization." Some people will not become sensitized until they have been repeatedly exposed to small amounts of allergens over several years. For instance, sometimes it takes many years for symptoms to develop in susceptible persons in the work place. Also, children with seasonal allergies, such as those to inhaled pollens, do not usually begin having symptoms until the fourth, fifth, or sometimes later years of life. It often seems as if a child suddenly develops an allergy out of the blue, but it is usually that enough exposures have finally taken place for sensitization. With seasonal allergies, this often takes several years, depending upon the amount of airborne pollens in a given locality.

The allergens that most frequently cause symptoms in children are substances to which there has been chronic exposure. These include foods and potential allergens in the home, e.g., animal danders, molds, and dust. This continuous contact allows for sensitization early in life. There are times, however, when sensitization takes place quickly—upon exposure to relatively large amounts of an allergen. Once sensitization occurs and the individual again comes in contact with the allergen, symptoms may develop. For example, persons allergic to bee stings will not have symptoms after the first sting but will manifest symptoms when stung again.

COMMON ALLERGIES IN SCHOOL-AGED CHILDREN

Allergies Affecting the Respiratory Tract

The most common allergies in school-aged children are respiratory allergies, with the principal manifestation being an allergic rhinitis, which can affect a child during a specific season or all year.

Seasonal Allergic Rhinitis

Cause. Seasonal allergic rhinitis usually occurs because of inhaled pollens. The child may be very sensitive to a large number of pollens or may be exquisitely sensitive to one particular pollen, such as ragweed pollen.

The most common sensitizing pollens are tree pollens, grass pollens, and various weed pollens. There are also airborne molds that have a seasonal pattern. Trees tend to pollinate in early spring, closely followed by grass pollination. Throughout most of the country, ragweed pollinates late in the summer or early fall. It is not uncommon for children with seasonal grass allergies to have significant exacerbations around Memorial Day and for children with ragweed hay fever to have symptoms around Labor Day. Many children who have fall allergies fortunately do not have spring allergies and vice versa.

Symptoms. The usual symptoms are an acute rhinitis, which is inflammation of the mucous membrane of the nose. There may be nasal obstruction, profuse discharge of clear, thin mucus, sneezing, itching of the eyes and nose, and tearing. Sometimes a bacterial infection of the nasal passages and sinusitis may follow because of insufficient drainage in the nasal passages. The swelling of the nasal tissues may block drainage of the ear into the back of the nose. This predisposes the child to the accumulation of fluid in the ears, leading to recurrent infections. Recurrent fluid in the ears can also lead to hearing problems. Some children with allergic rhinitis may also have exacerbations of their asthma and/or atopic dermatitis (see Eczema).

Skin Testing. Seasonal as well as other allergies can usually be determined by skin testing. This is done either by placing an allergen on the skin and then pricking or scratching over it (prick or scratch method) or by injecting the allergen under the skin (intradermal method). RAST (IgE antibody) testing can be done in cases in which there is severe skin involvement or a history of anaphylactic reaction. This involves a blood test in which an allergen is incubated with a sample of the patient's serum and the interaction of the allergen and IgE antibody is determined by radioactive counting.

Treatment. Treatment of allergies involves a class of drugs known as antihistamines. In cases where there is nasal obstruction, decongestants (which may be in some antihistamine preparations) may also be used. Some children with seasonal rhinitis can be treated adequately with steroid nasal sprays. Eye drops are often used to relieve the itchy, watery eyes. Avoidance of the allergen is the best treatment but is not always possible, as in the case of pollen allergies.

Symptoms that do not respond to medication may require hyposensitization, or "allergy shots." This treatment consists of giving the child very diluted concentrations of an allergen and gradually building up to a concentration that approximates natural exposure. This involves weekly injections and, unfortunately, is not effective in all patients. Hyposensitization is helpful in severe allergy cases and is most effective when using pollen extracts. The length of treatment is usually several years or throughout life.

No matter what mode of treatment is used, it is essential that there be collaboration with a physician. Many over-the-counter allergy preparations can be overused or used incorrectly and cause serious problems. Their use should be discussed with the physician. Among the most abused over-the-counter preparations are the nasal decongestant sprays. Their overuse causes a "rebound effect," with the effects of the medication lasting for shorter periods with increasing doses. This results in worsening and prolonging the nasal congestion.

It is important with the management of both asthma and allergic rhinitis that medications be geared to the child's school performance and activities. Medications, such as antihistamines, should be chosen so as to give adequate control of symptoms without causing significant impairment of intellectual function. When possible, medications should be used before exposure, for instance, before exercise or exposure to pollens. Medication taken before going outside to play in a field is helpful. Teachers should report to the school nurse any signs of drowsiness, listlessness, inability to concentrate, decreased attention span, or increased activity in the child. Certain other drugs should not be taken with antihistamines, even those bought without a prescription.

Chronic Perennial Allergic Rhinitis

Symptoms and Cause. Children with chronic perennial allergic rhinitis have exacerbations all year round. The symptoms are the same as those in seasonal allergic rhinitis. The usual causes of perennial rhinitis in school-aged children are what we consider to be household factors, the most common being animals, dust and dust mites, cockroaches in urban areas, and molds in areas that have significant moisture.

Often, the symptoms will worsen in the winter when the child spends more time in the house. In homes with hot-air heating systems, various allergens are circulated through the ducts and dispersed throughout the house. Also, heating in winter causes the air to dry out, which then dries out mucous membranes. This causes great discomfort and may exacerbate the allergy. Sometimes there is both a perennial and seasonal pattern to the condition, with the chronic rhinitis being exacerbated during times associated with seasonal pollens.

In some children, the symptoms of perennial allergic rhinitis are not severe enough to prompt parents to seek medical advice or even for them to recognize that there is a problem. The child may have a low-grade chronic rhinitis and nasal obstruction that receives little attention or brings about few complaints. Perhaps the child has gotten used to the symptoms and is not aware of the possibility of feeling better. A typical example is the child who may not notice significant problems when being around a pet, particularly if he or she is used to being exposed to animals. The child then goes away to camp—and away from the pet—and experiences the unfamiliar sensation of being able to breathe freely. When he or she returns home again, the symptoms recur. It is at such times that the family frequently recognizes that there is a problem and seeks medical help.

Sometimes the allergy cannot be determined through skin testing or an environmental history. In many situations, symptoms will result from irritant factors, such as cigarette smoke and other substances in the environment.

Treatment. The medications used are the same as those for seasonal allergic rhinitis, and the same precautions should be taken in using them. Allergy shots are not as effective for perennial allergies as they are for seasonal allergies. Environmental control as a mode of therapy comes into play frequently with perennial allergies. The area most concentrated on at home is the bedroom. Recommendations are usually as follows:

1. Keep the child's room between 60° and 65°F in the winter.
2. If the house has forced air heat (through a vent), place a filter of cheesecloth or gauze soaked in Lysol over the vent in the child's room and on the intake vent on the heating unit. Change daily.

3. If the room is dry, crack the window at night. If a vaporizer is needed, cool mist is preferable. Run for about two hours with the door closed, then shut it off. The continuous use of a vaporizer causes mold to build up in the machine as well as in the room.

4. The bedroom should be dusted at least every other day with a damp cloth. The room should be kept as clean and bare as possible. No stuffed chairs, loose clothing, or extra furniture should be in the room, as these collect dust. Also, posters, toys, and stuffed animals will collect dust.

5. Low-pile carpet or bare floors are preferable. All bedclothes and curtains should be washable, and no wool blankets should be used. Mattresses and boxsprings should be covered with an allergy-proof plastic cover that zips shut, and no feather pillows should be used. Dacron or foam pillows are acceptable.

6. No dogs, cats, or birds in the child's room.

7. Keep the child away from aerosol spray cans, perfume, paints, extermination fumes, and cleaners. These will cause the allergy symptoms to worsen.

8. Do not smoke around the child, in his or her room, or in the car. Smoke is extremely irritating to the mucous membranes and makes the allergic person very uncomfortable.

A frequent sore spot for children with perennial allergic rhinitis is pets. Generally speaking, there is a tendency for children with other allergies, and especially children with asthma, to develop sensitivity to fur-bearing pets. However, reactions vary, with children being sensitive to one kind of animal and not to another. Also, it should not be assumed that all children who have a chronic perennial rhinitis will have symptoms when being around animals. Contrary to popular belief, the allergen on the animal is not the fur. Poodles are no less allergenic than sheep dogs. People are allergic to the protein in the animal's saliva, urine, and dander (skin). As of this writing, there is no proven acceptable treatment of the pet to make it nonallergenic. Once again, the best treatment for pet allergy is avoidance. However, this method may cause a lot of problems with other family members. The second choice would be to confine the animal to one room, preferably the basement, or keep it outdoors. The animal does not have to be present in the same room to cause a problem. If it has passed through, it has left behind its allergen.

Insect Sting Allergies

The insects that most commonly cause allergic reactions are the Hymenoptera, which include bees, hornets, wasps, and yellow jackets.

Stings by these insects are often associated with a local reaction at the site of the sting. Some children will have a more intense than usual local reaction, including itching and swelling over a more widespread area. Then there are those who will develop varying degrees of systemic reactions that involve hives and, in very severe instances, hypotension, shock, and laryngeal swelling with difficulty in breathing. These latter are the manifestations of anaphylaxis and are indications for the use of systemic treatment. Anaphylaxis from insect stings is rare in children, although it does occur. In adults, it is more common and is more often associated with a fatal outcome. Children who have had an anaphylactic reaction to insect stings may be desensitized through injection of diluted insect venom. Desensitization for insect stings is a lifelong procedure. Insect allergies are determined through skin testing. Children who have had a severe reaction to an insect sting involving generalized swelling, hives, and/or wheezing may carry a kit which contains adrenalin. Syringes are often preloaded and injections should be given at the first sign of severe reaction. In addition to adrenalin, potent antihistamines such as Benadryl (diphenhydramine) are often used.

Routine treatment for any bee sting involves applying ice locally to the sting. Antihistamines other than Benadryl or Atarax (hydroxyzine) are usually not helpful. Cautioning children that brightly colored clothes and perfumes may attract insects will help them avoid these contacts. Trips to gardens and greenhouses or hayrides are not advisable for children with sting allergies. Any other outing may require some forethought, such as carrying adrenalin or other medication with the child.

After a child has been stung, it is often important to know whether the stinger remains in the skin. This may enable the physician to determine the identity of the insect. The honeybee is noted for leaving its stinger and is only able to sting once, whereas hornets, yellow jackets, and wasps can sting several times. It is important when obtaining a history to know which kind of insect has stung.

The bites of insects such as ants, mosquitoes, lice, sand fleas, and others may produce local allergic reactions. If there is a more severe reaction, Benadryl or adrenaline can be used. Anaphylaxis to these other insect bites is rare.

Allergies Affecting the Skin

Hives

Cause. Hives (urticaria) are fairly common in children and are characterized by large reddish areas with hard centers. Viral infections in children are among the most common causes of infrequent, transient urticaria. Hives are also associated with various foods, some medications, and, occasionally, with physical causes. The most common food allergies causing hives are those that include milk, eggs, wheat, peanuts, and seafood. With foods, the attack may come on immediately or be delayed as long as two to four hours. Some children are sensitive to aspirin and develop hives; others may develop hives secondary to exposure to animals and, occasionally, pollens.

A common physical cause of hives is cold. Hands may swell after grabbing onto something cold, or the mouth and lips may swell after ingesting cold substances. In addition, generalized symptoms may rarely occur with severe cold exposure. These symptoms include generalized urticaria and perhaps swelling of the face, feet, or hands. Some children develop a cholinergic urticaria, that is, a reaction to heat. It can follow sweating, extreme physical exercise, or emotional stress. Manifestations aside from hives include abdominal cramps, diarrhea, fainting, sweating, salivating, and headache. These physical urticarias are much more common in adults but do occur in children.

Treatment. Treatment for hives is generally an antihistamine, such as Benadryl or Atarax, and avoidance of the allergen. Symptoms of both cholinergic and cold urticaria often will respond to treatment with antihistamines, especially Atarax or Periactin (cyproheptadine), and avoidance of the allergen. Hives usually last 24 to 48 hours and most likely resolve on their own. When an antihistamine is used for comfort, it should provide relief in a few hours.

As long as the hives remain as skin manifestations, they are more of a nuisance than a threat. However, if hives become associated with the mucous membranes, and there is throat tightening and wheezing, more vigorous medical care is needed. This could include the chronic use of antihistamines or the availability of a preloaded adrenalin syringe.

Eczema

Cause. Eczema, or atopic dermatitis, can be a skin manifestation of an allergy usually found on the arms, legs, and neck. There is excessive dryness, flaking, cracking of the skin, and intense itching. It tends to flare up periodically, usually during the winter. Some of the more common exacerbating factors for eczema are food allergies (particularly eggs), pollens, animal danders, and the dryness of cold winter air.

Treatment. Treatment of eczema includes putting moisture back into the skin with a moisturizing cream such as Eucerin or Vaseline applied to skin that has been moistened. Steroid creams are used on the bad areas.

Soap should be mild (Dove is preferred) and only used every other day at bath time. The intense itching is often relieved by Atarax, a potent antihistamine. It is very important to watch the type of clothing these children wear. Lightweight cotton clothing, in layers if necessary, is best. Wool or wool blends are extremely irritating and will make these children miserable. Parents are cautioned against using scented creams and lotions and bubblebaths, as these will dry out the skin and make the condition worse. A more positive note is that children will usually outgrow their eczema, or at least the symptoms will become milder with time.

Gastrointestinal Allergies

Allergies to foods may present gastrointestinal symptoms (such as vomiting and diarrhea); respiratory symptoms (such as nasal congestion and/or wheezing); or skin manifestations (such as exacerbations of eczema or hives). The question of hyperactivity as a result of food allergies often comes up. That hyperactivity can be caused by foods or food additives has not yet been proven by scientific studies. We do know, however, that hyperactivity is not a manifestation of allergic reactions.

Cause. Food allergies in young infants are common, especially milk intolerance which may result from an early exposure to cow milk. Some children with significant food allergies have less difficulty as they grow older. This may be because as the gastrointestinal tract matures, it becomes less permeable or better able to degrade allergens before they can be absorbed into the system. In this case, it could be said that the child truly does outgrow an allergy. Many such children will have skin test reactions to certain foods but when challenged to those foods in a double-blind manner will not respond with significant symptoms.

Treatment. The most effective treatment for food allergies is avoidance. However, if the symptoms are mild, it is a good idea to challenge a patient periodically with the offending food to see if the symptoms have abated. If there are no symptoms after eating the food, there is no reason to continue restricting the food. There has been an overemphasis on food allergies with resultant restrictions. This can be dangerous, as children need certain foods to grow correctly, and their patterns for later eating habits are formed during childhood.

ANAPHYLACTIC REACTIONS

A systemic anaphylactic reaction is a potentially severe and sometimes lethal allergic reaction. Fortunately, it is uncommon in children. The systemic manifestations include hives, generalized swelling that can cause upper airway obstruction, and cardiovascular collapse. As in other allergic reactions, the patient must first be sensitized by a potentially offending agent. Drugs, particularly those that are injected; agents used in diagnosis (for example, dyes used in certain x-ray studies); allergen extracts for hyposensitization; foods; chemicals; and Hymenoptera stings have all been known to cause anaphylactic reactions. The best-known anaphylactic allergic reactions are those as a result of injected penicillin or bee stings. Treatment consists of administering adrenalin and monitoring blood pressure. A fall in blood pressure indicates shock.

SCHOOL LIFE

It should be recognized that children with allergies may have significant problems at school. These problems can occur for various reasons and differ according to the type of allergy. Children who have trouble with chronic runny or stuffy noses, chronic wheezing, or frequent abdominal symptoms because of allergies may find it difficult to concentrate in the classroom. If teachers are not aware that the problem lies in the child's symptoms and not in inherent abilities, the child may be thought of as less motivated and intelligent than he or she actually is.

We encourage allergy patients to attend school as regularly as possible. Very often the child is no more uncomfortable at school than he or she would be at home. Often the stimulation of the school environment will even take the child's mind off symptoms. Frequent absences will put the child behind in schoolwork, and the resultant poor grades and poor understanding of classroom work can build up a pattern of wanting to further avoid school, which has become associated with failure. Sometimes children are sent home from school unnecessarily, since it is felt that their symptoms are secondary to a cold.

Problems Related to Seasonal Allergies

Seasonal allergies can affect school performance during the two most crucial periods in the school year: the beginning and the end. The initial weeks of school coincide with ragweed pollination and the end of the year with tree and grass pollination.

Getting off to a good start is important to a child academically and socially. The beginning of the school year can be stressful under normal circumstances. Getting used to new teachers, new classmates, and new subjects and not feeling well for several weeks at a stretch can sometimes overwhelm a youngster. This is manifested in several ways. Schoolwork can lag just because the child doesn't feel well. Relationships with classmates can suffer, too. Children realize that classmates often stick by first impressions when it comes to choosing friends and teammates on the playground. Obviously, children who are not feeling well and who are coughing, sneezing, and constantly blowing their noses are not going to make a good first impression or be considered fun to be with or to have as competent teammates. This knowledge can upset the youngster.

Grass and tree allergies are manifested at the end of the school year, which coincides with examination time. Symptoms and side effects of medications may affect both studying for and taking exams. If class placement for the following year is largely determined by year-end tests, the child with spring allergies is put at a great disadvantage. It should be recognized that if the child did well all year, a sudden drop in performance or poor test scores may be a result of health problems and not because of lack of ability or motivation. Socially, the end of the school year is also meaningful to a child. That is when school outings, field days, and other celebrations are usually held, and these are frequently looked forward to and planned for all year.

Hearing Difficulties

In both seasonal and perennial rhinitis, airway obstruction can impair drainage, especially from the eustachian tubes in the ears. This may lead to difficulties in hearing and understanding, which will in turn lead to academic problems. When it is known that a child has allergies that could affect hearing, he or she should be given a seat near the front of the class, and teachers should make the effort to determine if the child can hear what is being said. This should be done without embarrassing the student. Often a clue can be gotten from facial responses to classroom activity or the answers to a few questions after class.

Classroom Embarrassment

Children displaying symptoms of asthma or allergy may have difficulty in breathing and may cough. This may be disruptive to the classroom and irritating to the teacher. Sometimes, as teachers well know, other classmates will join in on the coughing to further disrupt the class. This embarrasses the child who has unintentionally started it all. Such situations may be avoided if the coughing child is allowed to quietly leave the room to get a drink of water before the cough becomes persistent. The child's allergies should not be commented on during class period.

Participation in School Activities

The child with allergic rhinitis should be encouraged to participate in physical activities, but it should be acknowledged that certain activities may be restricted when symptoms are severe. Communication with parents and the child's physician can help in working out a plan to minimize the child's being left out of normal school activities. If a child's symptoms are pollen-related, allowing him or her to stay inside the school, or better yet to come back inside if symptoms become bad, is recommended.

A most important aspect of handling the child's allergy involves communication between teacher, parents, and physician. Parents should communicate with teachers about the child's allergic condition and medications to allow the teacher to have a more appropriate response to the child during a difficult period. When possible, teachers should let the parents know how the treatment regimen is affecting the child's performance. It is helpful for a school nurse to tell parents when the child is acting differently or if the symptoms have changed or worsened. Side reactions of medications or a change in symptoms or behavior may be more apparent at school than at home. The opportunity for comparison with other children and the structured class situation can offer insights that cannot be gained in the more casual home setting.

Some children may have symptoms of allergies in school that the parents are not aware of or that they have ignored. Children who are constantly sniffing, sneezing, mouth breathing, and showing other signs of respiratory difficulties should be reported to the school nurse who can then determine what, if anything, is being done to help the child. If the child is not receiving treatment, parents should be contacted.

Juvenile Diabetes

by Kenneth R. Lyen, M.A., B.M., B.Ch., M.R.C.P., D.C.H.

OVERVIEW

Childhood diabetes is a metabolic disorder caused by inadequate production of insulin. Insulin is a hormone, produced by the beta cells of the Islets of Langerhans in the pancreas, which regulates the metabolism of carbohydrates. In the normal digestive process, the carbohydrates in food are broken down into a sugar called glucose and carried to the various parts of the body by the bloodstream. Glucose is also produced from proteins and fats. When needed, glucose passes from the blood into the cells to be burned for energy. Insulin regulates the utilization of glucose and its production from carbohydrates, proteins, and fats. When insufficient amounts of insulin are produced, glucose cannot enter the cells, and proteins and fats are drawn upon as alternative fuel sources. The amount of glucose in the blood increases and, upon reaching a certain level, spills out into the urine (glycosuria). Fats are broken down into ketones, which are acidic and are excreted in the urine. Without treatment, the diabetic child will become very ill and eventually lapse into a coma.

Juvenile diabetes affects one child out of every 500 to 1,000.[1] It occurs about equally between girls and boys and is seen more frequently in whites than in nonwhites. Juvenile diabetes differs from adult-onset diabetes in several respects. As the name implies, onset is usually in childhood but may occur as late as the age of 30 and still be considered juvenile diabetes. The rate of occurrence is highest in children from 10 to 15 years of age.[2] The diabetic child is usually thin, whereas the adult-onset diabetic is often obese. The diabetic child lacks insulin throughout life and must depend on daily injections of insulin. A special diet is also required. With adult-onset diabetes, however, the pancreas continues to produce insulin but not enough to prevent blood sugar from rising at certain times, usually after meals. Treatment may take the form of diet and tablets (oral hypoglycemic agents), with no need for insulin injections. Some adult-onset diabetics do, however, need insulin injections.

Cause

In juvenile diabetes, for reasons not completely known, the number of beta cells of the Islets of Langerhans in the pancreas becomes greatly reduced. It is certain that there is a hereditary component to juvenile diabetes, not a simple transmission from parents to offspring but rather the inheritance of the susceptibility to diabetes. This susceptibility may be passed on by nondiabetic parents. What actually causes diabetes in the susceptible person? While the final answer still eludes us, we now believe that a defect in the body's immune, or defense, system may allow diabetes to develop in susceptible children under certain conditions. Normally, the immune system defends the body against the onslaught of infectious diseases; however, it may malfunction. In the diabetic, it is thought that the immune system turns against the body's own cells, seeking out and specifically destroying those cells that manufacture insulin. Such self-destructive behavior by the immune system is termed an "autoimmune response." Why this should happen in an otherwise healthy child is not yet known. It is of interest to note that many characteristics of the immune system, including the propensity to develop autoimmunity, can be inherited.

Another possibility is that diabetes is caused by a viral infection that damages the insulin-producing cells of the pancreas or triggers an autoimmune response that in turn causes the damage. The peak incidence of diagnosis of diabetes in childhood is in winter when the incidence of viral infections is highest. It must be emphasized that the possible role of viruses in causing diabetes is only a theory. Diabetes itself is *not* infectious.

Diabetes in children is not known to be caused by eating too much sugar nor is it related to the nutritional status of the child. Whatever the cause may be, the pancreatic cells are unfortunately so severely damaged that complete or permanent recovery is impossible. Although no cure is available at present, the disease can be controlled satisfactorily.

Symptoms

The onset of juvenile diabetes can be rapid (a few days) or slow (a few months), with the duration of symptoms before diagnosis being shorter with younger patients. A common symptom is increased frequency and volume of urination, accompanied by increased thirst. As the urine output increases, the child drinks large amounts to replenish fluids. A toilet-trained child may wet the bed, and an older child may get up frequently at night to void. In addition, there may be increased appetite accompanied by weight loss. Other symptoms are fatigue, irritability, moodiness, and a decline in scholastic achievement.

If the condition is allowed to persist, with the blood sugar rising and ketones being produced, the child becomes very ill and develops a complication known as "ketoacidosis." There will be dehydration, sometimes accompanied by nausea and vomiting, abdominal pains, and drowsiness. Eventually the child may fall into a coma. Unfortunately, it is all too common that medical counsel for the earlier symptoms is delayed until the child develops ketoacidosis.

Diabetes can be diagnosed by testing the urine and checking for a high blood sugar level (usually over 200 mg/dl).

Course

The insulin-producing cells in the pancreas do not suddenly stop production in the early stages of the disease. Within a month or two after the diagnosis, the pancreas may recover partially, and the insulin requirements of the patient may drop to 50 percent or less of the requirement deemed appropriate upon diagnosis. In rare instances, the newly diagnosed diabetic child may require almost no insulin at all during this period of remission or "honeymoon phase." Also at this time, the amount of insulin needed to control the level of sugar in the blood fluctuates. There is a danger of hypoglycemia (low blood sugar) when the amount of insulin given exceeds that which is necessary to keep the blood sugar at acceptable levels. This period is invariably transient, usually lasting about six weeks but occasionally lasting several months. Insulin requirements will again rise at the end of this phase, sometimes gradually and sometimes abruptly.

Retardation in growth, often associated with delayed puberty, occurs in 6 to 10 percent of diabetic children.[3] Any profound growth impairment should be regarded as abnormal and requires investigation. Menarche in diabetic girls is often delayed to about 13 years of age, but it does take place, and there are no later problems with fertility.[4] Shortly after menarche, diabetic girls tend to gain weight more easily and often become obese.

Although the life span of the diabetic child has been lengthened with the advent of insulin therapy, it is still shorter than that of the nondiabetic. It is too early to say whether recent advances in achieving better control have improved the outlook. Over the course of years, the poorly controlled diabetic is more likely to develop chronic complications which could affect the eyes, kidneys, nerves, and cardiovascular system. Kidney failure is the leading cause of death in juvenile diabetes, although it may not become apparent until 10 to 20 years after diagnosis. Blindness in young adults is a common result of diabetes. Diabetic retinopathy (disease of the retina) seems more common in persons whose disease has not been well controlled. All diabetics of 5 to 10 years from onset should have yearly retinal examinations for early detection of retinopathy. Heart attacks are another cause of death in diabetics later in life.

Psychological Aspects

There is much discussion about the psychological aspects of diabetes, both in children and in adults. Psychological factors such as stress can affect sugar and fat metabolism, probably to a large extent by causing the release of catecholamines. These hormones, secreted by the adrenal glands found above the kidneys, cause an abrupt rise in blood sugar levels. Stress can thereby render diabetic control more difficult because it causes unpredictable rises in blood sugar. Unfortunately, emotional pressures seem to be synonymous with our modern life-style and cannot be totally avoided. Exactly how best to minimize the consequences of feeling angry, frustrated, or depressed has been the subject of numerous debates and publications. The reason for the confusion may lie in the fact that different individuals respond to stress in different ways and that one form of treatment may work for one individual but not for another.

Childhood diabetes imposes a heavy responsibility on the patient and family. It requires daily commitments in such matters as assessing the urine or blood sugar levels and then deciding how best to manage the diabetes for that day. The child is placed under numerous rules and restrictions which include regular sleeping and waking hours, frequent urine or blood tests, insistence on eating all meals at set times, avoidance of "free sugars" such as ice cream and candy, and planned physical activities. There will inevitably be further restrictions at school.

There are several ways that diabetic children may react. Some feel depressed and withdraw from normal social contacts.[5] Having heard inaccurate accounts of diabetic complications, some children develop fear of treatment or fear of death. Other children feel anger and resentment at their condition and rebel by neglecting their treatment. Insecurity and self-pity are other reactions.

Adolescence is a particularly difficult time. Not only is the disease more difficult to regulate at this time because of the rapid growth spurt and monthly hormonal fluctuations in pubertal girls, but adolescents are trying to establish independence by ignoring impositions. They may fail to eat all snacks and meals, indulge in dietary indiscretions, or refuse to test the urine or blood. When parents capitulate to this behavior, it encourages even more manipulative behavior. All the reactions of the diabetic child should be dealt with sympathetically but firmly. It should be pointed out that the well-controlled diabetic, paying attention to a balanced diet and regular exercise, may be in better health than a nondiabetic.

A minority of diabetics have recurrent and seemingly intransigent problems. Some of these children use the threat of an acute diabetic complication to gain their own ends, while others have repeated episodes of ketoacidosis requiring hospitalization despite adhering to the prescribed insulin treatment. Therapy for these children is discussed in the section on treatment.

TREATMENT

Upon the diagnosis of diabetes, the child is usually admitted to the hospital where treatment is begun. Since the child is usually dehydrated because of the fluid loss from excessive urination, fluids are given intravenously, and insulin is replaced by injections. The efficacy of treatment is monitored by frequent checks of sugar in the blood and urine. During the 7 to 10 days that the newly diagnosed patient is usually in the hospital, the dose of insulin injected is adjusted according to the response of blood sugar. The patient's family and the patient, if old enough, are taught to cope with this lifelong disease.

The child whose diabetes is well controlled is usually absent from school for only a week or two after diagnosis. Follow-up as an outpatient may be required once every two to six months. Ideally, the diabetic child should be managed by a team led by one regular pediatrician specializing in diabetes, a family pediatrician, a nurse practitioner or a diabetes educator, a dietician, and the consultation services of a child guidance specialist for family emotional problems.

Most diabetic children need no further hospital admissions for diabetes, but a minority will be problematic and require several admissions during a year. Poor advice from physicians in adjusting insulin dosage, noncompliance on the part of the patient, emotional problems, and intercurrent infections are examples of factors that may jeopardize control resulting in hospitalization.

The mainstay of treatment is injected insulin. Other important adjuncts to treatment are diet and exercise.

Insulin

A fine balance between the amount of insulin given, food eaten, and exercise undertaken is needed to obtain optimal diabetic control. Adult-onset diabetes can sometimes be treated with tablets that stimulate the release of insulin from the pancreas and promote the action of insulin on body tissues. Unfortunately, the pancreas of a juvenile-onset diabetic is unable to produce almost any insulin except for a brief period shortly after diagnosis. Therefore, the diabetic child can only be treated by regular injections of insulin. Insulin cannot be given by mouth because the digestive juices in the intestines will destroy it.

Doctors try to achieve optimal control with the least imposition on the child and family. Injections are given once or twice daily; only rarely are more frequent injections needed routinely. The timing of once or twice daily injections is such that the school staff need not be involved. The first shot is given before breakfast; if a second is required, it is given before the evening meal at about 5:00 p.m. or 6:00 p.m. Injections are usually given by the parents to children under 12 years old. Because it is important for diabetic children to feel in control of their illness, as soon as they are mature enough, they are taught to give their own injections. Surprisingly, children get used to the shots, and many say that they do not hurt.

The standard insulin used in the U.S. contains 100 units of insulin per milliliter (U-100). There are three classes of insulin, based on duration of action. These are described below, together with the times when hypoglycemia is most likely to occur. The most common mode of insulin therapy is administration of a combination of fast-acting and intermediate-acting insulin given together in the same syringe once or twice daily.

Short-Acting Insulin

This is known as regular insulin, Velosulin (Nordisk-USA), Actrapid (Squibb/Novo), or Regular Iletin (Lilly) insulin. It starts acting within a half hour, has a maximum effect about two hours after injection, and lasts about four to six hours after injection. Hence, the time when hypoglycemia is most likely to occur is about two hours after injection, which is usually between midmorning and lunchtime. If a child has a second shot of insulin before dinner, hypoglycemia might occur between 7 p.m. and 9 p.m.

Intermediate-Acting Insulin

Other names for this form of insulin include Insulatard (Nordisk-USA), Monotard (Squibb/Novo), NPH, or Lente Iletin (Lilly) insulin. This type of insulin usually starts acting in one hour, has a peak action some four to six hours after the injection, and varies in duration from 10 to 24 hours. The most vulnerable period for hypoglycemia is from midafternoon to dinnertime. If a second injection of insulin is given before dinner, hypoglycemia might develop in the middle of the night. This is potentially dangerous because the child and parents are likely to be asleep, and the complication may escape detection for several hours.

Long-Acting Insulin

Also known as Ultratard (Squibb/Novo) or Ultralente Iletin (Lilly), this insulin does not start working until about four hours after injection and peaks in 12 to 18 hours. The total duration of action is between 24 and 36 hours. This type of insulin is the least frequently used.

Insulin Pump

The insulin pump has been introduced only recently. The child wears a small pump, and insulin is infused into the body through a tube and needle. The needle is inserted into the lower abdomen about a half inch under the skin and kept in place by elastic tape. The main advantage is that insulin can be provided according to the body's needs as determined by home glucose monitoring. A national trial is currently underway in the U.S. to determine if the continuous administration or frequent injections of insulin may prevent some of the long-term complications of insulin. A bolus of insulin is usually given before each meal. If sports or vigorous exercise are planned, the needle and pump should be removed.

Diet

Food raises the blood sugar; therefore, a balanced diet constitutes the second essential part of the child's treatment. The type of food, the timing, and the amount are all important factors in attaining good diabetic control. Diabetics are advised to maintain a meal plan that is reasonably consistent from day to day. "Free" sugars, such as those in candy, soft drinks, ice cream, cakes, cookies, jelly, and syrup, are to be avoided except during a hypoglycemic emergency. The caloric allowance and detailed dietary plans are negotiated with the patient and family and established on an individual basis. These children are taught to select their own food from the school menu or bring their own lunch. No special foods need be prepared in the cafeteria for the diabetic child. It is important for school personnel to understand that the delay or omission of a snack or meal may be dangerous, as it can lead to hypoglycemia.

Compliance to a given diet is usually poor, and this may stem in part from conflicting advice from pediatricians and dieticians. A further problem may arise in the female adolescent with an overconcern for slimming. Excessive reduction in food intake without concomitant reduction in insulin dosage can precipitate hypoglycemia.[6]

Exercise

Exercise is also considered an integral part of the child's treatment, as prolonged and strenuous physical exertion will lower blood sugar. All diabetics can and should be encouraged to engage in regular physical activities, preferably under supervision, and provided they are not potentially dangerous.

Family Therapy

Understanding family dynamics plays a critical part in formulating treatment strategies for children with behavior problems related to their diabetes. In the diabetic with behavioral problems who refuses to adhere to the diabetic regimen, the problem is best managed by meeting with parents and convincing them to present a united front. Disobedience should be countered by an agreed graded set of penalties. Misdemeanors in diabetic management should be treated no differently from any other transgression. For example, if a child breaks curfew by returning home late from a party, it may be appropriate to remove certain privileges, such as the use of the telephone. Similar age-appropriate measures can be used for the diabetic who persistently fails to test his or her urine or blood.

Diabetic children with psychosomatic problems often have poor school attendance and frequent episodes of ketoacidosis. Families of these children are frequently found to have the following features:

1. Emotional enmeshment or entanglement between family members.

2. Parents tend to overprotect the child and rarely allow activities outside the home.

3. Denial of any problems in the family except the medical problems associated with diabetic management.

4. Covert conflicts remain submerged and unresolved, resulting in stress and tension in the family.

5. Instead of resolving family problems, the parents are preoccupied with the patient's symptoms, which reinforces the patient's role as the

chronic invalid in the family and perpetuates the chronicity and severity of the illness.

The treatment of these children and their families is complex. The patient needs to be disengaged from the arena of parental conflict. Rarely, one may have to resort to the drastic measure of removing the child from the family environment, at least temporarily. Family therapy is based on teaching the parents and patient to understand their problems, to train them to go through the emotional stages of demonstrating their genuine feelings, and to find out how they might resolve some of their conflicts. A more complete account of this kind of family therapy is given in the book by Minuchin.[7]

SCHOOL LIFE

It is not uncommon to find diabetes intruding into the child's performance at school and also affecting the child's relationship with peers. This section will address the various ways diabetes can influence school life.

Academic Ability

Although intellectual performance is seldom affected to a large extent in most diabetics, there are several factors that can make the child fall behind in classwork.[8] Multiple hospital admissions can, of course, take the child from the classroom. Hypoglycemia induces drowsiness, irritability, and loss of concentration.[9] If a child's academic performance is uneven, it may be worth investigating whether the poor grades are occurring in subjects scheduled just before lunchtime when the risk of hypoglycemia is greatest. A snack before that particular class may bring about an improvement.

A recent study from Oxford[10] has shown that in 76 diabetic children, 29 percent were at least two years behind in reading compared with 19 percent of a control group. The children in the study who had poor diabetic control were more likely to be poor readers than those with good control. An increased incidence of behavioral disorders and psychosocial problems was also related to poor diabetic control. It may be that the self-control and organization required to follow the medical regimen for diabetes is good training for school performance.[11]

Psychosocial Aspects

School adjustment has been studied in children with diabetes. Gath et al.[12] found, in a study of 50 diabetic children and controls, that similar proportions of each group had a good adjustment at school, with behavioral and emotional problems no more prevalent in diabetic children than in nondiabetic children. This study did find a difference between the two groups in adjustment at home, with only 24 percent of diabetic children found to have a good adjustment at home compared with 62 percent of the nondiabetic children studied. They also found that mothers of diabetic children were more depressed and anxious than mothers of the controls. The emotional tone of homes of childhood diabetics reflected more conflict and strain than those of controls.

Physical Activities

The common school sports such as ice hockey, football, basketball, and skiing do not pose any special hazard to the diabetic. Some precautions should be taken, however. When a student is scheduled for gym or sports practice, either the insulin dosage should be reduced that morning or extra food eaten before the activity. During or after physical exercise, the diabetic may become hypoglycemic and require sugar immediately. The teacher should be prepared with some fruit juice, candy, or cookies. These students should carry sugar in the form of candy, sugar cubes, or specially prepared gels in a packet (Monogel) or tube (Instant Glucose, Cake Mate) or as powder in a packet (Glutose or Reactose) for emergency situations.

APPROACH TO THE CHILD WITH JUVENILE DIABETES

The schoolteacher can assume an important role in the life of the diabetic child, supplementing the part played by the parents and physician. Many children have inadequate home backgrounds, and in these cases, the teacher may play a more critical role in helping the diabetic child by providing emotional support. Understanding the medical nature of the disease is a prerequisite for helping the child achieve diabetic control and in avoiding acute emergencies. Appreciation of the anxieties of the diabetic child and the problems of pressure exerted by peers are of equal importance in helping the child adjust emotionally. In addition to academic guidance, the teacher fills an important role in career counseling.

It is important for teachers to provide the diabetic child with support and understanding without being overprotective. These children often know a great deal about their condition, and the teacher should pay attention to their needs while allowing them the benefit of the doubt in managing their own diabetes. School personnel may also have access to information about programs that may help the child grow in self-reliance and self-confidence. There are many excellent summer camps for diabetics, and parents should be informed of these when they are known to school personnel. Not only do they provide an enjoyable experience, but they expose children to others with diabetes so that they can learn how others cope. The addresses of diabetes camps can be obtained from local branches of the American Diabetes Association.

Inappropriate reactions by a teacher to a diabetic child in the classroom may vary from overconcern and overprotection to neglect and disregard. The diabetic child should not be unnecessarily restricted in any of the normal school activities. It is completely inappropriate for a child to be deprived of participating in a specific activity that is allowed by the physician and the family just because the teacher has particular fears about diabetes or does not have confidence in handling a situation such as hypoglycemia.

Singling out the diabetic child for special attention should be avoided. Few children like to be fussed over in front of their peers. Indeed, many diabetic children do not want their friends to know about their condition for fear of being considered different. The teacher should allow the child to have snacks and be excused for urine or blood tests as inconspicuously as possible.

Keeping the child in detention as a form of punishment is potentially dangerous because delay or omission of a snack or meal can lead to hypoglycemia.

Absences from School

Prolonged absence from school is unusual. If a child misses school often, the reason should be investigated. Some families become overprotective and unnecessarily restrict activities or allow patterns of hypochondria to develop. Teachers should inform the school nurse of frequent absences. It may be appropriate to contact or meet with the child's parents and physician, nurse practitioner, diabetes educator, or social worker involved with the child. From this meeting, a strategy may be formulated to help the child and family minimize the factors detrimental to school performance.

When absences occur, arrangements should be made for schoolwork to be made up, either through tutoring or take-home assignments. When teachers insist that work be made up for all days missed, and all assignments are handed in and then graded as rigidly as the work of other children, children who malinger to get out of schoolwork soon find this activity less satisfying.

Avoidance of Certain Activities

It may be useful to delve into the reasons why a child avoids participating in certain activities. Diabetic children are in a powerful position to utilize their condition to avoid those activities they dislike. They can pretend to experience symptoms of hypoglycemia, omit a snack and actually become hypoglycemic, and even precipitate genuine ketoacidosis by self-induced emotional arousal. There are examples of children who develop ketoacidotic vomiting during school exams.[13] These actions amount to "emotional blackmail" and are particularly difficult to manager, especially by teachers unfamiliar with the disease and who might be afraid of the life-threatening nature of these complications. When there are questions about a child's motives, a teacher or school nurse should confer with the parents or the child's physician about ways to determine which symptoms are genuine and which are contrived. Parents cannot know whether the child is using the disease to get his or her own way at school unless they are informed of it. If such manipulative patterns of behavior are allowed to continue through the school years, the child may not mature normally or develop the necessary scholastic or social skills for adulthood.

Career Guidance

The teacher will often be asked to advise students on the selection of a career. One study showed that many teachers and counselors were unaware of the vocational and educational opportunities available to assist diabetics.[14] Diabetic children should be encouraged to pursue their own fields of interest, but it should be borne in mind that they are barred or discouraged from certain occupations such as piloting aircraft, driving public service vehicles, high-rise construction, fire and police forces, merchant navy, and armed forces. In other areas, well-controlled diabetics can perform as well as others and should be encouraged in careers in areas compatible with their academic abilities and ambitions.

Diet

It is important to discuss the child's diet with parents, so that transgressions of the diet at school can be minimized. Although adherence to the prescribed diet will enable better diabetic control, this has to be balanced against the realities of childhood. Undue dietary restrictions could result in rebellion to the entire diabetic treatment strategy. In general, if diabetic control is satisfactory, a moderate degree of latitude in dietary regulation may be permitted. School parties, where cookies, cakes, and candies are a frequent part of the refreshment menu, are times when lapses may be permitted. It is helpful if the teacher inconspicuously has crackers instead of cookies, or fruit instead of candy, available for the diabetic child. When lapses become a daily event, parents need to be notified.

Daily Schedule

Scheduling of activities and classes must be considered in the light of the child's condition. Indeed, with proper planning there is nothing the diabetic child cannot participate in. For instance, if a sports event or a school outing is planned, the child could modify insulin intake and meals accordingly. Supervision is recommended if the activity is likely to be long or physically strenuous. When there is a change in the class routine, such as a class trip and during special school days, the diabetic child should be allowed to maintain his or her own schedule for lunch or a snack. Meals or snacks should not be delayed because of the danger of hypoglycemia. These children should not be assigned the last lunch period, nor should gym classes be scheduled just before lunch.

Lavatory Use

The diabetic child may need to go to the lavatory frequently, but if this becomes excessive (more often than once every one to two hours), the parents should be informed, as it may be necessary to adjust the insulin dose or have other measures taken. Older children may change their own insulin dose based in part on these symptoms of more frequent urination. If a child is required to test the urine or blood several times a day, the teacher should allow time for this and also make arrangements for privacy.

MEDICAL PROBLEMS THAT MAY OCCUR IN THE CLASSROOM

In childhood diabetes, the major medical problems that can occur during the school day have to do with fluctuations in the blood sugar, resulting in either a high level of sugar in the blood or an extremely low level of sugar. A child sent home with one of these problems should always be accompanied. It should be determined if someone will be at home to care for the child.

Hypoglycemia

Overdosage with insulin can lead to a drop in blood sugar (hypoglycemia or "insulin shock"). It is imperative to recognize it and treat it at once, as the consequences of delay may be serious. Very low blood sugar levels can cause seizures, which could result in brain damage.

Symptoms may include one or more of the following:

- inattentiveness, inability to concentrate
- daydreaming
- sweating
- hunger
- dizziness, lightheadedness
- pallor
- confusion
- inappropriate responses or behavior
- tremulousness
- seizure
- drowsiness
- coma

Symptoms differ from child to child, and it is important for parents to inform the teacher how their child usually behaves when this occurs. The child will probably look normal during an attack. The only clue might be lack of coordination, irritability, or behavior that is out of character. Occasionally, the behavior is quite bizarre: a highly publicized news report tells of a diabetic who was shot and killed by a police officer because his unusual hypoglycemic behavior was mistaken for a criminal activity.

Emergency treatment is as follows:

1. Give some form of sugar at once: candy, fruit juice, sugar cubes, or soda (not diet soda). The child may need some coaxing to eat or drink. Improvement should take place within 10 minutes.

2. The child should then be given additional food and can resume normal school activities.

3. If there is no improvement, call the parents or a physician.

4. If the child cannot take anything by mouth or is developing seizures, an injection of glucagon should be given intramuscularly as soon as possible. The school nurse should keep a bottle of glucagon available in the school medicine cabinet.

Ketoacidosis

Elevation of blood sugar may be a result of insufficient insulin or be provoked by infection or acute emotional stress. The blood sugar is unable to enter the cells, and the body tissues draw on other fuel sources for energy, such as stored fat and protein. When fat is converted into energy, some of it is broken down into ketones or ketoacids. These ketoacids build up in the bloodstream and may spill into the urine. One or more of the following symptoms are usually present:

- frequent urination
- excessive thirst
- dehydration
- drowsiness
- nausea
- vomiting
- heavy or labored breathing
- breath with sweet smell characteristic of ketones
- abdominal pains
- coma

Ketoacidosis does not come on suddenly or unexpectedly. It usually takes several hours to develop. The diagnosis can be confirmed by testing the urine for sugar and ketones, both of which should be high. The blood sugar will also be raised.

Treatment should include the following:

1. Drinking large volumes of sugar-free fluid, such as diet soda, water, or soup.

2. Insulin injection; additional regular insulin can be given after consultation with the parents or with a doctor.

3. Ketoacidosis may take several hours to abate. It is advisable to inform the parents so that the child can be taken home for treatment and observation.

Injury

If an injury necessitates hospital treatment, the child should be accompanied by a teacher or school nurse to the hospital and the physicians or nurses informed of his or her condition.

Minor injuries are treated in the conventional manner; that is, all cuts should be cleaned thoroughly and dressings applied. Infected wounds may take longer to heal in the poorly controlled diabetic than in other children.

FOSTERING CLASSMATES' UNDERSTANDING

Classmates have a strong influence on diabetic children's behavior. They may deliberately provoke them or unwittingly place temptations in their way, such as encouraging them to eat sweets or to play on after they have insisted that they must break for a snack. Diabetic children who must carry candy for hypoglycemic emergencies sometimes complain that their friends constantly deplete their supply. Peer pressure can be so great that diabetic children may face segregation if they do not comply. The solution to the latter problem is to have sugar in the form of a gel or powder, which does not look like candy.

Teachers can play a role in helping diabetic children stand up to group pressure. At the same time, they should speak to the class, explaining what diabetes is and enlisting moral support for the diabetic child. It may be worthwhile to invite speakers experienced in the management of diabetes to address the class. Individual troublemakers should be spoken to in private.

Since children spend a major portion of their time at school, the teacher can play a critical role, especially when it is integrated into the goals of the parents and physicians. The teacher with insight into the interaction of the child and family can exert a more effective influence on the emotional maturation of the child. Ultimately one hopes that the teacher can educate the diabetic child in the fullest sense of the word, to foster a more mature individual better equipped to face the outside world.

REFERENCES

1. C. J. Kyllo and F. Q. Nuttall, "Prevalence of Diabetes Mellitus in School-Aged Children in Minnesota," *Diabetes* 27 (1978): 57–60.
2. R. E. LaPorte, H. A. Fishbein, A. L. Drash, L. H. Kuller, et al., "The Pittsburgh Insulin-Dependent Diabetes Mellitus Registry—The Incidence of IDDM in Allegheny County, Pennsylvania (1965–1976)," *Diabetes* 30 (1981): 279–84.
3. J. D. Baum, "Clinical Management of Diabetes Mellitus," in *Clinical Paediatric Endocrinology,* ed. C. G. D. Brook (Oxford: Blackwells, 1981).
4. B. Weber, "Physiological Aspects of Diabetes Mellitus," in *Clinical Paediatric Endocrinology,* ed. C. G. D. Brook (Oxford: Blackwells, 1981).
5. D. P. Orr, M. P. Golden, G. Myers, and D. G. Marrero, "Characteristics of Adolescents with Poorly Controlled Diabetes Referred to a Tertiary Care Center," *Diabetes Care* 6 (1983): 170–75.
6. R. B. Tattersall and J. Lowe, "Diabetes in Adolescence," *Diabetologia* 20 (1981): 517–23.
7. S. Minuchin, *Families and Family Therapy* (Cambridge, MA: Harvard University Press, 1975).
8. D. W. Guthrie and R. A. Guthrie, "Diabetes in Adolescence," *American Journal of Nursing* 75 (1975): 1740–44.
9. C. S. Holmes, J. T. Hayford, J. L. Gonzalez, and J. A. Weydert, "A Survey of Cognitive Functioning at Different Glucose Levels in Diabetic Persons," *Diabetes Care* 6 (1983): 180–85.
10. A. Gath, M. A. Smith, and J. D. Baum, "Emotional, Behavioural, and Educational Disorders in Diabetic Children," *Archives of Diseases in Childhood* 55 (1980): 371–75.
11. S. Ahnsjo, K. Humble, Y. Larsson, G. Settergren-Carlsson, and G. Sterky, "Personality Changes and Social Adjustment during the First Three Years of Diabetes in Children," *Acta Paediatric Scandinavica* 70 (1981): 321–27.

12. Gath, Smith, and Baum, "Emotional, Behavioural and Educational Disorders," pp. 371–75.
13. A. L. Kinmonth, M. K. Lindsay, and J. D. Baum, "Social and Emotional Complications in a Clinical Trial among Adolescents with Diabetes Mellitus," *British Medical Journal* 286 (1983): 952–54.
14. B. N. Collier, "The Adolescent with Diabetes and the Public School: A Misunderstanding," *Personnel Guidance Journal* 47 (1969): 753–57.

RESOURCES

Suggested Reading

Baker, Lester, and Lyen, Kenneth. "Childhood Diabetes Mellitus." In *Diabetes and Obesity* edited by B. N. Brodoff and S. J. Bleicher, Baltimore, MD: Williams and Wilkins, 1982.

Chase, H. Peter, M.D. *Understanding Juvenile Diabetes*. University of Colorado Medical Center, 4200 East Ninth Ave., Container C233, Denver, CO 80262.

Craig, Oman, FRCP. *Childhood Diabetes and Its Management*. Stoneham, MA: Butterworths, 1982.

Travis, Luther B., M.D. *An Instructional Aid on Juvenile Diabetes Mellitus*. Austin, TX: American Diabetes Association, South Texas Affiliate, Inc.

Useful Addresses

American Diabetes Association, 650 Fifth Ave., New York, NY 10020.
Juvenile Diabetes Foundation, 23 E. 26th St., New York, NY 10010.

Diabetes Identification

Medic Alert Foundation, P.O. Box 1009, Turlock, CA 95380.

Identification cards can be obtained from the American Diabetes Association (address above); Ames Company (Division of Miles Laboratories, Inc., Elkhart, IN 46514); and Becton Dickinson (Becton Dickinson Consumer Products, P.O. Box 5000, Rochelle Park, NJ 07662).

Epilepsy

by Claire M. Chee, R.N. and Robert R. Clancy, M.D.

OVERVIEW

Seizures are a common symptom of neurological disorders affecting children and adolescents. A seizure is defined as a sudden, brief, temporary state of abnormal brain function due to uncontrolled electrical discharges in the brain. The seizure may be manifested as an abrupt disturbance of consciousness, muscle control, or body sensation.

Although the terms "seizure" and "epilepsy" are frequently used interchangeably, not all seizures are epileptic in nature. A seizure that is provoked by a medical disorder, such as low blood sugar, drug intoxication, or infection does not indicate a diagnosis of epilepsy. Neither does a single unprovoked seizure without recurrence. The diagnosis of epilepsy is reserved for recurrent (two or more), unprovoked seizures. Because of the stigmata and superstition generally associated with the term "epilepsy," the comparable term "seizure disorder" is frequently used.

Epilepsy can arise at any age, but there are three age periods during childhood when it is more likely to begin: under age two, from five to seven years of age, and at the onset of puberty. Approximately 80 percent of all epileptics are diagnosed before the age of 20.

Epilepsy is an "invisible" condition except when the seizures occur and is not required by law to be reported. For these reasons, the exact incidence of epilepsy is unknown. It is estimated that about four out of every 100 children have this condition.[1,2] The actual number of seizures experienced by epileptics can vary widely—from as few as two seizures in a lifetime to multiple episodes each day.

Most children with epilepsy can live happy and productive lives, particularly if they are free of co-existing neurological problems. It is imperative that the child, family, school, and physician work together to optimize attendance and performance in the appropriate classroom. This chapter will aid in the understanding of epilepsy and provide guidelines in developing relationships with epileptic children and their families.

Cause

In some children, recurring seizures are caused by an identifiable condition, such as asphyxiation at birth, tumor, injury to the brain, or meningitis. This is called "symptomatic epilepsy," in that the seizures reflect a serious nervous system insult. Affected children may display additional signs of the injury or disorder, such as paralysis, loss of hearing or vision, or cognitive impairment. In the remainder of children with epilepsy (about 80 percent), the exact cause of the recurring seizures cannot be determined even after an exhaustive neurologic evaluation. These children are said to have "idiopathic epilepsy." Children with inherited forms of epilepsy are usually included in this category, even though the cause is presumed to be a subtle derangement of brain structure or chemistry.

Course

Epilepsy is not necessarily a permanent condition. Many children will eventually enjoy a lifelong remission of seizures and not require anticonvulsants. It is difficult to predict precisely the outcome in a given individual, as many factors act together to determine the severity and duration of a seizure disorder. Probably the most influential factor is the classification of the seizures. Some forms of epilepsy are recognized as "benign," because the seizures are easily manageable with drugs and usually remit with the passage of time. Examples include petit mal epilepsy, simple febrile seizures, and an inherited form of focal seizures called Rolandic Epilepsy. Other factors that may play a role in determining the prognosis include the age of the child when the first seizure appeared, the length of time and number of drugs required to bring the seizures under control, the presence of other neurologic handicaps, such as mental retardation or cerebral palsy, and, possibly, the result of the EEG examination.

Many physicians will consider stopping anticonvulsant medication if the child remains entirely seizure-free on medication for four years, is intellectully and neurologically normal, and has no epileptic abnormalities on the EEG examination. An estimated 70 percent of children who satisfy these criteria will remain free of seizures after the drugs are discontinued. However the remainder will relapse and require the reinstitution of medications.

Classification

The most widely used system for classification is the "International Classification of the Epilepsies." In this scheme, the seizure disorder is classified by the kind of seizure the child has (clinical seizure type), cause of the disorder, and the results of the electroencephalogram (EEG, or "brain wave test").

Clinical seizure types can be broadly divided into two categories: "partial" or "generalized" (see Table 1). A partial seizure results from an abnormal electrical discharge in a limited portion of the brain. Consequently, the expression of the seizure is also limited. For example, it may be confined to an abnormal movement of an arm or a disturbance of vision. The two most common partial seizures seen in school-aged children are complex partial seizures (also called "temporal lobe" or "psychomotor seizures") and elementary partial seizures (also called "simple focal seizures").

Table 1. Commonly Seen Seizures in the School-Aged Child

Partial Seizures	
Elementary or Simple Focal (No change in consciousness)	Complex Partial or Temporal Lobe (Accompanied by some disturbance of consciousness)
(Either can spread and become generalized)	
Generalized Seizures	
Tonic-Clonic or Grand Mal	Absence or Petit Mal

Generalized seizures result from abnormal electrical discharges involving all portions of the brain simultaneously and often include a disturbance of consciousness or abnormal motor activity of both halves of the body. Common examples of generalized seizures are the tonic-clonic seizures (also called grand mal or major motor seizures) and absence seizures (also called petit mal seizures). Partial seizures occasionally spread from their limited area of origin to engage the entire brain and thus become "secondarily generalized" (see Figure 1).

Figure 1. Examples of Focal and Generalized Seizures

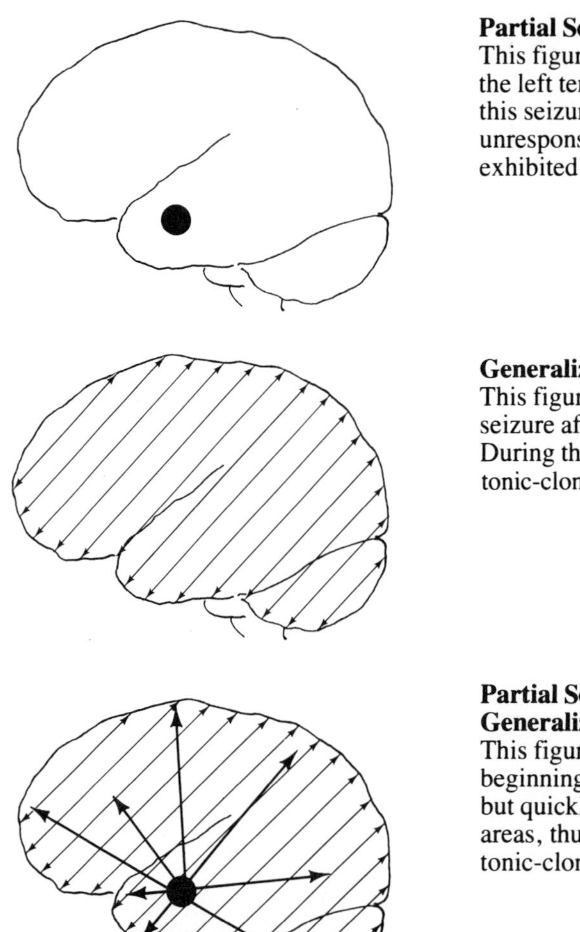

Partial Seizure
This figure depicts a seizure in the left temporal lobe. During this seizure the child was unresponsive, stared blankly, and exhibited lip smacking.

Generalized Seizure
This figure depicts a generalized seizure affecting the entire brain. During this seizure the child had a tonic-clonic seizure.

Partial Seizure with Generalized Spread
This figure depicts a seizure beginning in the temporal lobe but quickly spreading to all brain areas, thus provoking a generalized tonic-clonic convulsion.

CLINICAL SEIZURE TYPES AND FIRST AID PROCEDURES

Seizures are not painful, and the child retains no memory for most types of convulsions. To the onlooker, seizures may seem to continue for hours, but they actually persist for only seconds to minutes. They usually end spontaneously before medical help can be obtained. The most important role for the teacher is to remain calm, provide the student with appropriate first aid measures, appear accepting of the child during the attack, and reassure onlookers that everything is under control.

Medical help should be sought immediately under the following circumstances: (1) if the child has just experienced his or her first seizure or a new type of seizure; (2) if the seizure lasted longer than 10 minutes; (3) if the child suffered a series of seizures without regaining consciousness; (4) if the child was injured from the seizure; (5) if normal breathing has not resumed after the seizure; and (6) if the child requests it.

The most common clinical seizure types and first aid measures recommended for each are described below.

Complex Partial Seizures (Psychomotor or Temporal Lobe)

Manifestations

These partial seizures are called complex because their manifestations include a disturbance of consciousness, thought, or behavior in addition to possible involvement of the muscles or the senses. The seizure often begins in the temporal lobe or its connections and may last for several minutes. A warning or "aura" often announces to the child its impending onset. Dizziness, flashing lights, or an emotion, such as fear, are common examples of such auras. Although this seizure type may manifest itself in many different ways, the presentation tends to be consistent or stereotyped in each individual. Complex partial seizures may be accompanied by purposeless involuntary activities (called "automatisms"), such as lip-smacking, chewing, sucking movements, picking at clothes, wringing of hands, fumbling with articles, or pacing in circles. Other characteristic seizure activities might include the sudden cessation of ongoing activity with blank staring or a dazed facial expression and unawareness of or inability to respond to the environment. The child is not violent or aggressive during the seizure but may struggle or resist if forcefully restrained.

First Aid

Use a calm, reassuring voice when talking to the child but remember that he or she may not be able to fully understand or reply to your commands. Do not try to forceably hold or restrain the child or force anything into the mouth. This may provoke the child to struggle or resist. Allow the seizure to run its course and remove harmful objects from the child's path. Arrange for someone to remain with the student until he or she is fully awake and reoriented.

Elementary Partial Seizures (Simple Focal Seizures)

Manifestations

In simple partial seizures, there is a limited disturbance in motor activity or sensation without clouding of consciousness. Stiffening or jerking of one limb or one side of the body may occur, or there may be a tingling sensation in a similarly limited body region (sensory seizure). Simple focal motor seizures frequently begin in the face or a hand because these two areas have large representation in the brain (see Figure 2).

First Aid

Remain with the child. Since consciousness is preserved with this type of seizure, the student may be comforted and calmed by verbal reassurance. Do not attempt to restrain a body part (arm or leg) that is shaking or jerking because of seizure.

Figure 2. Organization of Muscle Control in the Brain

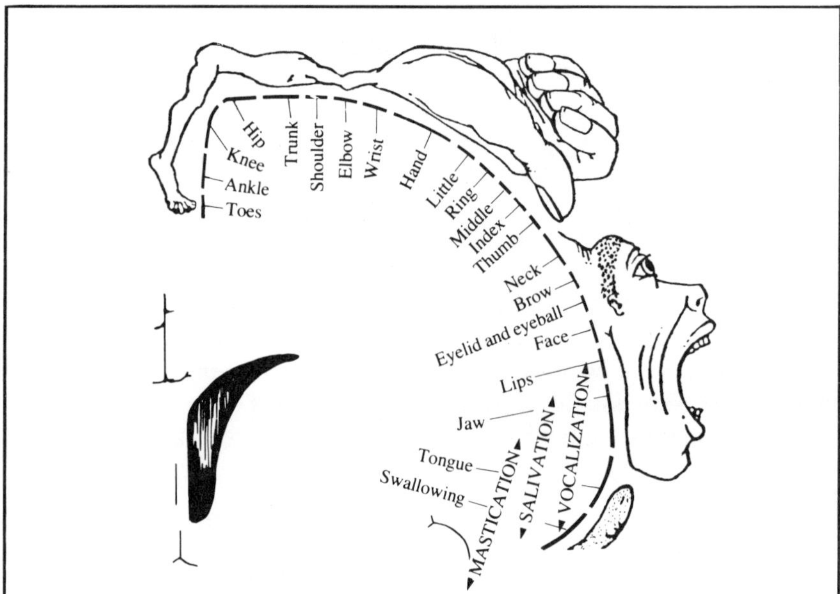

Depicts the organization of the muscle control area of the brain. Note the exaggerated representation of the face and hand. Focal seizures that begin in the motor control area commonly affect the face and hand.*

*Reprinted with permission of Macmillan Publishing Company from *The Cerebral Cortex of Man*, by Wilder Penfield and Theodore Rasmussen. Copyright 1950 by Macmillan Publishing Company renewed 1978 by Theodore Rasmussen.

Generalized Tonic-Clonic Seizures (Grand Mal or Major Motor Seizures)

Manifestations

This is the most dramatic and alarming type of seizure to witness. The youngster suddenly loses consciousness and falls to the ground. As air is forcefully expelled from the lungs, a groan or "epileptic cry" may be heard. The muscles first become rigid (tonic phase), and the back and neck may arch, followed by coarse, repetitive jerking movements of the arms and legs (clonic phase). The tongue may be bitten and bladder or bowel control lost. Breathing may become labored and, at times, momentarily cease. A pale or bluish complexion is then frequently noted. Tonic-clonic seizures usually last one to three minutes and are commonly followed by confusion, exhaustion, muscle fatigue, and headache. Immediate medical attention is necessary if the child passes from one seizure to another without regaining consciousness or if a single seizure lasts more than 10 minutes. Since this type of seizure is draining, the child may require rest for several minutes to an hour before being encouraged to resume school activities. Usually the student can continue the normal school day.

First Aid

Do not leave the child to go for help but provide the following first aid measures immediately:

1. Help the child into a lying position and put something soft under the head.
2. Loosen the child's collar or other tight clothing and remove eyeglasses.
3. Do not restrain the child's movements or attempt to force anything into the mouth.
4. Remove any hard or sharp objects from the vicinity of the youngster.
5. Remember that you cannot stop the seizure; it will run its course.
6. After the seizure is over, turn the child's head to one side to allow saliva to drain from the mouth. Do not give food or water until the student is fully awake.
7. If breathing does not resume after the attack, begin mouth-to-mouth resuscitation immediately.
8. Stay with the child until he or she is fully awake.

Absence Seizures (Petit Mal or Lapse Seizures)

Manifestations

The hallmark of the absence seizure is an abrupt alteration of consciousness, often accompanied by a blank facial expression, repetitive eye-blinking, and the cessation of speech or activity. Absence seizures may mimic simple daydreaming and can be aborted by calling to or touching the child. Absence seizures are typically brief (less than 30 seconds) and are not accompanied by falling or marked change of posture. The child may not realize that the seizure has occurred. If untreated, a child may have 50 to 200 or more "lapses" a day and, consequently, miss a significant amount of teaching. This type of seizure is relatively easy to diagnose by EEG and is usually brought under good control with medication. Some symptoms the teacher might detect in the classroom include frequent "daydreaming," inability to complete a sentence or follow a simple direction, and a blank stare.

First Aid

No specific first aid measures are required. The teacher should inform the school nurse and family of the occurrence. Once the child is on proper medication, these seizures generally will be under excellent control.

COGNITIVE, NEUROLOGICAL, AND BEHAVIORAL ABNORMALITIES THAT MAY COEXIST WITH EPILEPSY

The majority of children with seizure disorders are otherwise medically, neurologically, and behaviorally normal and function entirely well between seizures. However, a small number of children with epilepsy manifest additional signs of neurologic impairment and require thoughtful management from a multidisciplinary team to ensure their full personal and academic development. Compounding neurologic abnormalities are more likely to appear in children whose seizure disorders falls into the symptomatic category (see Cause).

Intellectual Status

The incidence of any cognitive impairment (IQ less than 70) among epileptics is estimated at 2 to 9 percent.[3,4] Severe mental retardation occurs in a much smaller percentage of affected children.[5,6] Reliable estimates of the incidence of more subtle learning disabilities, such as dyslexia or perceptual impairment, are unavailable but may approach 20 percent of the group.[7]

Physical Handicaps

Only a small percentage of children with seizure disorders have a motor handicap (cerebral palsy) severe enough to limit physical activities, such as running, climbing, or walking. Conversely, the incidence of epilepsy among children affected with cerebral palsy is reported to be as high as 35 percent, depending on the type of cerebral palsy.[8] The incidence of minor disturbances of muscle control (clumsiness or awkwardness) is unknown, but it may be higher than that of cerebral palsy. Less frequently observed physical handicaps include hearing or vision impairment that cannot be corrected with hearing aids or glasses.

Behavioral Characteristics

No specific personality profile has been described for school-aged children. However, considerable evidence suggests that behavioral problems appear more frequently in children with epilepsy compared with their counterparts with chronic nonneurologic illnesses.[9,10] Behavioral disturbances that can emerge include the attention deficit disorder (ADD), characterized by a reduced attention span, low tolerance for frustration, and, sometimes, hyperactivity. Some children have serious problems controlling aggression or hostility (verbal and sometimes physical) in response to seemingly trivial provocation. Drugs used to treat epilepsy may provoke the unwanted behavior in some patients with seizures.

Controversy surrounds the relationship between epilepsy and aggression and also the role of temporal lobe epilepsy in the predisposition to psychopathology or other behavioral disturbances. In adults with temporal lobe epilepsy (see Complex Partial Seizures), characteristic behavioral traits such as excessive negativism, apathy, withdrawal, humorless sobriety, dependency, and loss of sexual interest or appetite are sometimes described.[11] It is impossible to determine whether these behavioral traits result from the underlying neurologic injury that provoked the seizures or from the repeated minor disturbances of brain function caused by the recurring seizures. Also, a poor self-image and difficulties in obtaining employment may foster these undesirable personality characteristics.

MEDICAL EVALUATION AND TREATMENT

Diagnosis

A correct diagnosis of epilepsy rests heavily on a detailed description of the events that comprise the abnormal attack. Since the student may not recall the event and a physician is rarely present during an attack, the family or teacher is called upon to provide the details of the episode. The teacher who witnesses a seizure should take careful note of the sequence of events and later record them on paper. The physician will decide whether the abnormal attack represented a seizure. Children may demonstrate a variety of nonepileptic disorders that abruptly interrupt normal brain function, including simple fainting attacks, breath-holding spells, low blood sugar, daydreaming, or migraine headaches.

A medical evaluation for seizures includes detailed questioning and thorough neurologic examination of the child, the existence of prior neurologic disturbances, the use of prescribed or illicit drugs, and the presence of epilepsy in close relatives. This clinical evaluation is often supplemented by laboratory tests which might include blood tests, an electroencephalogram, and an x-ray examination (CAT scan).

Treatment

Anticonvulsants

The mainstay of the treatment of seizure disorders is the faithful daily administration of anticonvulsant (which literally means "against seizures") medications, with the ideal goal of completely eliminating seizures with no adverse side effects. This cannot be achieved for all children. If several types of seizures are exhibited or if seizure control is inadequate on a single medication, more than one drug may be needed. The amount of drug in the blood that is available to the nervous system can be determined by laboratory tests. Appropriate dosages have been established for each anticonvulsant to assure seizure control without risking overmedication. However, individual sensitivity to a given drug may vary, requiring adjustment of the dosage.

Until a few years ago, many anticonvulsants were administered three to four times a day. This required taking medicine during regular school hours, which placed an added responsibility on school personnel and constantly reminded the student of the chronic disorder. Now, many anticonvulsants can be given safely twice a day—in the morning and at night. When anticonvulsants must be given three times a day, an effort is made to schedule the third dose after school. Taking medications should become part of the child's daily routine. A parent generally gives the young child the anticonvulsant, but by adolescence, the responsibility should be the student's. Taking medicine each day can become a nuisance, and occasionally, the adolescent will rebel by refusal. Also, poor compliance can be an adolescent's way of controlling the environment and is generally not seen in children with a healthy attitude toward the disorder. Proper education by health personnel, a supportive family, and an understanding school system will provide the youngster with the empathy needed to cope with taking medications faithfully.

The type of seizure disorder largely determines the choice of medication. For example, phenobarbital, often effective in controlling grand mal seizures, has little value for petit mal attacks. Conversely, Ethosuximide (Zarontin) may completely abort petit mal seizures but has little efficacy in grand mal seizures. If a drug is ineffective or produces objectionable side effects, an alternative medication is chosen. Frequently used anticonvulsants are listed in Table 2.

Anticonvulsants can produce a wide variety of side effects. Side effects can range from an allergic reaction (fever, enlarged lymph nodes, and a skin rash) to an upset stomach, gum swelling, and increased facial or body hair—depending on the type of medication and duration of administration. Behavioral side effects are most common with barbiturates (phenobarbital, Mebaral, Mysoline). They may be brief and subtle or prolonged and dramatic. Some parents note a disturbance in mood, concentration, impulse control, and sleeping habits. Cognitive ability per se is not affected by phenobarbital,[12] but school performance could suffer if the behavior disturbance is severe. Individual variations in drug sensitivity make it impossible to predict which children will have side effects.

Excessive medication usually results in lethargy or somnolence, slurred speech, double vision, unsteady walking, tremors, or mental confusion. These symptoms will resolve when the drug is discontinued or the dosage reduced. The child with poorly controlled seizures who is on large doses of several medications in an attempt to reduce seizure frequency is most vulnerable to the development of drug intoxication.

Alternative Treatment Methods

Adequate seizure control is never achieved in some children despite multiple combinations of medication. In these refractory seizure conditions, alternative treatment methods, in addition to anticonvulsant therapy, can be tried. Success is usually limited, however. Hypnosis, relaxation techniques, biofeedback, and special diets are sometimes tried as an adjunct to conventional therapy but, again, are not recommended as the primary mode of treatment. In a selected small number of children who are incapacitated with uncontrolled seizures, neurosurgery may be helpful.

Table 2. Frequently Used Anticonvulsants

Trade Name	Generic Name	Common Use	Possible Side Effects
Dilantin	phenytoin	Most types of seizures except absence (petit mal)	Increased body hair, gum overgrowth, tremor, slurred speech, loss of coordination, double vision, confusion, upset stomach, acne
Luminal	phenobarbital	Most types of seizures except absence (petit mal)	Hyperactivity, lethargy, rash, drowsiness
Mysoline	primidone	Complex partial seizures (psychomotor, temporal lobe); tonic-clonic (grand mal)	Fatigue, drowsiness, loss of appetite, irritability, nausea, vomiting, dizziness
Tegretol	carbamazepine	Complex partial (psychomotor, temporal lobe), generalized tonic-clonic (grand mal)	Drowsiness, dizziness, rash, blurred vision, lethargy
Zarontin	ethosuximide	Absence (petit mal)	Hiccups, drowsiness, hyperactivity, nausea, vomiting, headache
Depakene	valproic acid	Absence (petit mal); tonic-clonic	Nausea, vomiting, temporary hair loss, indigestion, dizziness, sedation, weight gain, tremor
Clonopin	clonazepam	Absence (petit mal); tonic-clonic	Rash, lethargy, dizziness, nausea, vomiting, tremor, unsteadiness, drooling

Medical Alert Bracelets and Protective Helmets

A youngster with a seizure disorder should wear a medical alert bracelet or necklace providing pertinent information, such as the individual's name, address, diagnosis, physician's name, and emergency phone number. Adolescents who are reluctant to wear such a bracelet because it draws attention to their seizure disorder may agree to carry a wallet medical alert card.

A protective helmet, resembling a hockey helmet, can be useful to youngsters with persistent seizures who frequently fall and strike their heads. Parents can attempt to make the helmet as appealing as possible by decorating it with decals; however, to the child the helmet represents a glaringly visible stigma of the disability. It is generally accepted only by the very young school-aged child. Older children refuse to wear helmets because they are hot, unattractive, and provoke ridicule.

PSYCHOSOCIAL ASPECTS

In a very real sense, epilepsy represents both an acute and chronic disorder. The acute nature of the condition is reflected by the unpredictable and uncontrollable attacks of seizures that render the child temporarily helpless and incompetent. The chronic aspects of epilepsy include functioning despite the fear of an impending convulsion, taking medicine regularly, and interacting daily with a naive and sometimes unaccepting society. The child who has infrequent seizures has an especially difficult time accepting the diagnosis compared with the child who has numerous seizures, which reinforce the reality that the condition exists.

Many physicians confine their involvement to the immediate medical or neurologic aspects of the seizure disorder. What caused the seizures? What type of seizure did the child experience? What medication should be used? How effectively are the seizures controlled? The physician's attention is thus heavily focused on the acute aspects of epilepsy—the relatively brief but dramatic seizures. Less attention is directed to the quality of life between the seizures—the evolving process of personal adjustment and growth within the family, classroom, and society. Therefore, the child's needs in these areas must be satisfied by the informed collaboration of the child, the family, and the school.

Emotional Complications

The intrusion of a chronic, socially handicapping illness into the normal turmoil of growth and development may lay the foundation for future maladaptive behavior. Seizures occurring in the first and second decade of life frequently have a noticeable impact on the youngster's psychological development. This is a period of rich personal experiences and growth, when feelings of self-worth, acceptance, and confidence should emerge along with independence from strong parental supervision. The seizure disorder, however, will necessitate dependence on family, physicians, and medication. To lessen the conflict between dependence and independence, the child may passively submit to many unnecessary restrictions, sever close relationships, and become socially withdrawn, argumentative, or disruptive at school and at home. Also, the child comes to believe that the seizure disorder controls his or her life and dictates what he or she can and cannot do. Insecurity, anger, bitterness, frustration, a poor self-image and bleak expectations for the future may develop. Later, there can be secrecy regarding the disorder, as lack of understanding subjects the individual to discrimination.

Epilepsy can disrupt the development of competence in the child. Parents who want their child to be seizure-free sometimes become overprotective and keep their child from situations they fear may precipitate a seizure. For example, if they observe the child performing a task with difficulty, they may excuse the child from the task altogether. The child is thus deprived of an opportunity to become competent in that task. As this overprotection continues, the child misses the chance to develop the basic skills and confidence necessary for adulthood. As time passes, the parents realize that the child lacks the skills and self-assurance of his or her peers and begin to regard the child as incompetent. This attitude is transmitted to the child, further undermining self-confidence and the desire to acquire further skills.

Some epileptic children respond hysterically to the psychological stress of their disorder. Feeling unable to control their lives, they attempt to control the family environment through "pseudo" or false seizures. Subconsciously, this is done to gain parental attention but, instead, frequently leads to parental alienation. Additionally, adolescents with a long-standing seizure disorder newly brought under control may similarly develop false seizures because of their inability to cope with the demands or expectations of their seizure-free life-style. In most instances, these untoward psychological effects can be eliminated by appropriate psychiatric intervention.

Marriage and Employment

Childhood epilepsy may have long-term detrimental effects on employment and marriage. However, if the child has established independence and has feelings of self-worth, he or she will have the normal social contacts and experiences that form the basis for deep personal relationships and marriage. Long-term studies have shown that more men than women refrain from marriage because of their seizure disorder.[13] The likelihood of matrimony for women is good.

Three main factors affect the employment of epileptics: 1) the disorder and its associated neurologic problems; 2) the social adjustment of the individual; and 3) the prejudice of employers and coworkers. Some of these issues can be ameliorated by achieving optimal seizure control; realistic prevocational counseling and planning; and support by family, friends, and physicians. Some employers would not knowingly hire an epileptic for fear of an increased rate of accidents or absenteeism. Fortunately, many employers no longer discriminate against epileptics but judge applicants on the basis of their personal qualifications. If the epileptic has a healthy mental outlook and self-confidence, the chances of gainful employment are the same as those for the nonepileptic. Many studies of handicapped workers have shown that accidents and absenteeism are not problems.[14]

SCHOOL LIFE

Class Placement

The child should be placed in a regular classroom if seizures are infrequent and intelligence normal. This helps promote normal academic and social development. If a learning disability, behavior disturbance, speech impairment, lack of coordination, or vision or hearing deficit becomes apparent, appropriate therapeutic solutions should be explored. When needed, physical therapy, speech therapy, or special classroom placement should be made available without embarrassing or isolating the student from classmates. Professional counseling should be arranged for social or behavioral disturbances before they become deeply rooted (see Resources).

Athletics

Children with epilepsy can actively participate in most sports as long as their seizures are under reasonable control. This decision should be made in conjunction with the child's physician. Unnecessary restrictions can be more of a handicap than the disorder itself. Youngsters experience fewer seizures when they are active than when they are idle. If the youngster is experiencing frequent seizures, athletic energy can be channeled into noncontact sports, such as tennis, golf, and track. Also, students interested in sports but unable to participate could be official photographers, scorekeepers, and equipment managers.

Driver's Education

A driver's license, a sign of independence and impending adulthood, is a status symbol to the adolescent. Even noncompliant teenagers will usually adhere to their medication in order to be seizure-free and thereby obtain a driver's license. All states permit epileptics to drive if they are completely seizure-free for a specified number of years and can successfully pass the state driver's test. If the student is only under fair seizure control, only classroom driver's education can be permitted. If seizures remit later, the student will be permitted to obtain a driver's license. If it is apparent that the severity of seizures will prohibit the student from obtaining a driver's license, it is best to gradually prepare him or her for the restriction. The student should be given support by emphasizing that this goal may be reached in the future.

Water Danger

Submersion injury, whether it occurs in the bathtub, swimming pool, lake, or ocean, is a potential danger to the child with a seizure disorder. Generally this danger does not arise in the usual school setting, but guidelines are given here for class trips or overnight school outings.

Showers rather than tub baths are recommended. It is advisable for the faucet to have a safety device that permits the water to maintain a preset temperature to prevent scalding in the event of a seizure. This type of equipment can be purchased at medical supply centers. For tub baths, the water level should be kept low and the bathroom door left unlocked.

Swimming should only be permitted if the child is with a competent swimming companion and under the supervision of a responsible adult. Swimming in a pool is safer than swimming at the beach or in a lake. Scuba diving is discouraged. When boating, a safety jacket should be worn at all times.

Job Counseling

The interests, skills, and frequency of seizures of the student should be considered when assisting the youngster in selecting a career. If seizures are under perfect control, the epilepsy should not interfere with most future career goals. If seizures recur periodically, the student should not prepare for positions in careers that would endanger himself or herself or others such as surgery, commercial transportation, mountain climbing, heavy machinery operation, or high-rise construction. Alternative types of employment include business, government, computer science, photography, writing, education, and counseling.

APPROACH TO THE CHILD WITH EPILEPSY

A confident teacher with a knowledge of first aid and a matter-of-fact attitude will teach the students a positive attitude and will avoid becoming a terrified observer incapable of properly handling a situation involving a seizure. Lack of knowledge could foster the development of unwanted attitudes such as overprotection, segregation, and fear. These attitudes could cause the teacher to unintentionally regard the child as a "time-bomb" ready to explode at any moment. Rather than encouraging a good school experience, a teacher with such attitudes might send the youngster home after a seizure, rather than urge a return to class when appropriate, or needlessly recommend home tutoring. This can be avoided by collaboration with the child and the family.

It is the family's responsibility to inform the school nurse and homeroom teacher of the type of epilepsy, the frequency and severity of the seizures, precipitating factors, medications, and any physical limitations placed upon the child by the physician. The teacher should also learn to recognize auras and know the typical presentations of the seizure and the child's normal appearance following a seizure. A seizure data information sheet (see Figure 3) will provide a data base to explore important issues. If the teacher has questions pertaining to the child that the parents cannot answer, the parents should give permission for direct contact with the physician. In return, the teacher could review the anecdotal sheet (see Figure 4) and assure the parents that it will be filled out as needed.[15]

Expecting less than the epileptic child's best in classwork, behavior, and athletics is not in the student's best interest. Shielding these students from hard work, disappointment, or risk of failure shelters them and deprives them of the opportunity to master normal, healthy developmental dilemmas.

Academic competition and discipline is a normal, constructive part of school and should be experienced by the student with epilepsy. Some teachers may be too lenient, hoping to keep the epileptic child "calm" and fearing that the usual academic stress and tension will cause an increased frequency in seizures. Although prolonged or unusual stress can precipitate

Figure 3. Data Base for the Student with Epilepsy

NAME: ____________________ BIRTHDATE: ____________________

PARENTS: ____________________ HOME PHONE: ____________________

ADDRESS: ____________________ EMERGENCY #: ____________________

____________________ ____________________

(relationship and name)

PHYSICIAN: ____________________ PHONE: ____________________

Typical presentation and duration of seizure activity: ____________________

Likelihood and frequency of seizures occurring during school hours: ____________________

Known auras or factors which may precipitate a seizure: ____________________

Usual postictal period: ____________________

Recommended first-aid care: ____________________

Figure 3. Data Base for the Student with Epilepsy (continued)

Limitations, if any, specified by a physician: ______________________

____

____

____

Treatment—include current medication, dosage, and time administered; use of protective helmet: ______________________

____

____

____

Possible side effects: ______________________

____

____

____

Additional, pertinent information: ______________________

____

____

____

____

____

____

____

____

____

____

____

Figure 4. Anecdotal Record

NAME:____________________ DATE:______________

TIME:______________

Precipitating events and aura, if any reported:______________

Description of the seizure (if possible, record events in sequence; specify who observed the seizure):______________

Postictal phase (include level of alertness and length of time until full recovery; verbalized complaints):______________

Apparent injury sustained from the seizure:______________

First-aid care administered:______________

Disposition:______________

Other questions or concerns pertaining to the student (i.e., medication, behavior, school performance):______________

a seizure in a few epileptic children, the usual pressures of classroom expectations are not generally sufficiently potent. Failing to give constructive criticism, test under pressure, punish for misdeeds, or require recitation in class will only foster unnecessary emotional pressures by separating the student from classmates and labeling him or her as incompetent.

The epileptic child needs proper rest and should avoid extreme fatigue. This does not mean, however, that the child should have a shortened school day or should be excused from physical education.

Observation of the Child's Condition

School personnel can help the physician evaluate the effectiveness of anticonvulsants and choose those that interfere least with the youngster's behavior or learning ability. Occasionally, when a child begins taking medication or when the dosage is being adjusted, there will be transient side effects that could temporarily interfere with alertness. The child may seem fatigued and not as bright as usual. If persistent (more than three weeks) drowsiness, dizziness, restlessness, poor concentration, or other subtle changes are noted in the classroom, the family should be notified.

Do not assume that every fall, temper tantrum, fainting spell, or daydreaming episode is a seizure or that all lethargy or lack of classroom preparation is due to the side effects of anticonvulsants. Other causes for this sort of behavior should be considered. All children may daydream if they are bored or fail to do classwork if they are not motivated. Erroneous reports of seizures from school personnel can provoke unwarranted alarm and lead to unnecessary changes in medication.

Encouraging the Child to Communicate Concerns

The teacher should provide an opportunity for the child to communicate concerns over seizures, even if their occurrence is infrequent. The threat of an impending seizure can be a continual source of fear and anxiety. The seizure itself is not as frightening as the concern about the care that will be given during the seizure and the reaction of those witnessing the episode. The child should be assured that a responsible person will be close by and that peers will provide support, not ridicule.

For some children, seizures provide an opportunity to discuss their fears and concerns. If the student has missed school because of a seizure, be supportive when he or she returns to class. A kind remark, such as "Glad to see you back. We missed you," or "I heard you had a bad day yesterday. I'm glad things are better," can be very reassuring and will give the child the opportunity to discuss his or her feelings.

An occasional private conference with the youngster will offer the chance for the student to mention to the teacher any teasing, embarrassment, or mockery and give the teacher some hints as to what areas need to be covered in fostering student understanding. In addition, these meetings will encourage the student to seek advice should problems appear at a later date. It should be stressed to the student that these meetings are not primarily for "telling on" other students, but that the information gained can be used to help fellow students in interacting with persons with health problems. The child with epilepsy, of course, will benefit quickly from such improved attitudes.

FOSTERING CLASSMATES' UNDERSTANDING

Children with epilepsy must cope both with their seizures and the adverse attitude of much of society. Being labeled as "different" can affect the child's school performance and be frustrating psychologically, socially, and, later, economically. It is not uncommon for classmates to unwittingly reject the epileptic child. This problem can be ameliorated by educating these students about epilepsy. A thorough, open discussion with a concerned teacher could transform a traumatic incident into an enlightening and reassuring learning experience. The teacher should emphasize that epilepsy is not contagious, nor is it a sign of mental illness or low intelligence. It is important to foster the attitude that between seizures the child is healthy and like other children. If there is an epileptic student in the classroom, it is advisable to speak with the family prior to the seizure presentation. The epileptic child should not be identified. It should also be determined in advance whether or not he or she wants to be present during the classroom discussion.

A child coping with a seizure disorder will greatly benefit from the support of classmates. If the child is likely to experience a seizure during the school day, a "buddy system" can be devised. The classmates can actually be instructed in seizure first aid. Under the supervision of a teacher or nurse, a classmate may be permitted to stay with the child during the seizure as well as the period following the seizure.

REFERENCES

1. Epilepsy Foundation of America, *Statistics on the Basic Epilepsies* (Philadelphia, PA: F. A. Davis, 1975).
2. R. J. Gumnitz, *Epilepsy, A Handbook for Physicians* (University of Minnesota: Comprehensive Epilepsy Program, 1981).
3. *Statistics on the Basic Epilepsies*.

4. R. G. Ziegler, ''Impairments of Control and Competence in Epileptic Children and Their Families,'' *Epilepsia* 22 (1981): 339–46.
5. *Statistics on the Basic Epilepsies*.
6. S. Livingston, *Comprehensive Management of Epilepsy in Infancy, Childhood and Adolescence* (Springfield, IL: Charles C. Thomas, 1972).
7. Livingston, *Comprehensive Management of Epilepsy*.
8. *Statistics on the Basic Epilepsies*.
9. B. P. Hermann, R. B. Black, and S. Chhiabria, ''Behavioral Problems and Social Competence in Children with Epilepsy,'' *Epilepsia* 22 (1981): 703–10.
10. B. P. Hermann, ''Neuropsychological Functioning and Psychopathology in Children with Epilepsy,'' *Epilepsia* 23 (1982): 545–54.
11. J. Lindsay, C. Ounsted, and P. Richards, ''Long-Term Outcome in Children with Temporal Lobe Seizures. II: Marriage, Parenthood and Sexual Indifference,'' *Developmental Medicine and Child Neurology* 21 (1979): 433–40.
12. Gumnitz, *Epilepsy, A Handbook*.
13. Lindsay, Ounsted, and Richards, ''Long-Term Outcome in Children with Temporal Lobe Seizures,'' pp. 433–40.
14. *Statistics on the Basic Epilepsies*.
15. Gumnitz, *Epilepsy, A Handbook*.

RESOURCES

Useful Addresses

Information on laws, counseling, and research can be obtained from the following sources:

Educational Laws
Closer Look, Box 1492, Washington, DC 20013.

Employment Evaluation and Insurance Information
National Epilepsy League, 203 N. Wabash Ave., Chicago, IL 60604.

General Information on Specific Help
Bureau of Developmental Disabilities, Room 3070, HEW South Building, 330 C St., SW, Washington, DC 22201.

Patient Education Counseling
Epilepsy Foundation of America, 1828 L St., SW, Washington, DC 20036.

Research in Epilepsy
National Institutes of Health, NINCDS—Epilepsy Branch, Federal Building 114, Bethesda, MD 22014.

Suggested Reading

Epilepsy: You and Your Child—A Guide for Parents. Epilepsy Foundation of America, 1828 L St., SW, Washington, DC 20036.

Jan, J. E.; Ziegler, R. G.; and Erba, G. *Does Your Child Have Epilepsy*. Baltimore, MD: University Park Press, Baltimore, MD 21202.

Cardiac Disease

by Paul K. Woolf, M.D.

OVERVIEW

The degree of functional impairment secondary to heart disease in the school-aged child ranges from mild to severe, with considerable variability among patients with any specific diagnosis. The information presented here is only for general guidance. In order to formulate an appropriate approach for an individual child with heart disease, it is necessary to ascertain for that child exactly what symptoms and signs might be expected, the severity of that child's heart disease, what treatment is currently being used, and what the future plan is.

When the child with true cardiac disease (as opposed to a child with an innocent heart murmur) is identified, based upon his or her symptom complex, medical problems at school can be anticipated and appropriate medical and psychological support given. School staff should work closely with the child's cardiologist and pediatrician in assessing what medical and emotional support are required in the school atmosphere. Children with severe cardiac disease need considerable emotional support, even during the school day. Many times limitations must be enforced on a child who wants to participate in competitive sports despite advice to the contrary from the physician.

Incidence and Cause of Childhood Heart Disease

Heart disease in childhood can be divided into two major categories: congenital structural defects and acquired heart disease. Congenital defects are the most common, with a quoted incidence of 8 per 1,000 live births.[1] More than 90 percent of these babies will survive until adulthood.[2] In children with a congenital heart defect, it is generally only the heart that is affected. However, 20 to 30 percent of children with congenital heart defects have associated extracardiac birth defects. Most of these have a syndrome, that is, a constellation of defects. Many of these are associated with mental retardation of varying degrees. Among the most common are Down's syndrome (trisomy 21), Williams' syndrome, and Noonan's syndrome.

The cause and, when pertinent, the genetics of most heart defects in children are not completely understood. Ninety percent are thought to be caused by a not-as-yet-identified combination of environmental and genetic influences. Eight percent are felt to be primarily genetic in origin. Chromosomal abnormalities account for many of these cases. This group also includes syndromes with multiple anomalies and some specific congenital heart defects that are transmitted with high frequency from parent to child. The remaining 2 percent of defects are felt to be environmental in etiology, i.e., a result of prenatal fetal exposure to some environmental agent. Examples include maternal rubella infection, lithium use, and thalidomide use.

The incidence of acquired heart disease in children is difficult to assess. Common causes include bacterial and viral infections, as well as systemic, metabolic, or neuromuscular diseases.

In considering the incidence of heart disease in children, it must be noted that a heart murmur is not a heart disease. A heart murmur is a physical finding of an extra sound when listening to the heart. It may be "harsh," "swishing," "buzzing," or "blowing" in quality and may or may not indicate the presence of congenital or acquired heart disease. The incidence of "innocent murmurs,' that is, those caused by vibrations of *normal* heart structures, may be as high as 50 to 100 percent in normal children at some time in their lives. Innocent murmurs do *not* need special attention and should thus be differentiated from true heart disease by a pediatric cardiology examination.

NORMAL CARDIAC STRUCTURE AND FUNCTION

A basic appreciation of normal cardiac structure and function in children is important in understanding and dealing with heart disease in these youngsters. The heart pumps unoxygenated blood, returning from the body's organs, to the lungs. There this blood will receive oxygen, lose carbon dioxide, and return to the heart to be pumped through a series of vessels to supply oxygen and other nutrients necessary for the body's needs. The heart itself is composed of four chambers. The right-sided filling chamber (right atrium) receives the venous blood (blue) that is returning from the body's organs and tissues. Blood passes from the right atrium to the right-sided pumping chamber (right ventricle) across the tricuspid valve that prevents backflow. From the right ventricle, blood is pumped through the pulmonary valve into a vessel called the pulmonary artery, which carries blood to the lungs, where it is oxygenated. This oxygenated blood (red) then travels to the left-sided filling chamber (left atrium) and flows across the mitral valve into the left-sided pumping chamber (left ventricle), then across the aortic valve and out via the body's main blood vessel, the aorta. The right and left heart chambers, at both atrial and ventricular levels, are normally separated by walls (septa).

The heart is composed of three layers: an inner lining called the endocardium; a middle muscle layer, the myocardium; and an outer lining layer, the pericardium. In certain areas of the cardiac tissue, there is a complex specialized electrical conduction system that controls the rate and synchronous rhythm of contraction of the four chambers. By listening to the heart using a stethoscope, one is usually able to only hear sounds of closure of the four cardiac valves. These valve sounds usually occur in a regular fashion at a normal rate for a given age.

ABNORMAL CARDIAC STRUCTURE AND FUNCTION

Many varieties of acquired and congenital heart disease in childhood are responsible for a wide spectrum of clinical conditions and treatment needs. The most frequent manifestations of these defects are cyanosis, a bluish coloring of the skin, which indicates poorly oxygenated blood; congestive heart failure; and arrhythmias, which are irregular heartbeats or an abnormal rate of beating. The most common types of these and the specific problems associated with each will be discussed.

Congenital Structural Defects

Valve Deformities

The most common congenital heart defects are valve deformities and holes in the septa. Valves between chambers and vessels (see Figure 1) may be floppy (mitral or tricuspid valve prolapse) or may have an abnormal number of parts (bicuspid aortic valve). Such defects do not usually significantly affect heart function in childhood. Valve deformities may result, however, in a narrow opening (stenosis) or a leak with resultant backward flow (regurgitation). Significant stenosis or regurgitation as an isolated finding may result in mechanical stress to the heart chambers and subsequent congestive heart failure (see Symptoms and Signs). Pulmonary valve, aortic valve, mitral valve, or tricuspid valve stenosis or regurgitation may range from mild to severe and may progress in severity over time.

Figure 1. Normal Anatomy and Physiology

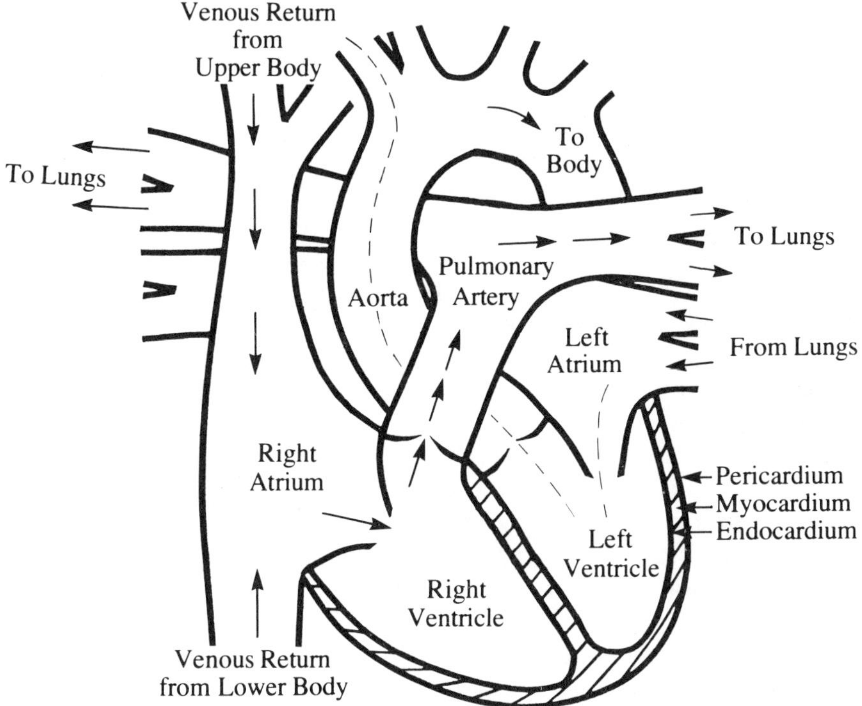

Surgical intervention is warranted if significant functional impairment is noted. The age at which repair is done and type of repair varies greatly from patient to patient, but eventual successful repair is the rule. An exception is aortic valve disease, which may result in residual valve or ventricular dysfunction. Artificial valve replacement for severe cases is often eventually needed, with persistence of symptoms until the child reaches adequate age or size for this procedure. Congestive heart failure as a result of such a defect may need medical therapy until the optimal time for surgery. A complete congenital closure of the valve (atresia) may be seen as part of a complex of several defects (see Complex Defects).

Septal Defects

Defects of the ventricular, atrial, or aorto-pulmonary (connections between the great arteries) septa are frequently encountered. These defects, if isolated, allow passage of oxygenated blood from left to right heart chambers with more flow to the lungs than is normal. Again, there is a wide spectrum of severity. Excessive blood flow to the lungs plus a mechanical stress to the heart chamber may not cause functional impairment or may result in severe congestive heart failure, requiring vigorous medical therapy or early surgical intervention to close the defect. Surgical results are usually excellent with normal life span or activity levels. One exception is a complete atrio-ventricular canal, which is a combined atrial and ventricular septal defect with valve deformities. This is frequently seen in children with Down's syndrome. In these children, residual defects or impairment of function is common.

Surgical repair of large septal defects frequently is necessary in the first two years of life. If defects are large and associated with elevation of pressure in the lung's blood vessels, failure to repair these defects at an optimal time may lead to irreversible thickening of these vessels, with a reversal of direction of flow (from right to left) through the defect and resultant cyanosis secondary to unoxygenated blood entering the aorta—called Eisenmenger's syndrome. Children with Eisenmenger's syndrome cannot be helped surgically and soon die of stroke, pulmonary bleeding, or heart failure, despite medical treatment. Fortunately, children with pulmonary vessel disease from simple cardiac defects are rarely seen in this modern era. However, poor medical care can result in this situation.

In contrast to other types of congenital heart defects, defects of the atrial and ventricular septa close spontaneously without surgical intervention in a significant number of cases. For this reason, children with these defects are frequently observed for a period of years before surgical correction is needed. These defects are not exceptionally large, not associated with congestive heart failure, and not associated with excessive flow and pressure in the lung's blood vessels. Small septal defects without functional impairment of the cardiac chamber or blood vessels may not need any surgical intervention.

Stenosis of Vessels

Stenosis of vessels also occurs frequently, most commonly affecting the aorta (coarctation). Infants with this defect can experience heart failure requiring immediate surgical repair. Infants undergoing surgery will frequently have a recurrent narrowing of vessels in childhood, requiring reoperation—usually with excellent results. Children with coarctation without heart failure may have high blood pressure, abnormal leg pulses, or an abnormal chest x-ray. They will frequently be repaired electively from ages four to seven years, usually with excellent results, although persistent high blood pressure may require medication.

Tetralogy of Fallot

The most common cyanotic disease of childhood is a combination of ventricular septal defect and stenosis of the pulmonary valve, known as tetralogy of Fallot. Obstruction of blood flow to the lung causes flow from the right to the left heart, resulting in cyanosis because unoxygenated blood enters the aorta. Medications are generally not useful, and surgical intervention is required early in childhood if either chronic or episodic severe cyanosis appears. Age of elective repair is usually one to two years. Results are usually very good and depend upon the degree of residual pulmonary stenosis, pulmonary insufficiency, and postoperative rhythm disturbances secondary to the surgical trauma to the heart. Complete repair of tetralogy of Fallot may be delayed in severe cases, and early temporary shunting performed to lessen the degree of cyanosis. This involves bypass grafts from the aorta to the pulmonary artery. Temporary procedures are performed with an eye to subsequent complete repair later in childhood, sometimes using artificial valves and tube conduits to replace structures of the heart that are too small.

Transposition of the Great Arteries

The most common cyanotic heart defect at birth is transposition of the great arteries, i.e., the aorta and the pulmonary artery. This is an abnormality of connection of the great vessels to the ventricles. The pulmonary artery arises from the left ventricle, and the aorta from the right ventricle, which is the opposite of the normal arrangement. This results in two separate circulations, operating in parallel rather than in series. Oxygenated blood recirculates through the lungs and unoxygenated blood recirculates through the body's organs and tissues. This defect requires intervention in the first year of life, with surgery to redirect blood flow at either the atrial or great vessel level. Results are usually very good, but one may see vessel obstruction, valve leaks, rhythm disturbances, or some combination of all in a given patient. Usually cyanosis is not a big problem postoperatively.

Complex Defects

Combinations of the above defects may be seen frequently, but a complete discussion is beyond the scope of this text. Complex types of defects, either cyanotic or with congestive heart failure from mechanical stress to the ventricle, may not be amenable to early surgical repair in infancy. These patients may require temporary procedures or the prolonged use of medications in an attempt to reach an adequate age or size for corrective surgery. It is important for anyone taking care of children with complex heart defects to understand the basic principles involved in their heart defect and the treatment plan.

Heart Rate Abnormalities

Rhythm irregularities, or heart rate abnormalities, may be caused by congenital abnormalities of the electrical conduction system. The most common dysrhythmias (abnormal or irregular heartbeats) are premature beats, arising either from the atria or the ventricles. These may be benign, requiring no therapy, but if they occur frequently or if many occur consecutively, cardiac function may be impaired. The most common dysrhythmia requiring immediate attention and therapy is supraventricular tachycardia, which is a fast beat originating above the ventricle. In the school-aged child, medication is usually required for control. Symptoms may include palpitations, dizziness, syncope, or chest pain (see Symptoms and Signs). A block in the electrical conduction system between the upper and lower chambers (complete heart block) can cause a cardiac contraction rate that is too slow. If symptoms described above are present, a pacemaker may be required to ensure sufficient rate of contraction. Dysrhythmias that cannot be controlled by one or several drugs in combination may be approached surgically with excision of abnormal electrical pathways. Antidysrhythmic medications each have their own particular side effects, which should be made known to any caretakers of a child with a dysrhythmia.

Acquired Cardiac Disease

Any or all of the three layers of the heart, endocardium, myocardium, and pericardium, may be affected by a variety of disease processes during childhood. The most common disease process is infection, either viral or bacterial in nature.

Endocarditis

The inner lining of the heart may become infected at any site in the heart (endocarditis) in children with or without congenital cardiac defects. Endocarditis may be a life-threatening infection, with significant stress to heart function; possible embolization (remote passage through blood vessels) of infected materials from the heart to other body organs; or dysrhythmias, if the site of the conduction system is involved. The illness requires bed rest, close medical supervision, and long-term intravenous antibiotics. Residual defects may be severe, requiring long-term medical therapy or surgical intervention.

Particular care should be taken to prevent endocarditis in children with structural defects. All children with congenital heart defects should receive prophylactic antibiotics at the time of procedures associated with bacteria entering the bloodstream, as recommended by the American Heart Association. This includes dental work and surgery involving the respiratory, genito-urinary, or gastrointestinal tracts. The child's physician and parents should be aware of the need for endocarditis prophylaxis.

Myocarditis

Viral infection of the middle muscle layer (myocarditis) may cause weakening of the heart muscle, with resultant congestive heart failure or dysrhythmias. Bed rest and a variety of medications may be required for a lengthy period. Heart function may improve after the acute infection, or it may remain the same or worsen. The early mortality rate is substantial. Even if the child lives through the illness, congestive heart failure can be severe and long-term. No surgical treatment is currently available except cardiac transplantation in selected cases.

Pericarditis

Bacterial or viral infection of the outer lining (pericarditis) can lead to fluid accumulation around the heart or thickening of this outer layer, with constriction of the heart. Clinical states can range from mild infection with only chest pain to severe infection with signs similar to congestive heart failure. Severe cases may require emergency surgery—this may be lifesaving if heart function is severely compromised. Bacterial pericarditis requires hospitalization for three to five weeks, with bed rest and intravenous antibiotics. Residual impairment depends on the severity of the initial illness and varies greatly from child to child.

Other Systemic Disease Processes

Similar functional abnormalities can be caused by inflammation of any or all three layers of heart tissue. Systemic lupus erythematosus, rheumatoid arthritis, mucocutaneous lymph node syndrome, polyarteritis nodosa, and, rarely in the modern era, rheumatic fever are examples of systemic inflammatory diseases that may affect the heart tissue. Mucocutaneous lymph node syndrome (Kawasaki's disease) deserves special note, in that the residual defect is unique. Children may be left with aneurysms (dilations) of the coronary arteries (the vessels carrying oxygen to the heart muscle itself) and thus risk developing adult-type myocardial infarctions. These children may require long-term medical therapy and close observation.

Many other systemic disease processes, including metabolic (glycogen storage), hematologic (thalassemia), oncologic (leukemia), or neuromuscular (muscular dystrophy), may involve disease of any of the three layers discussed. Management involves a combination of therapy of the underlying disease and of the resultant heart disease.

SYMPTOMS AND SIGNS OF HEART DISEASE IN THE SCHOOL-AGED CHILD

Manifestations of cardiac disease, whether it is congenital or acquired, may be grouped into several major categories. The characteristic appearance and frequently encountered complaints of the child with congestive heart failure, cyanosis, and other problems will be discussed.

Congestive Heart Failure

Heart diseases that cause either a mechanical stress to the pumping chambers or a weakening of the heart muscle may induce a state of congestive heart failure. This is a constellation of symptoms and physical signs secondary to the inability of the heart to supply the body's needs.

In the school-aged child, congestive heart failure may be secondary to a postoperative defect with significant, residual impairment; an inoperable complex cardiac defect; Eisenmenger's syndrome; dysrhythmia; or acquired abnormality of cardiac muscle function. There is inadequate oxygen and blood supply to the body's organs and congestion of organs, primarily the liver and lungs, secondary to a "back-up" of blood. Symptoms include breathlessness upon exertion, or even at rest in severe cases; decreased urine output with fluid retention; or an inability to lie flat. The physical signs include a faster-than-normal heart and respiratory rate, distressed pattern of breathing secondary to lung congestion, neck vein distention, abdominal swelling secondary to liver congestion, excessive weight gain, and occasionally, ankle swelling in the older child secondary to fluid retention. Growth is slow, and these children are frequently behind their peers in both weight and height. Children with defects involving increased blood flow through the lungs are prone to frequent episodes of pneumonia as a result of pulmonary congestion.

Medications are commonly part of the treatment regimen of this group. These may include digoxin to strengthen the force of cardiac contraction and diuretics to relieve some of the pulmonary and liver congestion. Also, electrolyte supplements may be needed to replace some of the sodium and potassium loss in the urine with aggressive diuresis. Children may be on multiple medications but still be severely limited in exercise capacity and slow in growth and development, without a real possibility of curative surgery. Other children may be able to undergo surgical repair at a later age, with medications used only as a temporary measure. Children with congestive heart failure may need help during their school day with administration of medications. They frequently need help in organizing travel from class to class. The use of first floor classrooms may be necessary if school elevators are not available. Alternate activities must be planned in place of physical education classes for the child with exercise restrictions.

The caretakers of a child with chronic congestive heart failure at school should be alert to the presence of respiratory distress, fluid retention, or decreased exercise tolerance. Digoxin may cause palpitations, vomiting, or dizziness if taken in excess. Dehydration may result from excessive use of diuretics. Abnormalities of blood potassium levels may cause muscle cramps, abdominal pain, or symptoms of dysrhythmia. Presence of significant symptomatology warrants notification of parents and appropriate medical personnel.

Cyanosis

Cyanosis is a blue discoloration of the skin and mucous membranes caused by inadequately oxgenated blood. It results from flow of blue (unoxygenated) blood into the left side of the heart or an abnormal connection of the vessels and chambers as previously described. A significant exercise intolerance may be present, and the co-existence of congestive heart failure is common. Children may suffer from loss of consciousness, dizziness, headache, or other neurologic complaints caused by inadequate oxygen flow to areas of the brain. Severe headache with fever is especially worrisome because it may be a sign of a brain abscess. Cyanotic children are especially prone to developing such abscesses because bacteria may flow from veins to arteries without being filtered by the lungs. Cyanotic children are also small for their age and may be developmentally delayed.

Cyanosis in school-aged children is generally caused by a congenital heart defect that is very difficult to correct or by an untreatable result of a heart defect which was not treated in time (Eisenmenger's syndrome).

Temporary surgical procedures designed to partially alleviate the cyanosis in a particular child may be tried on multiple occasions, but they tend to fail with time. Multiple attempts are needed for improvement. Complete repair is frequently not possible because of very complicated anatomic problems or excessively high mortality rates associated with surgery. Medications generally do not help.

Syncope (Loss of Consciousness)

Generally loss of consciousness is a warning signal of either neurologic, metabolic, or cardiac disease. Cardiac causes of syncope include dysrhythmia or aortic valve stenosis, leading to a sudden inadequacy of cardiac output for adequate brain function. Children with loss of consciousness at school should have vital signs (heart rate, respiratory rate, and blood pressure) checked immediately and should be referred for proper evaluation.

Palpitations

Palpitations are sensations of irregular or rapid heartbeats. They are generally a symptom of dysrhythmia. Heart rate and rhythm should be confirmed immediately and appropriate referral made. Dysrhythmias may be entirely benign, not requiring therapy, or may be significant. If accompanied by either dizziness, shortness of breath, loss of consciousness, or chest pains, palpitations require urgent evaluation with an electrocardiogram.

Chest Pain

Chest pain is a fairly rare symptom of cardiac disease in children. Left anterior chest pain may be seen in children with mitral valve prolapse, dysrhythmia, or rarely, in a child with a coronary artery disease leading to an inadequate oxygen supply to the heart muscle. If chest pain occurs at exercise, the child should be allowed to rest. Appropriate referral for evaluation should be made, with urgency dictated by the child's vital signs and severity of symptoms.

Summary

The above symptoms and signs frequently require pediatric or pediatric cardiology evaluation to assess the severity or degree of control of a child's heart disease. The majority of school-aged children with a heart defect will show no evidence of the defect. This includes the children with dysrhythmias well controlled by medication, those who have had corrective surgery for a defect with minimal residual problems, or those with mild defects who will never need surgical or medical intervention. Common defects in this category include small ventricular or atrial defects, mild pulmonary stenosis, mitral valve prolapse, or bicuspid aortic valve. These asymptomatic children, either on medications or in the postoperative state, may be prone to a sudden, unexpected event. Most important, careful documentation of their vital signs at the time of these events is needed, followed by appropriate referral for evaluation and possible therapy.

PSYCHOLOGICAL ASPECTS

The school-aged child with significant heart disease may manifest a variety of psychological problems. The presence of the symptoms described, leading to exercise intolerance, poor growth and development, and cyanotic appearance, all may contribute to the feeling of isolation from one's peers. Frequent absences from school can preclude good academic performance. Impending cardiac surgery or tests requiring hospitalization may cause great anxiety, leading to an increase in symptoms. Infantilization is common as a result of overprotection by parents.

Significant and obvious manifestations of symptoms indicate that the heart disease is a difficult one to correct. In these children, a fear of death is frequently present. The child with heart disease that does not cause any functional impairment, on the other hand, frequently is led to feel isolated from peers and is unnecessarily overprotected by parents. Children with innocent murmurs, who do not have any heart disease at all, are often wrongly labeled as having heart disease and treated differently from others.

A child with significant heart disease should be encouraged to be as active as possible, within limits of activities set by the child's physician. Creative assignment of nonstrenuous responsibilities during gym class is one way to give the child a feeling of involvement. An understanding but firm approach as to what the child can and cannot do is important. Teachers should try to encourage situations leading to social acceptance in the classroom. If the child is not feeling well, he or she should be encouraged to seek medical attention, but this should be done privately. Teachers and other caretakers should be sensitive to the presence of anxiety regarding impending cardiac surgery, diagnostic tests, or death, and discussions can be initiated in an appropriate setting. Sometimes, actual physical help with administration of medications or traveling from classroom to classroom may be necessary.

Because children with significant heart defects are surviving infancy with increasing frequency, an understanding of their medical and psychological needs is important for all caretakers. Also important is the identification of children who may have been wrongly labeled as having cardiac disease and the definition, with the help of their physicians and their families, of their true status. Once it is established that no cardiac disease exists, these children need no special care requirements.

REFERENCES

1. Forrest H. Adams and George C. Emmanouilides, eds., *Moss' Heart Disease in Infants, Children and Adolescents* (Baltimore, MD: Williams and Wilkins, 1983).
2. J. Manning, "Insurability and Employability of Young Cardiac Patients," in *Pediatric Cardiovascular Disease,* Cardiovascular Clinics Vol. XI., No. 2, ed. by M.A. Engle (Philadelphia, PA: F. A. Davis, 1981).

RESOURCES

Useful Address

American Heart Association, National Center, 7320 Greenville Ave., Dallas, TX 76231.

Juvenile Rheumatoid Arthritis

by Balu H. Athreya, M.D. and
Carrie Goren Ingall, R.N., M.S.N.

OVERVIEW

Juvenile rheumatoid arthritis (JRA) is one of the most common chronic diseases of childhood, affecting somewhere between 50,000 to 250,000 children in the United States. It is characterized by chronic inflammation of the joints. Inflammation of other parts of the body, such as the eye or the outer layer of the heart, can also occur. Most children with JRA experience only a slight disability, but a small percentage have severe cases that lead to joint destruction, deformity, and blindness. The cause of JRA is not clearly understood, although it has been suggested that an infection or a defect in the body's immune system may be responsible. There is evidence that heredity plays a role in some of the various subgroups of JRA, but the details are not yet clear. If one considers JRA as a whole, the incidence is much higher in females than in males. In one subgroup, however, 90 percent of the children affected are males.

Subgroups and Complications

JRA cannot be discussed as one disease, since there are five different subgroups, each with different manifestations and affecting different populations. *Systemic juvenile rheumatoid arthritis* affects children of any age and accounts for about 20 percent of all cases of JRA.[1] About equal numbers of boys and girls are affected. Systemic JRA is characterized by a high fever, which can persist for many months or even a few years. The fever usually comes on once or twice a day and lasts several hours. Commonly, it reaches 103°F, although it may reach 106°F. A child can seem very ill during the fever and surprisingly well when it goes away. Some children even feel well while having a fever. A rash is often associated with the fever. In the early stages, there may be no joint involvement, but the majority of children with systemic JRA will develop joint disease when the fever and rash subside. The liver, spleen, and lymph nodes are usually enlarged. The pericardium, the external layer of tissue surrounding the heart, may also be affected.

Sero-positive and *sero-negative polyarticular arthritis* are characterized by multiple joint involvement. In sero-positive JRA, a protein called the "rheumatoid factor" is present in the blood. Children with the rheumatoid factor (sero-positive) are most likely to have persistent arthritis for many years and a more destructive joint disease compared with those without the rheumatoid factor (sero-negative polyarticular arthritis). In both groups, the small joints of the fingers and hands and the weight-bearing joints, such as hips, knees, ankles, and feet, are involved. There may be a very low-grade fever, a mild anemia, and growth disturbances. From 80 to 90 percent of those affected are girls, and onset can occur throughout childhood.[2] About 35 percent of all children with JRA have these forms.[3]

Pauciarticular disease type 1 affects mostly (about 80 percent) girls[4] and usually appears in the first five years of life. Only three to four joints are involved, and the joint inflammation is not too much of a problem. Some of these children have an abnormal protein in the blood called "antinuclear factor," which is different from the rheumatoid factor. The most serious problem in this type is the involvement of the eye, which can lead to blindness. The fifth group of children, those with *pauciarticular disease type 2*, are mostly boys in their preteens. They also have less then four joints involved. Upon reaching adulthood, many develop ankylosing spondylitis, a type of arthritis that primarily affects the spine and hips. These two types account for approximately 45 percent of children with JRA.[5]

Diagnosis

There is no one diagnostic test for JRA. Because the symptoms (swollen joints, fevers) resemble those of other illnesses, such as infections and tumors, hospitalization is often necessary to rule out other illnesses. This is especially so in children with the systemic type. There may be numerous invasive and painful tests, such as bone marrow aspirations. Despite extensive work-ups, these children are often discharged without a definite diagnosis. The diagnosis of JRA cannot be confirmed unless the symptoms persist for more than six weeks. School personnel should be aware of the necessity of this waiting period so that they will not urge a change of physicians when it seems as if nothing is being done. Time is as important a part of the diagnostic process as are blood tests.

General Complications

Growth retardation and delayed sexual development are particular problems in children with multiple joint involvement, those with systemic features (fever, rash, enlarged lymph glands), and those few who are on steroid therapy. The child's growth may be slow when the disease is active but may accelerate during remissions. There also may be either overgrowth or undergrowth of the bone near the inflamed joints. One leg may grow longer than the other, resulting in changes in gait and posture and abnormalities of the spine. Another common finding is undergrowth of the jaw. Arthritis in the temporomandibular (jaw) joint limits the ability to fully open the mouth. Many younger children refer to the pain from this joint as an earache. Neck involvement is also common, characterized by stiffness and pain. In general, children with JRA are very stiff in the morning and do not reach their full range of mobility until late morning. Symptoms also vary from day to day. Weather conditions, such as cold, high humidity, and a fall in barometric pressure, can cause increased aches, pains, and stiffness.

Eye Disease

Eye disease is of concern in all children who have JRA but especially so in girls with pauciarticular arthritis who also have the antinuclear factor. This inflammation of the iris and ciliary body is referred to as "chronic iridocyclitis." The damage from the inflammation can be so severe as to impair vision or even result in blindness. The symptoms of impending eye problems may be very minimal. Redness, blurring of vision, or watering of the eyes when looking at light may be the only clues. It is important that all children with JRA have a "slit lamp" examination by an ophthalmologist at least once a year. Children with the antinuclear factor should have this examination every six months. It is not known why the eye becomes affected in JRA, but it is a significant problem and can be more disabling than the arthritis itself.

Course

The course of JRA is variable, even within each subgroup. Flares and remissions are common in all five varieties. Remissions may last for only a few weeks or may be permanent. Those with systemic disease that persists for more than two years after onset, those with multiple joint involvement, and those with the rheumatoid factor have the worst prognosis. Girls with multiple joint involvement without the rheumatoid factor have the best prognosis. Children with fewer than four affected joints usually improve over a period of from two to three years. However, the risk of eye disease is high in this group, and there is a tendency toward recurrent bouts of arthritis. In general, JRA usually begins to improve within two years of onset; if it persists beyond two years, it will probably last throughout life.

Most children with growth retardation catch up, while others continue to be small. Girls with delayed sexual development eventually get their menstrual periods.

Psychological Aspects

During the initial phase of the disease, children will often use denial to help them cope with illness. This is acceptable up to a point and is a necessary safeguard to psychological functioning in the face of the stress of illness. However, this denial sometimes leads to noncompliance with the medical regimen, refusal to talk about the arthritis, behaving as if the problem did not exist, and participation in activities that risk exacerbating the condition.

In a study involving 42 children from a pediatric rheumatology clinic, it was found that children with arthritis had more psychological problems than children who served as controls.[6] Surprisingly, children with recognizable and severe handicaps seem to have fewer psychosocial problems because they are accepted without question as handicapped and treated with consideration of their limitations. In contrast, children who truly have aches, pains, and stiffness with no obvious physical deformity are sometimes pushed to perform as normal children when they really cannot.

It has also been noted that children with JRA do well intellectually but perform poorly in social settings. Psychosocial problems often stem from the fact that JRA is characterized by flares and remissions and sometimes even a day-to-day variability. This variability can disrupt social relationships.

Peer reactions become increasingly important as the child gets older. Children between the ages of 10 and 17 are often self-conscious about the disease and afraid to tell peers they have JRA for fear of rejection and of appearing different. They may tell classmates untruths about their disability rather than make explanations. For example, a child with a flare-up of arthritis may tell friends that his or her bike is broken rather than say riding is impossible because of knee pain. Some children who find out that they cannot keep up physically with their classmates withdraw into a shell.

Some studies suggest that severe stress in life at times aggravates the condition.[7] However, there has been no firm evidence that this is so. Family problems, such as divorce and marital separation, as well as the hospitalization of a parent because of serious illness, were the most frequent problems mentioned. In another study, a high frequency of broken homes was observed among children with JRA.[8] Considering how common single-parent families are, it is hard to know how significant the association is.

THERAPY

The aims of treatment are to preserve joint function, take care of manifestations of the disease in systems other than joints, and plan for the growth and development of the child. Support for the family and the child in coping during the most trying periods is also important. Juvenile rheumatoid arthritis is usually treated by general pediatricians in consultation with adult rheumatologists. Pediatric rheumatologists are available only in large medical centers. An ophthalmologist should perform all eye examinations and treat eye disease, if present.

Medication

The most frequently used drug is aspirin, which is given in large doses to achieve and maintain a specific therapeutic level in the blood. Aspirin, an anti-inflammatory drug, helps control inflammation around the joints in addition to controlling fever and pain. The most important role of aspirin in the treatment of JRA is its anti-inflammatory properties; it should be taken even when there is no pain or fever. Missing even an occasional dose may delay progress. While taking large doses of aspirin, children may develop stomach irritations, vomiting, and ringing in the ears. Rarely, they will have bleeding from the stomach. The other major side effect of aspirin is its effect on the liver, which occasionally leads to abdominal pain, vomiting, and jaundice. When liver toxicity occurs, the child may also have severe bleeding, particularly nosebleeds. Even small doses of aspirin can cause children to bruise easily because of its effect on the platelets. However, this is not a major difficulty.

Although the controversy has not yet been settled, concern about the relationship between aspirin and Reye's syndrome has led more and more physicians to prescribe some of the newer drugs to children with JRA. These are called nonsteroidal anti-inflammatory drugs, the most common of which are Tolectin, Indocin, and Naprosyn. They all act in the same fashion and have fewer side effects than aspirin, although they may also cause stomach irritation, headache, skin rash, and kidney injury.

Children who do not respond to these medications are given one of the long-acting, or slow-acting, anti-rheumatic drugs. One is gold, which is generally given as an intramuscular injection. Although oral gold is available, it is not yet licensed. D-Penicillamine is another useful medication given orally, but it has serious side effects. Another drug in this class is hydroxychloroquine, which has serious side effects on the eye. When these medications are used, physicians will require laboratory tests every week or two.

Eye disease as a result of arthritis is usually treated with eye drops to dilate the pupil and control the inflammation. This treatment almost always controls the problem, but the eye disease must be detected early. Occasionally, surgery is needed.

Giving medicines around the clock for a number of years presents a major problem in compliance. Patients tend to use drugs sporadically, especially when the disease persists for over a year. When a child is given aspirin, well-meaning friends and relatives, as well as parents and patients, do not see how it can actually work, since it is so common, inexpensive, and can be gotten without a prescription. "You mean, there's no medicine, *just* aspirin?" is a frequent reaction, especially when a child seems very disabled by the disease. People often question the parents about the safety of high doses of aspirin. In some children, compliance is better when one of the new medicines that is costlier than aspirin is given.

Physical Therapy

The purpose of physical therapy is to preserve joint motion, maintain muscle strength, and help the child carry out the activities of daily life. Usually children with morning stiffness are advised to take a warm tub bath in the morning. Ideally, physical therapy exercises are done following the bath, although this is difficult to accomplish if the child has an early school schedule. Exercises should be done twice daily. The time spent varies according to the severity of joint involvement. Sometimes these exercises may take up to 30 minutes. Therapeutic exercises involve moving the affected joints through their range of motion and strengthening the muscles around affected joints. Preferably, a physical therapist should arrange the home program, teaching the child and offering supervision. Children are more likely to follow a program of age-appropriate activities, such as riding bicycles and big wheels and swimming, rather than routine exercises.

Provision of Psychosocial Support

Independence is encouraged and stressed to parents. Allowing as much independence as possible, with subtle supervision, helps these children feel some control over the disease, which, in many respects, controls their lives. It is important to reinforce coping mechanisms that will help the child develop a positive self-image. Adolescents are helped to cope with changes in body image and to become responsible for their own health care. Teenagers with chronic illness can benefit by meeting others with similar problems. This decreases the feeling of isolation that is common to children with any chronic illness.

Play therapy is also a means of providing psychosocial support. Through play therapy, the child uses various media for expression, such as role-playing or clay, and is encouraged to verbalize fears and concerns.

Some medical facilities provide education programs about the treatment and the disease and organize parent support groups.

Unconventional Remedies

Although there is no cure for arthritis, some families continue to "shop" for a physician who might promise a cure. They may also be attracted to fad remedies, especially if the child had endured months or years of daily medicines and exercises. Some unconventional remedies may be harmless, but they are usually expensive and give false hopes. They also prevent the family from following the medically prescribed treatment and delay improvement. It is important to know that some misrepresented remedies could contain ingredients that have toxic side effects. Families should be wary of claims that promote food or vitamins as a cure. Many are costly, and some forms of diet therapy using high doses of vitamin A may be dangerous. Research scientists have not found any foods or nutrients that cause arthritis, make it worse, or cure it.

SCHOOL LIFE

Academic Performance

JRA is a disease of the joints, not of the mind. Children with the disease may be smaller in stature than most of their classmates, but their potential for academic performance is not diminished. However, the mechanics of the school situation, such as the distance between classes, present problems that could affect scholastic achievement.

A variation in how the child feels within the school day may result in inconsistent performance. The student may do extremely well in one or two classes but may seem quiet and disinterested in others and may not even complete assignments. This causes tension between the student and teacher. For example, a history teacher, knowing that the child gets good grades in other subjects, may wonder if the student is really trying in history class. The student, in turn, may feel misunderstood by the teacher. Nonaccusatory communication with the student and parents is essential in finding out the student's usual pattern of well-being so that poor academic performance during certain times can be addressed appropriately (see Approach to the Child with JRA).

Physical Activities

Physical activity is important throughout the year. Children with JRA can play outdoors even in cold weather if they are dressed warmly. They should be encouraged to take part in physical education classes, with certain limitations, but should not be pushed beyond their limits. Ideally, these children should be allowed to set their own limits on a daily basis. A child may be able to participate fully one day and only minimally the next because of the intermittent nature of the pain and stiffness. Allowing for these variations can be difficult in a school setting. Also, many physical education programs require that the student participate at the speed set by the class or not at all. A modified physical education program would be excellent for these students. Emotional problems can be intensified when a student must either be left out or extend himself or herself beyond the limits set by the disease.

As a general guideline, activities that require total body movement, such as swimming, are most beneficial. Children with JRA should be cautious about participating in contact sports and should not do so without their physician's approval. Activities should also be avoided that put stress on an arthritic joint when it is inflamed or when there is restriction of range of motion. For example, a child with wrist, shoulder, or elbow involvement should not do push-ups, handstands, and other exercises that stress these joints. Headstands should be avoided. If the knees are affected, activities that require repeated knee-bending should be avoided. Most children with JRA limit their own physical activity appropriately; therefore, they should be encouraged to find their own tolerance level to activity.

APPROACH TO THE CHILD WITH JRA

The key to psychosocial well-being with chronically ill children is to encourage them to live as normally as possible. Children with JRA are no different in that they must clearly be expected to perform to their potential and not be given preferential treatment inappropriately. However, there are appropriate allowances that must be made if these children are to function at their best at school.

Parents have remarked that the best time for the child's learning or play seems to be from midmorning to early afternoon. Stiffness and soreness is most often a problem in the early morning and fatigue a problem in the late afternoon. In children with fevers, the fever tends to rise in the afternoon. In a self-contained classroom, the teacher may be aware of the child's limitations during these periods. If the child has several teachers, a guidance counselor can assist in making up a suitable schedule. The most demanding classes should be scheduled during the middle of the day, leaving the beginning and end for less challenging activities.

Writing for periods of more than 15 or 20 minutes may be difficult for children with arthritis in the wrists and fingers. Thus, giving oral examinations, allowing the child to answer questions by tape recorder, and permitting breaks during exam periods may be appropriate. Prolonged sitting may cause stiffness and sore joints in the child with hip involvement, so the child should be free to walk around to lessen discomfort. To minimize the class's awareness of the problem, a teacher might designate the child as the class messenger.

Children with severe arthritis will find it difficult to carry books from class to class and from school to home. They should be given an extra set of books to be kept at home and be allowed to store the necessary books for each class in the classroom. The child should have permission to leave class a few minutes early to allow time to get to the next class, lunch, or the bus without risk of being pushed in crowds.

Some children are teased for having to take medicine in the middle of classes. This sometimes leads to poor compliance. If a teacher notices that a child has neglected to take a scheduled medication, a private reminder is appropriate. The teacher might also plan a way for the child to leave the classroom inconspicuously to take medicine.

A child's morale is helped when teachers offer support by recognizing the variations in how he or she feels, encouraging a positive attitude, and advising the child to take one day at a time. A brief remark such as "It must be hard for you. Yesterday you felt fine, and today your knees are swollen" will convey the feeling that the problem is understood.

Whenever there is a prolonged absence or patterns of attendance change, the school nurse should question the family as to the reason. The child may have been hospitalized or perhaps kept home necessarily. Children with systemic JRA may miss a lot of school, especially in the early stages of the disease when fevers are high and fatigue and irritability are common. However, once the child has begun treatment and all other possibilities for fever, such as viral and bacterial infection, have been excluded, the child can return to school. Parents sometimes need periodic reassurance that if a child feels fairly well, he or she can attend school with a JRA-related fever. Occasionally a child's symptoms will worsen and absences will increase because the family cannot afford to continue to purchase the medication needed. This possibility should be investigated when the child begins to miss school.

Failure to motivate the child toward academic and career goals is inappropriate, since the majority of children with JRA go into remission by adulthood. It is tragic for a child to overcome a serious illness only to be faced with overcoming educational deficits that have accumulated during the years of illness.

Motivation must be given not only in the classroom but when the child is absent. If a child must miss school for a prolonged period, parents and school personnel should work together as soon as possible to formulate a homebound program that will keep the child up to date with the class. For short-term absences, make up work should be given and done. A child may be too uncomfortable to attend a full day of school but could do the assignments at home. For this work to be meaningful, it should be evaluated by teachers as critically as work done when the child is actually attending class.

Allowing the child to fall into patterns of blaming JRA for all failures and for not participating in classroom activities is a mistake. Teachers cannot always know when pain is real and when the child may be avoiding something unpleasant or intimidating. When it is suspected that the child really could perform, it is helpful for teachers to focus on specifics rather than generalities. Both parents and children tend to be less defensive when specifics are given and when specific goals within a subject are worked toward. "He's not working as well as he can" or "She's not trying to learn fractions" are general statements that seldom produce positive results. Chances for success are greater when statements are made such as "John needs some practice with fractions, especially in finding common denominators" or "Kim needs to read more carefully so that she gets enough information to answer questions at the end of the chapter."

Responsibilities can be assigned to children who do not voluntarily participate in classroom activities. Requesting opinions in class discussions can help involve a withdrawn child. Teachers can encourage interaction with peers by arranging for the child to participate in activities that require group interaction but not physical activity. Examples are committees to plan class trips or class parties. Also, games, such as computer games and chess, can be planned in which the affected child can take part and have as much chance of winning as unaffected classmates.

MEDICAL PROBLEMS THAT MAY OCCUR IN THE CLASSROOM

In children with systemic JRA, fevers and rashes could occur during the school day. If other possible sources of infection have been ruled out, children who feel they can function at school should not be sent home. This situation can be planned for by discussions with the child, the parents, and the doctor. The child is not presenting a danger to the other children by being in school with a fever or a rash. If the question comes up, reassurance should be given that the illness is not contagious.

Some side effects from medication may occur during the school day. There may be nosebleeds, stomachaches, and vomiting in a child who is taking aspirin or Tolectin. When these occur, the parents should be contacted and advised to call their physician. Signs of salicylate (aspirin) toxicity are deep, heavy breathing and drowsiness, although these are problems that occur more often in acute aspirin poisoning than in chronic aspirin toxicity. Also, heavy breathing is much more often a symptom in younger children than in those of school age. However, if a child on aspirin breathes heavily or becomes drowsy, a physician should be contacted. The child may have to be taken to a hospital emergency room.

Children being treated for iridocyclitis with eye drops that dilate the pupils may have problems reading letters on the chalkboard or with other schoolwork. If a teacher notices the child having vision problems or having red or watery eyes, the parents should be contacted to establish whether the child has had the slit-lamp examination.

FOSTERING CLASSMATES' UNDERSTANDING

A proper attitude displayed by the teacher toward a child with a chronic illness offers the best assurance of the child's being accepted by classmates. An explanation of the nature of the disease and the reason for certain necessary privileges, such as allowing the affected child to stand up and stretch, may reduce the anxieties and jealousies of classmates. However, this must be done in a sensitive way. Arranging for affected children to perform important functions will make them more acceptable to their classmates. One child with JRA served as a trainer for a sports team, since he had learned so much about physical therapy through his own physical therapy program. Assigning "helping roles" to classmates, such as carrying books for an affected friend, may make them feel useful and teach the satisfaction of helping others.

Children with JRA should be encouraged to share their feelings about their disease. A child may be approached privately about the possibility of presenting the facts about JRA in a health class and bringing visual aids to help explain the disease. This kind of project can help a child's self-image as well as foster an understanding of his or her health problems among peers.

REFERENCES

1. J. G. Schaller and R. J. Wedgwood, "Rheumatic and Connective Tissue Diseases of Childhood," in *Nelson Textbook of Pediatrics,* 12th ed., ed. Richard E. Behrman and Victor E. Vaughan, III. Senior Editor Waldo E. Nelson (Philadelphia, PA: W. B. Saunders, 1983), pp. 564–72.
2. Ibid.
3. Ibid.
4. Ibid.
5. Ibid.
6. E. R. McAnarney, I. B. Pless, B. Satterwhite, and S. B. Friedman, "Psychological Problems of Children with Chronic Juvenile Arthritis," *Pediatrics* 53 (1974): 523–28.
7. R. Rimon, R. H. Belmaker, and R. Ebstein, "Psychosomatic Aspects of Juvenile Rheumatoid Arthritis," *Scandinavian Journal of Rheumatology* 6 (1977): 1–10.
8. M. J. Henoch, J. W. Batson, and J. Baum, "Psychosocial Factors in Juvenile Rheumatoid Arthritis," *Arthritis and Rheumatism* 21 (1978): 229–33.

RESOURCES

Suggested Reading

Brewer, Earl J.; Giannini, Edward H.; and Person, David A. *Juvenile Rheumatoid Arthritis*. 2nd ed. Philadelphia, PA: W. B. Saunders, 1970.

Giesecke, Linda; Athreya, Balu; and Doughty, Robert. *Thanks to You, The Child with JRA Will Succeed in School*. Children's Seashore House, Rheumatology Dept., 34th St. and Civic Center Blvd., Philadelphia, PA 19104.

Williams, Gordon F. *Children with Chronic Arthritis*. Littleton, MA: PSG Publishing Co., 1981.

Useful Addresses

American Juvenile Arthritis Organization, 3400 Peachtree Rd., NE, Atlanta, GA 30326.
Arthritis Foundation, National Office, 3400 Peachtree Rd., NE, Atlanta, GA 30326.

Systemic Lupus Erythematosus

by Balu H. Athreya, M.D. and Carrie Goren Ingall, R.N., M.S.N.

OVERVIEW

Systemic lupus erythematosus (SLE) is characterized by inflammation of the blood vessels supplying various parts of the body, such as the skin, the membranes in the joints (synovium), the heart, the brain, and, most important in this condition, the kidney. Inflammation, which is the usual response to infection, occurs even though there is no infection. The inflammation in SLE is caused by an abnormality in the immune system. Normally, antibodies are produced to fight infectious agents and foreign substances in the body and to act as the body's defense system. In lupus, as in other "autoimmune diseases," antibodies are produced that attack and damage the body's own tissue. Certain types of antibodies are commonly seen in patients with SLE, although not exclusively. These antibodies are called antinuclear (ANA) and antideoxyribonucleic acid (anti-DNA), and they react with various nuclear materials in cells. Antibodies that react with other components, such as red and white blood cells, are also found.

Cause

The actual cause of SLE is unknown. Current opinion is that at least three different factors are involved: genetic, hormonal, and environmental. Studies of the immune system of patients with SLE have shown that certain cell or tissue types (called Human Leukocyte Antigen or HLA) and complement deficencies are associated with this disorder. Both HLA and complement are components of the immune system that are inherited. Therefore, certain people have a genetic abnormality that predisposes them to having lupus. There is usually a very strong history of lupus in families of children with lupus.

Lupus is more common in females than in males. There is evidence from animal experiments that hormones are involved in modifying the severity of the disease, but the mechanism is not clear.

The environmental factors associated with lupus include sunlight and drugs. In a susceptible person, it appears that a stimulus, such as a specific drug or sunlight, might initiate the process. Though infections may be another initiating factor, no particular organism has been associated with SLE. Lupus that occurs as a side effect of certain medicines is not as common in children as in adults. This is because many of the drugs that produce lupus are not used in children but in adults with cardiovascular disease. When it does occur, however, drug-induced lupus is less severe than lupus that is not induced by drugs.

Course

The onset and course of SLE are variable. Onset most commonly occurs during the second decade of life. There may be periods of increased disease activity and periods of remission. Some patients will enter a complete remission while others continue into adulthood with this disease. With recent advances in early diagnosis and management, more than 80 percent of children with SLE survive more than 10 years after diagnosis, with some having various levels of disability. The major causes of death are kidney disease and various types of infections.

Population and Incidence

SLE occurs about eight times more frequently in girls than in boys. In adults, the ratio is even greater (9:1). The disease seems to be more common in blacks, with more black women than men being affected. Although the incidence of SLE is unknown, it begins in childhood in 20 percent of cases.

Major Complications and Symptoms

Symptoms of lupus may begin suddenly or slowly and gradually. With sudden onset, early symptoms are a rash and kidney, heart, or brain disease. Gradual onset is characterized by fever, weakness, arthritis (inflamed joints), and rash. The fever may not be high but may be sustained. There may be malaise, aches and pains, and loss of weight. Several types of rashes are seen in SLE. The most common are flat, pink lesions over various parts of the body. The typical rash, which seems to be especially prominent after exposure to sunlight, usually appears over the face, often in a butterfly pattern. In these children, light seems to induce release of DNA from skin cells, which in turn leads to anti-DNA antibody production. These children may also develop purpura, which are small reddish lesions caused by bleeding into the tissues. Hair loss may occur. Children with SLE may also develop sores in the mouth and nose. Arthritis is an extremely common symptom. However, unlike the arthritis in rheumatoid arthritis, it does not lead to permanent disability, although it may be uncomfortable.

Lupus involves different systems of the body in different people. Symptoms and complications depend on the parts of the body involved. With heart involvement caused by inflammation of the outside layer (pericardium) and muscle (myocardium) of the heart, there may be fever, chest pain, difficulty in breathing, fast heart rate, and heart failure.

Kidney disease may be present without any symptoms early in the course of the disease. Routine examination of the urine in a patient suspected of having lupus may show protein, red blood cells, and various types of casts. Kidney disease may also be manifested by reduced urine output and swelling of various parts of the body. Kidney biopsy is done almost routinely by some physicians, since recognizing the type of kidney lesion has some value in predicting the course of the disease. The type of treatment, and how aggressively it is followed, may depend on the types of kidney lesions. Kidney biopsies are examined under special microscopes.

The lung disease of lupus behaves like pneumonia, except that an infectious organism, such as bacteria, is not involved. A lung biopsy may show inflammation of the blood vessels. Large amounts of fluid may accumulate between the lungs and their lining (pleural sac), resulting in breathing difficulty. Cough and shortness of breath are common signs of many different kinds of lung disease in lupus.

Abdominal pain is also fairly common and can result either from the disease or from the medications. In severe SLE, there may be bleeding from the gut and inflammation of the pancreas.

Involvement of the blood vessels of the brain and central nervous system may lead to neurological or psychiatric symptoms. The neurological symptoms may include seizures, inability to sense with or move a particular body part, and spinal cord problems. Psychiatric manifestations include hallucinations, loss of memory, and personality changes. For example, these children may suddenly do poorly in school, become forgetful, and get careless about their appearance. Some children may go into a coma if they are very ill.

Prognosis

Children with lupus can expect to grow into adults, although there may be some restriction of activities. Most can continue with their education, become employed, marry, and have families. The prognosis in lupus depends in a major way on the presence and severity of kidney disease.

Psychological Aspects

A child with lupus, like any child with a chronic illness, may have problems accepting the disease. Soon after diagnosis, when there is disbelief, doubt, and fear, the child may behave differently from before. He or she may be more tired and become disinterested in schoolwork. In addition, because of frequent visits to physicans and admissions to hospitals, he or she may fall behind in some lessons. The use of medications, such as corticosteroids, may affect the personality. Since these drugs also alter the appearance, emotional problems are common and understandable, particularly in girls who become obese and develop facial hair and acne. Psychological defenses, such as anger as a response to these disfiguring effects of treatment, lead to poor compliance with medication. Poor compliance, in turn, aggravates the disease, which perpetuates the cycle.

THERAPY

Appropriate Medical Care

Lupus is a relatively rare disorder in children, and the complications can be serious. Drugs used for treatment can have serious side effects. For these reasons a rheumatologist should be involved in the care of children with SLE. Around the time of diagnosis, frequent visits to the hospital are necessary, particularly in the presence of heart, central nervous system, or kidney disease. Adjustments of medications are essential, since treatment varies with each individual. Most physicians try to adjust medications without hospitalization, but untoward side effects and lack of disease control may necessitate a hospital admission. The child may have to be seen in clinic once or even twice a week. However, once the disease is under reasonable control, appointments may be made every six to eight weeks. Since SLE is characterized by acute flares, and since these children may develop side reactions to medicines, they may have to be admitted to the hospital periodically.

Medications

Since we do not know exactly what causes SLE, there is no drug that specifically offers a cure. Because the symptoms of SLE are caused by inflammation of blood vessels, a number of medications can be used to control either the effects of the inflammation or the inflammation itself.

The usual drugs for the management of fever and arthritis are aspirin or one of the newer nonsteroidal anti-inflammatory drugs, such as Tolectin or Indocin. Aspirin and nonsteroidal anti-inflammatory drugs can produce stomach irritation and easy bruising in some people. Tolectin and Indocin can cause headaches, particularly in the morning. Diarrhea is another side reaction of some of these drugs.

For diseases characterized by involvement of the heart, lungs, kidneys, or brain, medications classified as corticosteroids are used. One type of corticosteriod, prednisone, is used in fairly large doses in life-threatening situations. If prednisone in full dose does not work over a period of six to eight weeks, if a patient develops serious side reactions to corticosteroids, or if the disease is rapidly progressing, another type of drug that suppresses the immune system may be used. These drugs—Imuran and Cytoxan—are very potent and are also used in the treatment of cancer. Although lupus is not a type of cancer, some of the anticancer drugs have been found to be useful in treating SLE.

Prednisone produces various changes in the body, such as excessive hair growth, weight gain, puffiness, muscle weakness, cataracts, and high blood pressure. Children on corticosteroids may also develop stomach irritation and bleeding. Corticosteroids can produce mood swings, but this is more common in adults than in children. Certainly, children can become euphoric and eat more than usual. They can also become talkative and giddy, without realizing it.

The skin disease of lupus often responds to hydroxychloroquine. In addition, drugs to treat specific symptoms, such as phenobarbital for seizures, drugs for high blood pressure, and antibiotics for infections, are used when needed.

SCHOOL LIFE

Academic Performance

In most cases, SLE itself does not affect learning ability and academic performance. However, the fatigue and malaise that are present when the disease is active may affect the child's ability to complete assignments and/or attend school for the entire day.

In the presence of involvement of the brain, the child may suddenly experience academic problems because of loss of memory (particularly for recent events) and inability to concentrate. At these times, there may be difficulty with reading, writing, and coordination. All these problems may be a result of the disease process and not of any behavioral abnormality. Teachers and school nurses should notify parents if any of these problems arise. Increasing the child's medication, as advised by the physician, will usually ease the symptoms.

Psychosocial Aspects

One of the greatest psychosocial problems of children with lupus, especially adolescents, is the change in body image. When the disease is active, a facial rash and other skin discoloration is often present. Children with kidney involvement may have swollen hands and feet. Medicines can cause puffiness of the face, thinning of the hair, acne, and excessive hair growth. There is also anxiety about the disease itself, especially when it is active. The child may not only have fears about the outcome of the disease but may be worried that he or she will have to miss school or will be rejected by peers. These fears, combined with changes in body image, can lead to feelings of isolation, which is reinforced by the fact that many of these children nap after school for two to three hours, thereby missing after-school social activities.

Physical Activities

Children with lupus should be encouraged to participate in activities appropriate for their age and take part in most physical activities to their tolerance. They should be permitted to set their own limits on a day-to-day basis because the nature of the disease is such that some of these children will be more tired or have more symptoms on some days than on others. There may even be a variation of symptoms within a given day. If the heart or lungs are involved, stair climbing may cause shortness of breath, and an elevator should be used.

Environmental Factors

Since lupus is in the category of diseases that involve arthritis as a symptom, some children with SLE may experience morning stiffness.

Dampness and cold weather may also cause discomfort. Although there are no scientific data proving that dampness and cold weather cause joint pain, many children with SLE complain of worsening symptoms when the weather changes to these extremes. Each child is different and therefore should be encouraged to seek his or her own level of tolerance to weather conditions.

Some of these children have difficulty with the small blood vessels in their extremities during cold weather. Their hands and/or feet may become blue, cold, and painful for several seconds or even minutes. They are instructed to wear warm gloves and not to remain outside for extended periods of time. Moving the affected extremity in a circular motion helps to restore blood flow; affected areas should not be put in hot water.

Prolonged exposure to sunlight can precipitate a flare-up of lupus. Those who are sensitive should apply Number 15 sunscreen to exposed areas when in the sun for more than a few minutes. If a child's skin is sensitive to fluorescent light, he or she should not be seated in the classroom directly under a light fixture, since this may cause a flare-up of the disease.

APPROACH TO THE CHILD WITH LUPUS

Several situations may arise in the classroom that can best be handled if they are anticipated. To prevent fatigue, a student could have his or her four major subjects broken up by a study period during which he or she could rest in the nurse's office. If there is a second study period in the day, it could be scheduled last so that the student could have the option of going home early. Access to an elevator is often helpful in conserving energy. If joint symptoms are problematic, allowing the student to leave class a few minutes early to get to the lunchroom or to the next class on time is helpful. If a student with lupus is having kidney or heart symptoms, he or she may be on medicine that necessitates frequent trips to the lavatory. Attention should not be called to this during class or in front of other children.

When disease activity requires long absences from school, someone from the school should contact the family to see if homebound tutoring is appropriate. Most children become very anxious about their schoolwork when they are absent and would welcome help so that they do not fall behind. In general, the prognosis for this disease is good, and children with lupus should be prepared academically and socially to function as active members of society. Career or vocational guidance is encouraged.

Communication with the child, the family, and the health care team liaison will do much to help the child adjust to and cope with school life. Also, it is helpful for school personnel to convey understanding and concern without pity.

MEDICAL PROBLEMS THAT MAY OCCUR IN THE CLASSROOM

There are several signs of disease activity that may be noticed by teachers. A rash in a butterfly shape on the face or discoloration of face, ears, and extremities may signify activity of disease. Makeup can be suggested to cover the facial rash.

Nausea and vomiting may be a sign of lupus or a drug reaction, or it may merely be due to the common problems of "upset stomach" that children get. If a child is vomiting, a parent should be notified and encouraged to contact the child's physician. It is important to differentiate between a flare-up of the disease and the onset of an illness, such as a common virus. The child should be sent home if fever is greater than 100°F, and parents should be advised to seek medical attention.

Shortness of breath is also a sign of disease activity. If this occurs at school, the teacher should ask the child if he or she has experienced this before and then advise medical follow-up. The school nurse should be notified so he or she can follow up with a phone call to parents. During this time, any means of helping the child conserve energy makes the school situation more bearable. For example, another child could carry books for the patient, or an elevator could be used.

Although seizures are very rare in lupus, their occurrence is possible. The child may say he or she feels "funny" or lightheaded and then demonstrate jerking movements of the arms and legs. Stay with the child while someone else seeks medical help. It is important that the area where the child is having a seizure be made safe so he or she does not get hurt. Do not try to put anything in his or her mouth. Try to estimate the duration of the seizure. Remember: a seizure cannot be stopped once it has begun. A safe environment is the key.

If the child's feet swell, the legs can be elevated during prolonged periods of sitting. Ask the child privately if the doctor knows if he or she is having this problem. Swelling will probably decrease with treatment.

FOSTERING CLASSMATES' UNDERSTANDING

Classmates should be informed that the rash is not contagious. Young children who ask what is wrong with a friend who has lupus can be told that he or she has a problem with whatever organ is affected and that the disease, unlike measles or chicken pox, is not contagious. Classmates are often afraid that they, too, will become sick.

When adolescents ask about a peer who has lupus, one might try to explain that their friend has something wrong with his or her blood vessels. Since blood vessels are in every organ, that could provide a foundation for further explanation. No matter how the explanation is worded, it is important that (1) an explanation be given, not avoided; (2) that it be presented in as positive and truthful a way as possible (i.e., "Mary is taking medicine that will help her, but the medicine is causing her face to look puffy. She probably feels self-conscious.") while allaying the underlying fears of the person who is asking; and (3) that it suggests some way that the classmate can help (i.e., "You can help Mary by getting her milk for her at lunch, so she doesn't have to stand in line. This way maybe her feet won't swell as much.").

RESOURCES

Suggested Reading

Carr, Ronald, M.D., Ph.D, and Jameson, Elizabeth S., J.D. *Lupus Erythematosus: A Handbook for Physicians, Patients and Their Families*. Lupus Foundation of America, Inc., Patient Relations Education Committee, 1982.

Epstein, Wallace V., M.D., F.A.C.P., and Clewley, Gina, M.S.W., L.C.S.W. *Living with S.L.E.* Dept. of Medicine and Social Work, University of California at San Francisco, 1976. May be ordered from Millberry Union Bookstore, 500 Parnassus Ave., San Francisco, CA 94143.

Gibbas, Donna, M.D. "Some Thoughts on Lupus in Childhood." In *Lupus Erythematosus: Selected Topics, Vol. 3*. Atlanta Chapter, Lupus Foundation of America, Inc., 1982.

Useful Addresses

American Lupus Society, National Office, 23751 Madison Street, Torrance, CA 90505.

Lupus Foundation of America, National Office, 11673 Holly Springs Dr., St. Louis, MO 63141.

Cystic Fibrosis

by Robert Wilmott, M.D., Barbara R. Burroughs, R.N., M.S.N., and David Beele, M.S.W., A.C.S.W.

OVERVIEW

Cystic fibrosis of the pancreas, previously called "mucoviscidosis" but now known simply as "cystic fibrosis," has only been clearly recognized since the late 1930s. Cystic fibrosis affects the exocrine glands, which are the glands that discharge their secretions via ducts to internal or external surfaces of the body. In this disorder, the mucus is abnormally thick and sticky, and other glandular secretions are also highly concentrated. It is not clear if the defect is the same in all organ systems.

Although cystic fibrosis is the most common serious inherited disorder to affect Caucasians, the basic cause of the disease remains unknown. However, much is known about the problems that result from thick mucous secretions characteristic of this disorder. These abnormally viscous (concentrated) secretions cause blockage of the ducts from the glands, such as those in the pancreas, so that other glandular secretions are reduced or cannot get out. For example, digestive juices from the pancreas cannot get into the small intestine where they are needed to digest food. Thick, sticky mucous secretions are also found in the intestines and liver. In the lungs, there is difficulty in clearing secretions from the bronchial tree, and this is associated with an increased susceptibility to infection. Sweat and salivary glands produce secretions that contain large amounts of salt. The abnormally high concentrations of salt in saliva have no clinical significance, but the high concentrations of salt in sweat, up to three to four times what is normal, can lead to excessive salt and water losses, dehydration, and heat prostration.

The most detailed studies have been on the salivary and sweat glands. Sophisticated studies of isolated human sweat glands have demonstrated that there is reduced reabsorption of sodium and chloride molecules by the lining membrane of the gland.[1] Why the mucus in cystic fibrosis is excessively thick is uncertain. Perhaps a defect of salt and water movement similar to that in the sweat and salivary glands results in secretions which do not contain sufficient water. Studies of the composition of the mucus have shown abnormalities of its chemistry.[2]

Inheritance

Cystic fibrosis is clearly inherited as an autosomal recessive disease. This was demonstrated by a large study of affected families.[3] Both parents of cystic fibrosis patients carry an abnormal gene for the condition on a nonsex (autosomal) chromosome. To inherit this disorder, the infant must receive an abnormal gene from each parent. Since each parent has a pair of genes and passes along only one to the child, it is possible for a child to receive a defective gene from one parent and a normal gene from the other. This would make the child a carrier, like the parents. It is also possible for the child to receive normal genes from both parents. When both parents are carriers, with each pregnancy the mathematical probabilities are one in four that the child will have cystic fibrosis, one in four that the child will be normal, and one in two that the child will be a symptomless carrier.

At the present time, there is no test for the cystic fibrosis carrier state, making it impossible to identify couples at risk and to provide genetic counseling. Certain biochemical tests do show statistically significant differences between cystic fibrosis patients, cystic fibrosis carriers, and normal people, but there is too much overlap between the three groups for such tests to be clinically useful. There are similar problems with prenatal diagnosis. Much research is directed toward developing a test that would identify cystic fibrosis babies early in pregnancy. Given the severity of cystic fibrosis and its incurable nature, the goal of this research is to enable clinicians to make the diagnosis early in pregnancy so that families who already have a child with cystic fibrosis can decide whether or not to continue with the pregnancy.

Incidence

The incidence of cystic fibrosis is approximately 1 in 2,000 among U.S. whites.[4] The incidence is much lower in blacks, Orientals, and Native Americans. An incidence of about 1 in 100,000 has been calculated for Orientals,[5] and approximately 1 in 17,000 has been suggested for American blacks.[6] Carrier frequency can be calculated from the incidence of the disease, and it is estimated that 4 to 5 percent of U.S. whites carry the gene.[7]

Course

The natural history of cystic fibrosis is so variable that it is difficult to summarize it briefly. There is great variability in severity of symptoms and pattern of disease even within families, so cystic fibrosis does not "breed true."

More and more patients with cystic fibrosis are diagnosed within the first one or two years of life. At the Hospital for Sick Children in London, it was observed that 80 percent of patients are now diagnosed within the first year. Symptoms usually develop in infancy even in patients who do not exhibit meconium ileus as new borns. Many young patients will present with a cough, which is dry at first but is characteristically repeated and harsh. Findings on physical examination are usually normal at this age, although there may be increased respiratory rate, barrel-shape deformity of the chest, or persistent indrawing of the spaces between the ribs with respiration. The results of listening to the chest with a stethoscope are usually normal. In such patients, especially if the mother is worried about the stools, a sweat test should be done. As the children grow older, they develop more persistent respiratory infections, particularly once they become colonized with the germ *Pseudomonas aeruginosa*. Periodic hospital admission for intravenous antibiotics and intensive chest therapy is eventually necessary for most patients.

The outlook for patients with cystic fibrosis has improved over the years. When the disease was first recognized in the late 1930s, approximately 80 percent died within two years of birth. The latest British figures show that now 17 percent survive to age 16, when they are transferred to adult centers.[8] This figure is similar to that from cystic fibrosis centers in the United States, Canada, and Australia. In childhood, males and females with cystic fibrosis do not differ significantly in survival rates. However, a difference emerges at the time of puberty, and particularly good survival rates have been described in Canadian males who participated in a study using Canadian children with cystic fibrosis as the sample population.[9] The reason for this difference is thought to be hormonal, as the male is probably helped by his increased muscle mass and chest development after puberty.

There are differences in prognosis according to age of onset of respiratory disease as well as according to sex. Some patients develop symptoms very slowly, and they may not come to medical attention until their teenage years. If the clinical course has been good until this time, such patients often continue to do well, as do other patients with few or mild symptoms and little disability from their disease. By contrast, the outlook is poor for children who have severe recurrent respiratory infections at an early age.

Infant Screening and Diagnosis

Several methods have been evaluated for screening for this disease in newborn babies. The original method was a chemical dip-stick test to detect increased amounts of protein in a newborn baby's bowel movement. This method is useful for children of families who already have a child with cystic fibrosis, but it is too inaccurate for application to large populations. An important criticism of the stool test is that it will detect only those children with cystic fibrosis who have pancreatic disease; 20 percent of patients have no such pancreatic involvement. Also, there is a 15 to 20 percent rate of false positive results. The accuracy of the stool test can be increased by combining it with further chemical analysis of the stool. New screening methods using dried blood spots are currently being evaluated.

The diagnosis of cystic fibrosis is always confirmed with the sweat test, which uses the principle that sodium chloride concentrations are increased in babies with cystic fibrosis.[10] The sweat test involves collection of sweat that is then analyzed biochemically. Although it is occasionally difficult to interpret the results in patients with borderline values, this test is very reliable and forms the standard for making the diagnosis of cystic fibrosis in children before puberty. After puberty the normal sweat electrolyte values have a wider range, which makes interpretation more difficult in older children.

CLINICAL MANIFESTATIONS AND TREATMENT

The child with cystic fibrosis is best treated at one of the cystic fibrosis centers established by the national Cystic Fibrosis Foundation. These centers have multidisciplinary teams which include physicians, nurses, social workers, nutritionists, and physical therapists. Some children with cystic fibrosis are treated by private physicians, especially in remote areas where special facilities are not available. However, it is difficult to provide comprehensive care outside a large medical center.

The time involved in the treatment of the patient with cystic fibrosis represents a major commitment for both the patient and family. Clinic visits are usually necessary every two to three months and may require a day of absence from school. For many families, the clinic visit requires a two- to three-hour drive in each direction. More demanding is the daily time commitment for physical therapy and the administration of enzymes. It takes approximately 20 minutes to perform chest percussion and postural draining, and this may have to be done two or three times a day. Some children do not take medications or enzymes well, imposing an additional strain on their parents.

Clinical symptoms of cystic fibrosis usually appear early in life, although they are not always recognized as being a result of cystic fibrosis. The most striking manifestation is in the newborn with intestinal obstruction from thick, sticky bowel contents (meconium). This may require surgery as well as an extended hospitalization. Later in infancy, children experience either recurrent respiratory infections, persistent diarrhea, failure to gain weight, or a combination of all of these symptoms. Less common presenting symptoms include recurrent polyps in the nose, prolapse of the rectum, anemia, low protein levels in the blood, enlargement of the liver, diabetes mellitus, infertility in the male, and heat prostration. Parents sometimes recognize a salty taste when kissing the baby and seek medical advice. Patients may present later, in the teenage years, with a history of a persistent productive cough and wheezing, which has been diagnosed as asthma.

Major Complications

Lung Disease

The typical symptoms of recurrent lung disease in cystic fibrosis patients include a persistent cough, recurrent wheezing, increased respiratory rate, pneumonia, and persistent production of yellow or green sputum. At birth, the lungs of cystic fibrosis babies are normal anatomically, but there is an increased risk of pulmonary infection, particularly with the bacteria *Staphylococcus aureus, Hemophilus influenzae,* and *Pseudomonas aeruginosa*. While staphylococcal and hemophilus infections frequently respond to antibiotic treatment, pseudomonas infection, once firmly established, is rarely eradicated.[11]

Increased Susceptibility to Infection. Cilia, which are minute hair-like structures on the surfaces of cells lining the air passages (bronchi) of the lung, move in a wave-like manner to propel mucus, bacteria, and foreign particles, such as smoke and dust, toward the throat where they may be coughed up. Reduced clearance of mucus and particles from the lungs has been described in cystic fibrosis and may account, in part, for the increased susceptibility to pulmonary infection. In patients with cystic fibrosis, the clearance rates are similar to those of adults with chronic bronchitis. Whether this is the result of a primary basic abnormality remains unanswered. Microscopic studies have revealed normal cilia and mucous glands, although the mucous glands increase in number after infancy. A recent study found that the coordination and beating of hair cells from the nose of cystic fibrosis patients was normal; these investigators suggested that reduced mucociliary clearance is probably the effect of abnormal mucus or an inhibitor of cilia.[12] The rate of secretion of mucus appears to be increased, but this has not been shown to be a basic defect. Thus, it may be the result of chronic infection, causing inflammation which in turn causes excess mucus production. It has been shown that the composition of airway mucus is abnormal, but whether mucus in the lungs is abnormally sticky in young patients who have not yet developed pulmonary infection is uncertain.

Studies of the bacterial pathogens (disease-causing organisms) in cystic fibrosis do not reveal a pattern that explains the unusual susceptibility to infection. Patients are infected by strains of *Staphylococcus* and *Hemophilus,* which are commonly pathogenic. Patients are initially free from *Pseudomonas aeruginosa* infection, but they eventually develop persistent colonization with this organism in up to 60 to 90 percent of cases.[13] Infection with common, or garden, varieties of *Pseudomonas* predominates in the early stages, but later the patients become infected with characteristic strains, which synthesize a complex slime substance. These strains are called "mucoid *Pseudomonas aeruginosa.*" This strain of *Pseudomonas* is rarely found in other disease groups, but its significance in cystic fibrosis is not fully understood, although the mucoid substance may inhibit the lung's defense against infection. There is no evidence of a primary abnormality of antibodies, white cells, or other immunological systems in the blood of cystic fibrosis patients, but there may be a defect of the white cells responsible for engulfing and digesting bacteria in the lungs.

Impaired Pulmonary Function. Patients develop airflow obstruction, which initially affects the small air tubes in the lungs and which may appear at a very early age. The persistent obstruction to small airways eventually leads to increased lung volumes with gas trapping changes which are similar to those of asthma. Later pulmonary complications include coughing up blood because of infection in the lung and collapse of the lung because of an air leak into the pleural space from a ruptured area of overinflation or from a ruptured abscess. Eventually, recurrent pulmonary infection leads to congestive heart failure because of the high resistance to blood flow through the scarred and infected lungs. Progressive pulmonary disease and congestive heart failure are the eventual causes of death in most children with cystic fibrosis.

Pulmonary Function Studies. Pulmonary function studies are used to measure the progress of lung disease in cystic fibrosis. These children may demonstrate increased lung size on the chest radiographs (x-rays) even as infants. In cystic fibrosis, pulmonary function data and the chest radiographs correlate well with one another. As most of the illness and mortality in cystic fibrosis result from the chronic obstructive lung disease, it is possible to use pulmonary function data, chest radiographs, and clinical history to assign a score to the patient that reflects clinical severity. This score is a somewhat subjective measure, and it should be used with caution. It may be helpful in counseling families about expectations for physical activity for the child, need for rest and special treatment, or whether limitation of activity is indicated at all. It can provide a rough measure of life expectancy, but even persons with severe disease may remain stable and function surprisingly well for long periods, making predictions of this sort hazardous and generally not helpful.

Treatment. To treat the lung disease of cystic fibrosis, the patient receives regular chest physical therapy involving postural drainage and chest percussion two or three times a day. Chest percussion is clapping with cupped hands on specified areas of the chest to loosen mucus so that it is easier to cough up. This is usually done in conjunction with postural drainage, which involves placing the person in various positions to facilitate drainage of mucus through gravity. After percussion in each position, the child is asked to cough. Parents are generally responsible for the treatment. Older patients are taught and encouraged to do some of the treatment themselves but still need help for hard-to-reach areas. Adolescent and young adult patients may have mechanical percussors prescribed for them to facilitate independence, although it is not clear whether these mechanical aids are as effective as manual treatments.

The child and one family member must arise early to do the treatment, which usually takes 20 minutes. Since many children cannot eat immediately after treatment because of coughing and the possibility of vomiting, it may require getting up an hour before the rest of the family to be able to get to school on time.

When patients develop symptoms of coughing, fever, or sputum production, they are treated with antibodies based on results of sputum cultures. Some patients are treated with continuous antibiotics, usually the sicker patients who have had persistent symptoms and who seldom go long between infections.

Gastrointestinal Disease

Pathological changes of varying degrees occur in secretory cells and exocrine organs all along the alimentary tract. The degree of involvement varies from one type of gland to another. The most affected glands are those with long narrow tubes such as those in the pancreas and liver. Possibly the thick, sticky secretions block these longer tubes more easily, and this causes dilation of the glandular sacs before the obstruction. Eventually, there is scarring and destruction of the organ. The pancreas shows the most changes in function and structure; these become evident early after birth, hence the name "fibrocystic disease of the pancreas."

Impaired Digestion. Eighty percent or more of patients have impaired digestion of food.[14] The most important aspect is impaired function of the pancreas, which causes reduced absorption of fat, protein, carbohydrate, and fat soluble vitamins. Because protein and starch are inadequately digested, meat fibers may appear in the stools, and starch may be detected by special tests. Fat is incompletely digested and excessive amounts are excreted in the stools, making them characteristically oily, bulky, pale, and offensive in odor. Impaired digestion also results in slow weight gain, a large appetite, and abdominal distention. Poor nutrition is often associated with poor growth and delayed skeletal and sexual maturation. A small proportion of cystic fibrosis children have rectal prolapse, which is probably caused by the combination of diarrhea, poor nutrition, and persistent coughing.

Intestinal Obstruction. The intestine is sometimes affected in the newborn by thick, sticky bowel movements, which can completely obstruct the intestine, producing a surgical emergency. This condition is called "meconium ileus." Later in childhood, patients can develop similar symptoms from blockage with hard, incompletely digested material in the bowel. This condition is called "meconium ileus equivalent."

Treatment. The treatment for these gastrointestinal problems is replacement of pancreatic enzymes (in the form of granules or powders) combined with vitamins, and a diet rich in calories. Some cystic fibrosis centers recommend limitation of dietary fat, but others find fat a useful source of calories so long as sufficient enzymes are present for its digestion. In the small proportion of patients with persistent diarrhea or abdominal pain, adjustment of the enzyme dosage usually results in improvement, but further investigations are sometimes necessary. The management of abnormal digestion in cystic fibrosis is usually straightforward and effective.

Liver Disease

A small proportion of patients with cystic fibrosis have liver disease caused by blockage of the small bile tubes. This causes areas of scarring and inflammation in the liver around the bile ducts. In most patients this process is mild and without major symptoms. In approximately 3 percent of children with cystic fibrosis, there is progressive liver disease that may eventually result in cirrhosis.[15] This liver disease is more common in older patients. The earliest signs are an enlarged liver with abnormal results upon biochemical tests of liver function. Some patients have abnormal blood-clotting times because of deficiency of the clotting factors normally made by the liver. This problem is corrected by vitamin K, a clotting factor. If the liver disease progresses to severe scarring and cirrhosis, patients develop an increase in the pressure of the venous system draining the intestines (the portal veins). This complication is called portal hypertension, and it is relatively serious because it is associated with hemorrhage from dilated vessels in the esophagus and stomach. Fortunately, gastrointestinal hemorrhage is uncommon. If it occurs, patients need hospitalization, blood transfusions, and measures to stop the bleeding.

Genito-Urinary System

The reproductive system is normal in the female cystic fibrosis patient. In the male, there is abnormal formation of the tubes that carry the spermatazoa from the testes to the urethra, the tube in the penis. Most structures composing the male reproductive system are poorly formed, including the seminal vesicles, the vas deferens, the epididymis, and the small tubes that drain the testes. The appearance of the testes is normal upon microscopic examination until puberty, although they are sometimes small and poorly developed in older patients. Testicular function is normal from a hormonal point of view, and therefore, a young man can anticipate a normal puberty unless it is delayed by nutritional factors. However, the semen contains either no spermatozoa, or very few, in the majority of cases. Most males with cystic fibrosis are infertile and semen analysis is recommended for those considering marriage.

Sweat Glands

All patients with cystic fibrosis sweat excessively, losing large amounts of salt and water. In temperate climates, these losses are not excessive, but in hot weather, heat prostration can result. This can be avoided by using extra sodium and by drinking copious amounts of fluids. It is seldom necessary to supply salt in the form of tablets, except in very hot climates. Patients are generally encouraged to take liberal amounts of salt as seasoning as well as to eat pretzels or saltines in hot weather. Cystic fibrosis patients also benefit from the use of air conditioning at home and in the car.

Upper Airways

Sticky infected secretions are found more frequently than normal in the nasal cavities, sinuses, and middle ears in cystic fibrosis children. The lining membranes of the upper respiratory tract are often congested and inflamed, and many patients with cystic fibrosis have persistent low-grade sinus infections. If these cause headache, facial pain, or fever, the patient should be treated with antibiotics. Most patients have abnormal sinus x-rays, and treatment should be prescribed only when there are symptoms as well.

Nasal polyps occur with an increased frequency, and they are probably caused by persistent infection of the upper airways. Polyps are produced by overgrowth of the lining membrane of the nose and sinuses. They are small, silvery-white growths in the nose resembling small bunches of grapes and they are rare in childhood except in cases with cystic fibrosis. They are usually removed surgically, although they tend to recur and sometimes are best left alone.

Growth and Nutrition

The growth of cystic fibrosis patients has improved considerably with modern management. With adequate enzyme replacement, most children will grow well unless they have severe respiratory infection. Severely affected children are short and thin for their age, and they eat poorly. Growth may be so slow that puberty is delayed until the middle or late teenage years, which in turn, delays the pubertal growth spurt. Therefore, intensive nutritional support with high calorie dietary supplements is used, along with overnight nasogastric tube feeding in some cases. Hormone therapy is sometimes used for markedly delayed puberty. This must be done under careful medical supervision, as it may reduce the eventual height by inducing an earlier puberty with cessation of growth.

Modern nutritional therapy combines a nutritious diet, enzyme replacement, and vitamin supplementation, and it is rare to see evidence of vitamin deficiency. In most cases twice the regular dose of a multivitamin preparation, such as Poly Vi Sol, is adequate. Increased losses of fat in the stools cause the loss of fat soluble vitamins, which are vitamins A, D, E, and K. If the blood clotting time is abnormal, vitamin K supplementation is prescribed. Vitamin K is also prescribed for children receiving frequent courses of antibiotics, as these inhibit vitamin K synthesis by intestinal bacteria. Some centers supplement with vitamin E, although it is contained in most multivitamin preparations. Vitamin E levels are reduced in patients with cystic fibrosis, and a small number of patients with neurological disease from vitamin E deficiency have been described.

PSYCHOLOGICAL AND PSYCHOSOCIAL ASPECTS

Coping Mechanisms and Stresses within the Family

Patients with cystic fibrosis, their siblings, and parents are exposed to an increased level of stress which relates to family relationships, occupation, finances, and medical prognosis. The degree to which family members are affected will depend on their resources and strengths as well as on the age at which the diagnosis is made, the severity of the disease, and the presence of other medical or family problems. The greatest impact of cystic fibrosis occurs at the time of initial diagnosis. If diagnosis has been delayed for some reason, or if a misdiagnosis has been made, the parents often feel a combination of anger and guilt. At diagnosis, the parents of older patients may have such feelings as depression, denial, self-pity, and shock. It is not uncommon for parents to feel guilty that they have passed on this disease to their child.[16]

Denial is a common mechanism of defense utilized by parents and children in coping with an illness such as cystic fibrosis. Many caregivers, and others who know the child and family, are sometimes overconcerned that a patient or parent is using too much denial. Actually, it is a very necessary and useful mechanism; healthy denial is to be desired. Initially, denial will appear to be an avoidance of accepting and beginning to deal with cystic fibrosis on the part of the parents. However; denial often allows people time to slowly accept the impact of the disease without causing a major emotional crisis. During this initial period of denial, a family can begin to develop various family and financial supports and resources. If the denial lasts too long, and the parents do not comply with the medical regimen because they don't believe the diagnosis is correct, then it is no longer healthy. In fact, it can cause medical and emotional harm to the patient.

After an initial period of denial and anger, the family usually starts to accept the diagnosis, and they become more constructive in planning the future management and in adjusting their lifestyle. Thus, they move from the "confrontational phase" to the period of "long-term adjustment."[17] Parents are usually very anxious about the possibility of losing their child during the early confrontational age, but once the treatments have helped, and once they have accepted the diagnosis, they usually move into a phase in which they are able to cope with the stress while maintaining self-esteem and ability to handle problems. During this phase of the disease, parents tend to underplay symptoms and problems and to deny the long-term outlook. As mentioned, denial is a natural defense mechanism, but it is maladaptive if it results in a refusal to bring the child for care or in not giving medications or not doing prescribed treatments. Overprotectiveness, while a common initial response by parents who have a child with a chronic disease, should be gently discouraged as it may interfere with the child's emotional, social, and, possibly, physical growth and development.

Anxieties and Stresses in the Patient

The patients who feel stress most severely include those who are diagnosed late in childhood or during adolescence. These patients must make major changes in their daily habits, and they face destruction of hopes for their lives. Patients near or at puberty have anxieties about delayed sexual maturation resulting from the illness, and they are at increased risk.[18]

The patient with cystic fibrosis who has seen a brother or sister die from the disease is more vulnerable to its stresses, even if the death occurred before the birth of the patient.[19] Patients whose mothers have given birth to a normal baby, or whose parents adopt a healthy child, may see the other child as a substitute for themselves. Serious marital problems or a broken marriage expose the cystic fibrosis child to more stress than usual. The family support system is also weakened in families who have moved away from their immediate relatives.

Cystic fibrosis patients often develop severe psychosocial problems during adolescence when there is a strong need for peer acceptance and for feelings of normality. The physical stigmata of cystic fibrosis, such as delayed development of sexual characteristics, small stature, barrel-chest deformity, teeth stained by antibiotics, and persistent, productive cough, all combine to make it difficult for the child to conceal the disease. In addition, the frequent hospital visits and the need for ongoing treatment with chest percussion or mist inhalations give an appearance of chronic disability. Patients may react negatively to their parents, doctors, and nurses at this time. Rebelliousness against medical treatment is often helped by allowing the child to assume increased responsibility for his or her own care. Older patients may encounter difficulty in finding an occupation, difficulty in achieving independence from their families, and difficulty in forming friendships with the opposite sex. The prospects of infertility in the male and the serious physical threat of pregnancy to the female with advanced cystic fibrosis provide further areas of stress.

Results of tests of psychosocial adjustment in older cystic fibrosis patients have revealed successful separation and independence from parents by most and the importance of work as a source of self-esteem and compensation for an impoverished social life.[20] These results also confirmed those of Boyle et al. regarding distress about appearance, social isolation, and use of denial and minimization as coping mechanisms.[21]

The adolescent patient should be supported and encouraged toward independence. Adolescent patients with cystic fibrosis need good counseling about school needs, occupation, birth control, marriage, and parenthood. In spite of their problems, many patients do well and live very full lives. It has been suggested that such patients have a preoccupation with death, but this is probably unfounded. A recent study of English adolescents with cystic fibrosis found that they had remarkably little disability, probably because of the judicious use of denial.[22]

SCHOOL LIFE

Learning Ability and Attendance

Academic performance and learning ability are normal in children with cystic fibrosis. School attendance is normal in younger children with milder disease, but it is affected later on. When this happens, the teacher may help by providing classwork, such as guided reading or essay projects, which can be completed at home or in the hospital. Some children miss so much school that home tutoring is recommended, although this should be avoided as much as possible.

Each time a child is admitted to the hospital for intravenous antibiotics, he or she will be absent from school from 10 days to 3 weeks. Many children's hospitals provide classes during these hospital admissions. Hospital teachers may need to communicate with the school teachers to plan the patient's schoolwork; at other times, it may be helpful if the school sends work home.

Necessity to Leave the Classroom

A persistent cough may be present, which is annoying to the child and can be distracting to the class, but it is not infectious. Smoke, particularly cigarette smoke, and dust, such as chalk dust, may irritate inflamed airways and produce bouts of coughing. Exposure to such irritants should be avoided. When necessary, the child should be allowed to leave the room for a drink of water. Some children may need special consideration regarding bathroom privileges, as they may need to leave the room suddenly to avoid an "accident" or the expulsion of embarrassing and offensive-smelling gas. This may result from failure to take enzymes or the need for an adjustment in enzyme dosage. Dietary indiscretions may also cause the problem.

Medications

Most patients require pancreatic enzymes with meals, and some need to take antibiotics; opportunities should be provided for taking these medications. Chest percussion is not usually done during the school day unless the school specializes in children with medical handicaps.

Physical Activities

Physical training programs to improve muscle strength may result in improved pulmonary function and clearance of mucus from the airways. Patients should be able to undertake physical activities normally when there is minimal or no lung involvement. Exercise is helpful in children with mild pulmonary disease, as it will make them breathe deeply, which may improve pulmonary function and clearance of mucus. Patients are advised to participate as much as possible in gym, jogging, soccer, or any physical activity that they enjoy. However, children with more advanced pulmonary disease may be unable to take part in gym, athletics, or similar activities, and they should be excused from exercise that makes them short of breath. They should be encouraged to participate in sports and physical activities within the constraints of their disease.

The cystic fibrosis center can be expected to counsel the patient and family as to what constitutes a reasonable amount of exercise for the individual child.

Career Guidance

Career guidance is very important to cystic fibrosis patients who are often physically limited as young adults. They must decide between technical training and a college education, and they must choose occupations that are within their current and projected physical ability. Many patients seem to be attracted to the medical field because of their considerable contact with hospitals and caregivers. A student with cystic fibrosis may feel that he or she will not live long enough to make career planning necessary. Such an attitude should be discouraged by guidance counselors, who should present a positive program to the student. In one case, such a student "frittered away" his time until he was 26, at which point he decided to plan for a way of supporting himself.

Sources of financial support and training should be explored through state bureaus of vocational rehabilitation. Financial constraints from the cost of the illness over the years may prohibit higher education without financial aid. If the student wishes to attend school away from home, guidance counselors can be helpful in identifying schools near cystic fibrosis centers. Some colleges have special programs for medically handicapped students.

Peer Relationships

Relationships with other pupils may be difficult for cystic fibrosis patients who are chronically disabled. Classmates or workmates may misunderstand the significance of the chronic cough or thin appearance. This may lead to embarrassing questions or even to discrimination. However, most patients make friends, receive support from their peers, and have fairly good social relationships. It is important for others to understand that the cystic fibrosis patient does not carry infections that are hazardous to normal people and that they cannot transmit the disease.

APPROACH TO THE CHILD WITH CYSTIC FIBROSIS

Cystic fibrosis is one of the few remaining common childhood diseases that result in death. Most patients know that their lives will be shortened even if they are unable to discuss it openly. It is inappropriate to question these children about their feelings too forcefully, as great harm can be done by exploring areas that are better left alone. On the other hand, the child's questions should be answered as sensitively as possible. Answer the question that is asked without including a lot of information that is not asked for. Refusal to discuss an issue or displaying behavior that indicates avoidance of the subject can make the child feel that the disease is somehow shameful or disgusting. This does not mean that you must always come up with answers. It is never out of order to simply say "I don't know" when a question is asked that you do not feel qualified to answer, either because of limited medical knowledge or lack of training in psychosocial areas. To guide the student toward an appropriate person to answer such questions may be helpful.

Teachers and school nurses can communicate directly with personnel at cystic fibrosis centers if they need information on both medical and psychological areas. Most important is that the child knows that he or she is being heard and that there is an honest attempt to obtain answers, if not necessarily give them.

It is inappropriate to reveal to classmates without permission from the child and family that a child has cystic fibrosis. Recent publicity given to cystic fibrosis through national fundraising has increased the awareness of the disease and has provided more information to the general public, which includes students. Many students do not have the understanding or the sensitivity to handle such information. In one case, a child was teased by classmates because of television publicity about cystic fibrosis. Classmates taunted him with the fact that he would die before they would. This boy reported these problems and was appropriately counseled. Other children might not be as vocal and might suffer considerable anguish because of such teasing. Teachers who learn of similar incidents occuring with their students should communicate with the cystic fibrosis center so that attention can be given to the child's feelings.

Cystic fibrosis patients should be treated as normally as possible. Look at the child first in light of what is expected of all children in terms of growth and development as well as intellectual function. Often problems perceived as related to cystic fibrosis are simply problems common to children at a particular age and developmental level. Try to see the whole child, not just the child's disease. Most patients require few concessions in the classroom (as outlined above) and should be subject to the same rules of discipline as other students. Children who are allowed to "get away" with poor behavior because of their illnesses only feel all the more anxious and insecure.

Encouraging an optimistic attitude is beneficial. Patients should not be allowed to feel that they are fighting a losing battle with their disease. They must be encouraged to assume that they are destined to do well, to eventually take up a useful occupation, and probably to marry, even though, unfortunately, in some cases this will never be realized. However, these negative aspects have to be played down, and patients should be given support, reassurance, and hope. At the same time, they should be allowed to discuss their medical problems. Questions should be answered as honestly as possible. Open discussion of patients' hopes and fears with parents, school teachers, and health care workers is encouraged. Most patients will open up only to one or two trusted individuals and to these people falls the responsibility of giving honest yet hopeful answers. Teachers should be alert to behavior that indicates problems, such as depression, agitation, inability to concentrate, and acting out and should report their concerns to parents and health care workers.

When medical complications worsen, or when the exacerbations become closer and closer together, children should still be encouraged to function as well as they possibly can. It is helpful to determine from the child's health care team what is realistic in terms of activity and expectations for achievement. At this stage of the disease, it is appropriate to present short-term, reachable goals that have a real possibility of being met. This allows the student opportunities for success. However, a certain amount of "risk-taking" is needed. The child should be allowed to attempt some goals even if failure is anticipated, as the child's morale may be improved if he or she feels that, like other students in the class, he or she is expected to tackle challenging tasks.

More difficult is the child who is obviously dying and who has reached the stage in which school attendance is becoming more and more sporadic. An attempt should be made by the child's caregivers to counsel the patient openly without destroying hope. Whereas the ideal may be emotional and intellectual preparation for dying, with acceptance as the final goal, this may not always be realistic or even kind. Insistence upon talking to a patient about his or her impending death may break down defenses needed to cope with the final days or months, particularly if it is done by someone unskilled in speaking with patients who are terminally ill. It is difficult to summarize what should be expected from these children at this point in the disease. In a nutshell, they should be expected to give the best performance they can with fair allowance made for physical or emotional disability. As far as possible, they should continue with the normal curriculum and take examinations in the same way as their classmates.

Some patients manage to keep up with their classwork and even to graduate from high school during the last year of their life. These students tend to focus on such goals in a very concrete fashion. Their ambitions to pass examinations or to graduate may help them focus on carrying out their treatments and give them the will to give the best fight that they possibly can. Most patients try to live life to the full and will perform well if given the chance. One 18-year-old patient who coped successfully recently summarized her feelings on the challenge of living with cystic fibrosis: "Some may feel I am fighting a losing battle, but I will not go down without the best fight I can possibly give. My family, friends, and self-respect have never allowed me to give up. I live each day as if it were my last. We are born for a reason; my goal is to be able to leave behind some little special something as a result of my life."[23]

Teachers and school nurses can communicate directly with personnel at cystic fibrosis centers if they need information on both medical and psychological areas. Most important is that the child know that she or he is being heard and that there is an honest attempt to obtain answers, if not necessarily give them.

MEDICAL PROBLEMS THAT MAY OCCUR IN THE CLASSROOM

The chief medical problem associated with cystic fibrosis is the development of respiratory infection. This usually comes on gradually in the form of a flare-up of a smoldering infection. It seldom occurs suddenly in the classroom. If the patient develops a severe fever, chest pain, shortness of breath, or other worrisome symptoms, the family should be contacted and asked to arrange medical care. More common is the situation in which children are sent home from school unnecessarily, sometimes against the parents' wishes. Many children with more advanced chronic pulmonary infection have recurrent fevers. This should not be an indication for sending the child home if the fever is relatively mild and something that the family is used to dealing with.

FOSTERING CLASSMATES' UNDERSTANDING

The attitudes of teachers and school nurses considerably affect the attitudes shown by classmates toward children with chronic diseases. Fortunately, a supportive approach is usually provided in most places.

There is widespread misinformation about cystic fibrosis, and it helps if misunderstandings can be dispelled. However, although honesty is the best policy, much discretion is needed when dealing with issues of death and dying in discussions with classmates.

The cystic fibrosis patient may need support in dealing with some of the hurtful comments made by other children. In general, cystic fibrosis children show much courage in dealing with their disease, and they deserve their classmates' respect. It may not be realistic to expect young children to recognize all that their classmate is going through and to demonstrate empathy, but junior and senior high school students should be able to understand this concept. Tactful comments and guidance toward such understanding can benefit the patient as well as contribute to a growing maturity among classmates.

Patients in the terminal stages of the disease may wish to continue attending school, and this might be difficult for their friends to accept. Recently a patient managed to stay in school until days before her death. She completed all the requirements for graduation, which in itself was an important goal. She was helped considerably by the morale boost of an achievement award. With her oxygen cylinder, she could drive her car to visit friends, and she was able to perform well in class. Some of her close friends would help carry books and the oxygen cylinder, but she asked for little in the way of special consideration. Such patients are a delight to work with and a fine example to all.

REFERENCES

1. J. A. Mangos, "Microperfusion Study of the Sweat Gland Abnormality in Cystic Fibrosis," *Texas Reports on Biology and Medicine* 31 (1973): 651–63.
2. T. F. Boat, P. W. Cheng, R. N. Iyer, D. M. Carlson, and I. Polony, "Human Respiratory Tract Secretions: Mucous Glycoproteins of Nonpurulent Tracheobronchial Secretions, and Sputum of Patients with Bronchitis and Cystic Fibrosis," *Archives of Biochemistry and Biophysics* 177 (1976): 95–104.
3. D. M. Danks, J. Allan, and C. M. Anderson, "A Genetic Study of Fibrocystic Disease of the Pancreas," *Annals of Human Genetics* 28 (1965): 323–56.
4. A. D. Merritt, B. L. Hanna, C. W. Todd, and T. L. Myers, "Incidence and Mode of Inheritance of Cystic Fibrosis," *Journal of Laboratory and Clinical Medicine* 60 (1962): 998–99.
5. S. W. Wright and N. E. Morton, "Genetic Studies on Cystic Fibrosis in Hawaii," *American Journal of Human Genetics* 20 (1968): 157–69.
6. L. L. Kulczycki and V. Schauf, "Cystic Fibrosis in Blacks in Washington, D.C.," *American Journal of Diseases of Children* 127 (1974): 64–67.
7. R. E. Wood, T. F. Boat, and C. F. Doershuk, "Cystic Fibrosis: State of the Art," *American Review of Respiratory Disease* 113 (1976): 833–78.
8. R. W. Wilmott, S. L. Tyson, R. Dinwiddie, and D. J. Matthew, "Survival Rates in Cystic Fibrosis," *Archives of Disease in Childhood* 58 (1983): 835–36.
9. Cystic Fibrosis Foundation, *Report of the Patient Registry Volume 1978* (Rockville, MD: Cystic Fibrosis Foundation, 1980).
10. Wood, Boat, and Doershuk, "Cystic Fibrosis: State of the Art," pp. 833–78.
11. Ibid.
12. J. Rutland and P. J. Cole, "Nasal Mucociliary Clearance and Ciliary Beat Frequency in Cystic Fibrosis Compared with Sinusitis and Bronchiectasis," *Thorax* 36 (1981): 654–58.
13. A. C. Hyatt, B. E. Chipps, K. M. Kumar, E. D. Mellitts, P. S. Lietman, and B. J. Rosenstein, "A Double-Blind Controlled Trial of Anti-Pseudomonas Chemotherapy of Acute Respiratory Exacerbations in Patients with Cystic Fibrosis," *The Journal of Pediatrics* 99 (1981): 307–11.
14. Wood, Boat, and Doershuk, "Cystic Fibrosis: State of the Art," pp. 833–78.
15. Ibid.
16. B. C. Hilman, "The Impact of Chronic Disease on Patients and Their Families. Feelings and Their Medical Significance," *Ross Timesavers* 21 (1979): 9–12.
17. A. T. McCollum and L. E. Gibson, "Family Adaptation to the Child with Cystic Fibrosis," *The Journal of Pediatrics* 77 (1970): 571–78.
18. Hilman, "Impact of Chronic Disease on Patients and Their Families," pp. 9–12.
19. W. F. Gayton and S. B. Friedman, "Psychosocial Aspects of Cystic Fibrosis," *American Journal of Diseases of Children* 126 (1973): 856–59.
20. G. D. Strauss and D. K. Wellisch, "Psychosocial Adaptation in Older Cystic Fibrosis Patients," *Journal of Chronic Diseases* 34 (4) (1981): 141–46.
21. I. R. Boyle, P. S. di Sant'Agnese, S. Sack, F. Millican, and L. L. Kulczycki, "Emotional Adjustment of Adolescents and Young Adults with Cystic Fibrosis," *Journal of Pediatrics* 88 (1976): 318–26.
22. E. M. Bywater, "Adolescents with Cystic Fibrosis: Psychosocial Adjustment," *Archives of Disease in Childhood* 56 (1981): 538–43.
23. Hilman, "Impact of Chronic Disease on Patients and Their Families," pp. 9–12.

RESOURCES

Suggested Reading

Burton, Lindy. *The family of Sick Children: A Study of Families Coping with Chronic Childhood Disease*. London and Boston: Routledge and Kegan Paul, 1975.

Clinical and Social Factors in the Management of CF: A Brief Self-Teaching Review for Students in the Health Professions. Professional Education Program, Cystic Fibrosis Foundation.

Debuskey, Matthew, ed. *The Chronically Ill Child and His Family*. Springfield, IL: Charles C. Thomas, 1970.

Psychosocial Aspects of Cystic Fibrosis: A Model for Chronic Lung Disease. New York and London: The Foundation for Thanatology and Columbia University Press, 1973.

Talking with Children with a Life-Threatening Illness, Emotional Aspects of Life-Threatening Illness in Children. Cystic Fibrosis Foundation, 6000 Executive Blvd., Suite 309, Rockville, MD 20852.

A Teacher's Guide to Cystic Fibrosis. Cystic Fibrosis Foundation, 6000 Executive Blvd., Suite 309, Rockville, MD 20852.

Useful Address

Cystic Fibrosis Foundation, 6000 Executive Blvd., Suite 309, Rockville, MD 20852.

Medical Aspects of Childhood Cancer

by Fredric Serota, M.D. and Anna T. Meadows, M.D.

OVERVIEW

Cancer is a group of diseases with the common characteristic of an abnormal proliferation of cells, which ultimately affects the functioning of the organ involved. Cancer cells, unlike the cells of benign tumors, invade surrounding tissue and can metastasize, that is, spread from one part of the body to another.

The types and anatomic distribution of cancer in children differ greatly from those in adults. The most common sites involved in adults are the breast, lung, colon, rectum, uterus, prostate gland, bladder, pancreas, stomach, and ovary. In children under 15 years of age, the most common cancers are, from the most to the least common, leukemia (cancer of the blood-forming tissues); tumors of the central nervous system; lymphoma (cancer of the lymphatic system); neuroblastoma (tumors arising from the nerves); soft tissue sarcomas (tumors composed of a substance like embryonic connective tissue); kidney tumors; bone tumors; and other miscellaneous malignancies.[1,2] Leukemia accounts for approximately one-third of all new childhood malignancies, and cancers of the central nervous system account for one-fifth.[3,4] The incidence of specific types of cancer varies with the age of the patient, perhaps reflecting periods of childhood during which certain tissues proliferate, such as occurs during the adolescent growth spurt when bone tumors are most common.

In this section, the broad aspects of childhood cancer and its treatment are covered, followed by specific information on the most common childhood cancers. This information is offered to provide school staff with some understanding of the multiple nature of cancer and the treatments required to offer the greatest chance of remission and cure.

Incidence of Cancer in Childhood

In the first year of life, congenital malformations are the leading cause of death. Thereafter, cancer is the most common disease that causes death in children. However, accidents account for four times as many deaths in this age group as cancer. The annual incidence of cancer in children under 15 years of age is 12 per 100,000 white children and 10 per 100,000 black children.[5] The reasons for this racial difference in incidence are not known. Each year 7,000 new cases of childhood cancer are diagnosed in the United States.[6] What these figures mean to the individual child is that the risk of getting cancer from birth to age 15, which is considered the end of childhood, is about one in 600 to 700.[7]

The incidence of cancer in children is not increasing, although it may appear to be. This is because modern therapy has resulted in a decrease in mortality and morbidity from infections, diarrhea, dehydration, and common childhood illnesses. Also, more sophisticated and accurate diagnostic techniques can detect cancer in children whose illnesses formerly might have been attributed to other causes.

Cause

The causes for childhood cancer remain unknown in most cases. However, some things are known about possible factors, such as environmental and host factors, that may predispose a child to develop cancer.

Environmental Factors

Although certain environmental exposures are associated with tumors in humans, only a few have induced cancer in children. This may be in part because children are not usually exposed to the carcinogens that adults may encounter at work or through dietary or smoking habits. Also, it generally takes several years for cancer to develop after exposure to carcinogens. Certain exposures in childhood have given rise to cancers in young adults. For example, ionizing radiation, when administered in childhood, may induce acute and chronic leukemias, thyroid cancer, and perhaps other cancers that occur during early adulthood. There may be an increased frequency of cancer related to drugs containing radioisotopes, to immunosuppressive therapy after kidney transplantation, and to certain anabolic steroids given for aplastic anemia. Large doses of stilbestrol given to pregnant women to prevent spontaneous abortion have been associated with cancer of the vagina in their daughters 14 to 22 years later.[8]

Viruses have been implicated in the origin of some animal cancers but, with only two exceptions, have not been known to cause human malignant diseases. The exceptions are the Epstein-Barr virus in Burkitt's lymphoma in Africa and in nasopharyngeal carcinoma in Asia and the hepatitis B virus in liver cancer. Studies have not demonstrated that viruses causing animal cancers can be transmitted to humans.

Host Factors

There is evidence that some children are more susceptible to the development of cancer than others. Children with certain genetically transmitted or congenital disorders are particularly susceptible to certain forms of cancer. For example, the probability that a child with Down's syndrome will develop leukemia is about one in 200 or about 10 times the normal rate.[9] There is also a higher than usual risk of developing leukemia in two other genetically transmitted diseases—Bloom's syndrome and Fanconi's aplastic anemia.[10] Lymphomas are associated with inborn disorders of the immune system. Other tumors, such as Wilms' tumor, are associated with disorders of growth excess, such as hemihypertrophy, or overgrowth of one extremity or one side of the body. Wilms' tumor is also associated with aniridia, the absence of the iris. As can be seen, the genetic disorder and the cancer that has the potential to develop are specific to each other.

Certain other childhood cancers aggregate in families more often than can be expected by chance alone, and for some, specific chromosomal changes have been identified in the tumor cells and/or in the somatic (body) cells. A great deal of research is going on in these areas, since these rare patients may provide clues to the primary cellular basis for malignant transformation.

TREATMENT

Treatment for the various childhood cancers has changed rapidly, and survival has greatly improved. For some diseases there is still room for even greater improvement, as current therapy is not yet able to cure all children with cancer.

Current regimens designed for the cure of childhood cancer depend on multiple modes of therapy, which include drug therapy along with radiation and surgery. Almost all children with cancer receive some form of drug therapy. Childhood cancers are more sensitive and responsive to drugs than are adult cancers. Also, most childhood cancers tend to metastasize (spread) early, necessitating systemic treatment in addition to localized treatment, such as surgery or radiation. Chemotherapy is even used when there is no apparent spread of tumors that have been removed surgically—this is called adjuvant therapy—to eradicate cancer cells that cannot be detected by current means but may be assumed to be present by past experience. It has been shown that combinations of drugs are often more efficacious than any single drug and that rates of recurrence of surgically removed tumors can be minimized by adjuvant therapy with either radiation or chemotherapy. The side effects of such intensive treatment require supportive care. In fact, these forms of treatment have only been possible during the last decade because of the availability of the newer methods of supportive care, such as broad-spectrum antibiotics, intravenous nutrition, special blood component therapy, and psychosocial support. These measures have been a major factor in permitting increasingly more intensive and therefore more effective treatment for cancer.

The intensive treatment of childhood cancer is best undertaken at a medical center with the facilities to deal not only with the disease but with the psychological and social problems of the illness. Ideally, a team approach should be used. The pediatric oncologist (specialist in the treatment of childhood cancer) should work with a pediatric surgeon and radiotherapist and specialists in hematology (disorders of the blood), infectious diseases, pathology, neurology, nephrology, cardiology, endocrinology, and genetics. Nurses and social workers experienced in the care of pediatric cancer patients are an essential part of this team. Special support facilities within the hospital should include clinical laboratories capable of responding to emergencies and able to perform blood counts and bone marrow examinations, to identify infectious organisms, and to test for sensitivities to various antibiotics. A blood bank equipped to supply all necessary blood components is essential. Specialists in intensive care with modern monitoring equipment are often required.

The following is a general discussion of the various modes of treatment available. When appropriate, more specific information will be given in the section dealing with various types of cancers.

Chemotherapy

Until the past decade, chemotherapy was used for relief of symptoms and, at best, gave a few additional years of life. However, it is now well established that chemotherapy alone can cure certain patients with leukemia, Hodgkin's disease, and non-Hodgkin's lymphoma. In addition, the cure rates for these diseases have been increased through combinations of chemotherapy and radiation. The use of chemotherapy in combination with surgery and sometimes with radiation has significantly improved survival rates in patients with Wilms' tumor (kidney turmor), rhabdomyosarcoma (cancer of the muscle tissue), Ewing's sarcoma, and osteosarcoma (both tumors of the bone). Chemotherapy may be used to treat the bulk of the disease, as in leukemia, but it is used most effectively as an adjunct to surgery and/or radiation therapy to eradicate small or microscopic metastases or residual disease.

In general, drugs used to treat cancer work by inhibiting the growth of rapidly dividing cells. All cancer cells divide without regulation or control. Certain normal populations of cells undergo rapid renewal and are also affected by chemotherapeutic agents. This is especially true of the blood-forming cells and intestinal and hair cells. The result of effects on blood cells are anemia from a low red blood cell count, an increased susceptibility to infection from a decreased white blood cell count, and bleeding because of a decreased number of platelets. Hair loss is a common side effect, as are vomiting, diarrhea, and malabsorption of nutrients from the gastrointestinal tract. The manner in which drugs are administered—that is, the timing and dosage—is arranged to maximize the effect on the tumor while minimizing toxicity to the patient.

By combining drugs that affect cells in different ways, increased eradication of the tumor population may also be achieved with a minimum of toxicity to the patient. Two or more agents may be more effective because they block metabolic processes concurrently, having an additive effect. Other agents may be used to prevent repair by the cell of the damage done by the first agent. A drug may increase the sensitivity of the cell to the damaging effect of a second agent, or second or other agents may prevent relapse by producing additional lethel effects on the cell population.

Corticosteroids are used in combination with other drugs in the treatment of leukemia, lymphomas, and brain tumors. Corticosteroids are never used for the duration of treatment, only for the first month or two and then for another month or two in the case of a relapse. Some of the side effects are a round, cherubic face, fluid retention, an increased appetite, and hyperactivity. These changes in appearance and behavior reverse themselves when treatment is stopped.

Therapeutic regimens must be designed for overkill of malignant cells, since failure to eradicate all tumor cells will undoubtedly result in recurrence of the disease. A major problem is that some tumor cells become resistant to the drugs currently in use, leading to a relapse of the disease under treatment. A great deal of research is under way to determine how these cells become resistant.

Radiation Therapy

Ionizing radiation damages the nuclear materials in the cell, DNA and RNA, in several ways, including breaking the genetic strands and damaging the chemical bases that provide structure. The cells then lose their ability to divide and proliferate. The amount of radiation necessary to adequately treat a given cancer depends on its cell type. Radiation therapists are skilled in delivering radiation for a maximum effect on the tumor while sparing normal tissues. Modern computerized equipment can deliver the radiation beam to a pinpoint, minimizing the toxic effect on surrounding tissue. Radiation is often used in conjunction with surgery to treat and/or remove localized or circumscribed tumor masses.

Sometimes children who have had radiation do not feel well and have a poor appetite, fever, or weakness. Side effects differ according to the site to which the treatment was directed. A child may experience periods of intense sleepiness two months after radiation treatment to the brain for leukemia or a brain tumor. He or she may even have to be awakened in class. If the radiation has been directed toward the abdomen, there may be vomiting, diarrhea, or other gastrointestinal symptoms. A sore throat or difficulty in swallowing may result from radiation to the neck. These symptoms are transient, however.

Treatment of Infections

Therapy directed at tumor control often compromises the patient by altering many of the body's normal defense mechanisms. Infections remain the leading cause of death and the most frequent cause of serious complications in childhood cancer. The treatment of infection should be specific to avoid undesired complications. Repeated examinations, cultures, and x-rays may be necessary to determine the site of an infection, the organism responsible, and the proper treatment. Repeated episodes of fever in a patient undergoing cancer chemotherapy or radiation therapy may necessitate hospitalization for observation and antibiotic treatment.

Simple, good hygiene often provides protection from life-threatening infection. Careful attention should be given to any break in the skin whether induced by trauma during play or under sterile conditions such as surgery. Dental and oral hygiene should also be carefully monitored.

Although the child with cancer tolerates most viral infections, such as the common cold or gastrointestinal infections, with few or no resultant problems, more serious viral infections may occur. Most children are protected from common childhood illnesses, such as measles and mumps, by inoculation during infancy and boosters thereafter. Therefore, exposures to these illnesses are of no concern. Inoculation for chickenpox is not yet generally available; children undergoing treatment for cancer are at risk for developing a severe case of chickenpox. Children who have not had chickenpox and are exposed to it while attending school should receive special gammaglobulin treatment. Their parents should be notified if an exposure has occurred. Immunizing children who are undergoing treatment for cancer with live viral vaccines, such as those for polio or measles, in a mass immunization program, as often occurs in the school system, is not recommended.

Proper Nutrition

Proper nutrition plays an important role in sustaining the patient until antitumor therapy has controlled the underlying malignancy. In general, patients in sound nutritional condition are better able to cope with the intensive therapy required to control cancer. Malnutrition may result from the tumor growth itself and from infections, alterations in taste and smell, and, occasionally, changes in the absorptive capability of the gastrointestinal tract caused by chemotherapy and radiation therapy. Loss of appetite, nausea, vomiting, and diarrhea secondary to treatment also cause malnutrition. Treatment may have to be stopped or modified when these side effects are severe. Many centers use intravenous feedings as an adjunctive therapy. Special diets have been devised by nutritionists experienced in working with children undergoing cancer treatment. The families of such patients are usually well counseled in the special needs of their children.

Blood Component Therapy

The ability to deliver specific blood components has been a major breakthrough in the management of childhood cancer. Current techniques allow the administration to patients of red cells, which carry oxygen; granulocytes, which fight infection; and platelets, which are small cells that are part of the blood's clotting system. Also, concentrated gammaglobulin preparations that provide protection against a variety of viral agents such as measles and hepatitis are now available. The development of modern techniques for detection of certain types of hepatitis has reduced the risks associated with transfused blood products. Even so, the administration of blood or blood components is not without risk because not all types of hepatitis can be detected in advance and other infections may be transmitted through blood. Patients transfused repetitively may become resistant to certain types of blood products and not be able to receive any benefit later when such a transfusion may be lifesaving.

Alternative Therapies

From time to time, reports of new, exciting treatments appear in the press or on television. These are sometimes touted as the breakthrough everyone has been waiting for; some even border on quackery. Before advocating such treatment, one needs to be assured that it has been thoroughly investigated in a scientific manner and that it is better than what is currently thought to be the best therapy. Unfortunately, families may be offered false hope while competent treatment is delayed. Most modern cancer centers, during the initial parent education sessions, discuss alternative therapies. The facts supporting each possible mode of therapy and the inherent toxicities are discussed and compared. In the most optimal situations, families are included in all treatment decisions.

Time Required for Treatment

A child is often initially hospitalized when a malignancy is discovered to determine the extent of the tumor and the tissues involved, to plan a course of treatment, and to educate the family and child as to what is involved and what to expect. Once treatment gets under way, it is usually continued on an outpatient basis. Both radiation and chemotherapy can be given to outpatients. Most physicians now believe that a child belongs at home as much as possible.

The frequency and duration of visits to the hospital or outpatient clinic will vary depending upon the tumor type and the treatment protocol. Sometimes several visits to the outpatient clinic per month with periodic readmissions to the hospital for reevaluation of progress are necessary. Treatment for solid tumors is usually shorter than the treatment for leukemia. With solid tumors, the length of treatment is usually six months to two years; with leukemia, it is usually from two to five years.

COMMON TYPES OF CHILDHOOD CANCERS

Leukemia

Leukemia, the most common malignant disease in children, involves the blood-forming tissue located primarily in the bone marrow. The leukemias are named according to the white cell line that is proliferating out of control. Lymphocytic leukemia arises from cells of the lymphoid line; myelocytic (or granulocytic) leukemia arises from cells of the myeloid line; and monocytic leukemia involves cells of the monocytic line. Normal white cells provide the body's defense against disease and foreign substances. The various white cell lines perform different functions in this effort. In leukemia the proliferation of abnormal white blood cells can interfere with the bone marrow's capacity to produce normal blood cells. Normal white cells, red blood cells, and platelets become deficient. (Platelets are small cells that circulate in the blood and are active in the prevention of bleeding.) Complications such as anemia, infection, and bleeding therefore result. In addition, children with leukemia are often in pain because of the pressure of the multiplying malignant cells within the marrow cavity of the bones.

Types of leukemia can be differentiated by the appearance of the cells under the microscope and by the way they take up certain chemical stains. The most common leukemia in children is acute lymphocytic leukemia, which accounts for about 80 percent of all leukemia in children.[11] Acute nonlymphocytic leukemia is primarily myelogenous and accounts for about 15 percent of the total.[12]

Children of all ages are affected. The peak age for acute lymphocytic leukemia is reached between three and four years of age. Acute myelocytic leukemia occurs uniformly throughout childhood, and its occurrence increases in adolescence.

Clinical Manifestations. The clinical manifestations of acute leukemia are variable and nonspecific and usually appear two to six weeks before the diagnosis is made. Bone discomfort and joint pains may have been evident even earlier. The child with acute leukemia often experiences one or more of the following symptoms: easy fatigability, lethargy, fever, bleeding and easy bruisability, enlargement of the lymph glands or abdomen, and bone pain. Physical examination reveals irritability, pallor, rapid heart rate, bruising of the skin, bleeding from the gums and nose, fever, infection, and enlarged abdominal organs or lymph nodes. Abnormal cells are generally seen on a blood smear from peripheral blood, but, in some cases, the peripheral blood cells may appear normal. Diagnosis is then made by examining a specimen obtained from the bone marrow. Other disorders such as infection, rheumatoid arthritis, rheumatic fever, collagen vascular diseases, infectious mononucleosis, certain viral infections, and aplastic anemia may mimic leukemia and, at times, make diagnosis difficult.

Treatment. Hospitalization is generally required for the initial evaluation and institution of therapy. Physiologic imbalances brought about by the disorder are corrected, and blood products are administered as necessary. When infection is present, appropriate antibiotic treatment is given. If there is bleeding, the cause is determined, and specific therapy instituted. Baseline function of all vital organ systems is determined.

The mainstay of treatment, chemotherapy, is used to induce and then maintain a complete remission. Combinations of two or more drugs are significantly more effective than a single drug. Generally, leukemic cells can be eliminated from the peripheral blood and bone marrow in four to six weeks. Modern treatment strategies involving several modes of therapy have lengthened the first remission so that 50 percent of patients with acute lymphocytic leukemia can remain disease-free for periods of greater than five years. Many of these children will be cured. Prior to the era of modern therapy, half of the patients with acute lymphocytic leukemia could be expected to have a recurrence in the central nervous system. For this reason, presymptomatic treatment of the central nervous system is given with either cranial irradiation and methotrexate directly into the spinal fluid or methotrexate alone. This has virtually eliminated this problem. Treatment continues for two and a half to three years, long after any sign of leukemic cells is present.

Although treatment has been highly successful in children with acute lymphocytic leukemia, the same is not true for patients with acute non-lymphocytic leukemia. While remissions can be achieved in 60 to 70 percent of patients, the median duration of remission is short, and only 20 to 40 percent will achieve prolonged remissions.[13]

Patients with siblings who have identical tissue types are undergoing experimental therapy with bone marrow transplantation. In this approach, the patient's own bone marrow and leukemia are destroyed using very aggressive radiation and chemotherapy. New bone marrow is injected from a tissue-type identical sibling, thus providing normal blood-forming tissue. The results to date are encouraging, but it is too early to know whether these encouraging results can be maintained.

Brain Tumor

Brain tumors are the second most common malignancy in children, accounting for approximately 21 percent of all cancers in young people.[14] After the first year of life, during which these tumors are rare, the incidence of brain tumors is evenly distributed. There are several types of tumors, and these receive their designation according to their location and the tissue composition of the tumor. This section will include general information on the intracranial tumors. Further information is given in the next chapter.

Clinical Manifestations. Most of the symptoms are due to increased intracranial pressure, which results from blockage of the spinal fluid. Headache is usually the first symptom. At first there is only pain in the morning, which is relieved as the child moves about. Later there may be loss of appetitie, nausea, and vomiting. These also are at first manifested only in the morning. Other symptoms include awkwardness of motion, double vision, the inability to look upward, and stiffness of the neck with head tilting. The child may become drowsy, be in a stupor, or become comatose. Sometimes seizures occur. Symptoms that may be particularly noticed in the classroom are indifference, a diminished attention span, apathy, restlessness, confusion, and forgetfulness. Personality changes could include moodiness, teariness, irritability, and antisocial behavior. When considering these symptoms in school children, it must be remembered that brain tumors are extremely rare, and these symptoms are more likely to have other causes.

Diagnosis and Treatment. Although the presence of a brain tumor can often be strongly suggested by physical examination and medical history, tests should be done to confirm the suspicion and locate the tumor. The most common studies used now are computerized tomography (CT) scan, myelogram (x-ray study of the spinal cord), and spinal fluid examination.

The treatment for brain tumors is complete surgical removal if possible. When the size and/or location of the tumor makes this impossible, as much of the tumor is removed as feasible. Irradiation to retard further growth is usually administered when removal is incomplete or impossible. In tumors that appear to be completely removed, irradiation is used to prevent recurrence as a result of microscopic remains of the tumor. Chemotherapy has proven useful in prolonging the disease-free period in certain types of tumors. Corticosteroids are used to manage swelling of brain tissue and to reduce the symptoms of increased pressure.

The prognosis for children with brain tumors primarily depends upon the type of tumor, the degree to which surgical removal is possible, and the extent to which further growth or recurrence can be retarded or prevented by irradiation. Some tumors have the property of recurring even after the patient has had optimal treatment. On the other hand, in some types, progression tends to be slow even after only partial excision. Survival rates for the same type of tumor may vary, depending on the findings upon microscopic examination of the tumor. Excellent results have been reported for children with certain types of brain tumors. For example, there have been reports indicating that 95 percent of children with one type of tumor, juvenile cerebellar astrocytoma, were alive 25 years after surgery.[15] With other tumors, however, there is a less favorable outlook, and survival may be limited to a year or two.

Lymphoma

This group of malignant diseases affects the lymphatic system, which includes a network of vessels that are interrupted by clusters of nodes. This system also includes the lymphocytes (a type of white blood cell) and the spleen, tonsils, and appendix. Through the vessels flows a clear fluid called lymph. The nodes act as a filter system and a barrier to the spread of infection.

The lymphomas are grouped into two categories: Hodgkin's disease and the non-Hodgkin's lymphomas.

Hodgkin's Disease

Hodgkin's disease is characterized histologically by infiltration of the involved or diseased lymph nodes with a cell called the Reed-Sternberg cell. Many normal-appearing white blood cells are also present. This disease is quite rare in childhood and its incidence increases with age. Boys are three times more likely than girls to develop this tumor. Curiously, the incidence of childhood Hodgkin's disease in socioeconomically under-developed countries is higher than in the more affluent societies.

Clinical Manifestations. The patient usually has a lump, swelling, or mass caused by an enlarged lymph node, most frequently found in the neck. Nodes may also be found under the arm or in the groin, chest, or abdomen. In most instances, the enlarged nodes are not painful or tender and may grow quite large before they are noticed. The rate of growth of the lymph node mass is very variable. Some enlarge rapidly in a few days; some may be present for as long as two years. Such nodes have been found to wax and wane in size, occasionally associated with cycles of tenderness or fever. Nonspecific clinical manifestations may include weakness, fatigability, loss of appetite, weight loss, sweating, fever, and itching. Fever may occur in a third to half of patients and may be continuous or cyclical. In advanced disease, there may be fevers and sweats.

Diagnosis. A definitive diagnosis requires biopsy of a lymph node. It is important to determine the extent of the disease so that a proper course of treatment may be formulated. This is done by "staging" studies to determine the extent of involvement. Localized disease is designated as Stage I or II and more disseminated disease as Stage III or IV. X-rays may reveal enlarged lymph nodes both within the chest and the abdomen. The newer techniques, such as ultrasound and computer-assisted x-rays, have proven to be even more sensitive than routine x-rays in delineating the extent of disease. Scans or x-rays of the skeletal system may reveal bony involvement. Depending upon the patient's clinical status, abdominal surgery may be performed to determine the extent of disease in the liver, spleen, and nodes below the diaphragm.

Treatment. The treatment selected depends upon the extent of disease. Radiation therapy is the treatment of choice for localized disease in older individuals. The doses needed to destroy cancer cells in involved nodes are likely to produce significant growth problems in young children. Therefore, lower doses are now used, combined with chemotherapy. Chemotherapy is also used for disseminated Hodgkin's disease, with combinations of drugs being more effective than single drugs. The combinations of drugs most frequently used are nitrogen mustard, vincristine, procarbazine, and prednisone (MOPP) or adriamycin, bleomycin, vinblastine, and imidizole carboxamide (ABVD). Other treatment programs that are variations of these highly successful regimens are under investigation.

There has been a dramatic improvement in the outlook for patients with Hodgkin's disease since modern diagnostic and therapeutic approaches have been used. At present, the five-year survival rate for Stage I and Stage II (localized) disease is approximately 90 percent and for Stages III and IV better than 65 percent.[16] The majority of these patients will be permanently cured of this once inevitably fatal disease. This, of course, assumes a meticulous diagnostic evaluation including proper staging and the proper selection and skillful administration of radiotherapy and/or multidrug chemotherapy.

Non-Hodgkin's Lymphoma

The term "non-Hodgkin's" refers to all malignant lymphomas aside from Hodgkin's disease. In children these disorders are markedly different from Hodgkin's disease with regard to the anatomic extent of disease at diagnosis, rate and manner of progression, incidence of leukemic conversion (spread to the bone marrow), central nervous system involvement, and response to irradiation and chemotherapy. Some of these lymphomas may spread rapidly within days to weeks, with a progression rate as high as that in any human malignancy. Two-thirds of children have extensive spread of the tumor at the time of diagnosis, but the majority are now able to be cured because of the use of multiple-agent chemotherapy, sometimes combined with radiation.

Clinical Manifestations. Lymphadenopathy (swollen lymph glands), usually painless, is the most common presenting complaint. The lymph nodes involved may be either in the neck, chest, or at other sites. In some cases, only the gastrointestinal tract is involved. The complete blood count is usually normal except when leukemic transformation has occurred.

Treatment. Since the pattern of spread of non-Hodgkin's lymphomas is unpredictable and does not follow the more orderly movement from one contiguous lymph node site to the next, as in the case of Hodgkin's disease, radiation therapy is only moderately useful. However, the use of multiple drugs in the treatment of all children with this disease has increased the cure rate in local disease to greater than 90 percent and in advanced disease to approximately 70 percent.[17]

Neuroblastoma

Neuroblastoma is a malignant tumor of embryonic neural tissue and may arise from any site where neural tissue is present. After brain tumor, neuroblastoma is the most common malignant solid tumor in childhood (leukemia is a malignancy of blood). Although this tumor may occur throughout childhood and rarely in adults, it is predominantly a tumor of early childhood. More than half the cases occur in children two years of age or younger, and about 90 percent occur before school age.[18]

Clinical Manifestations. Signs and symptoms produced by neuroblastoma are largely attributable to compression of organ structures by the primary tumor or its metastases (tumor spread). The more common initial evidence of disease is usually a mass. In approximately half the patients, the tumor arises in the abdomen. Pressure by the tumor on the kidney, ureter, or bladder may cause obstruction to urination. Similarly, the mass can arise within the neck and appear much like a swollen lymph node. The tumor may occur in the chest and become quite large before the patient has problems with breathing. There may be complaints of pain in the neck, back, abdomen, pelvis, or legs caused by the pressure of the tumor. As one can see, neuroblastoma is typically a silent tumor in its early stages. Metastases may occur very early. In many cases the first signs and symptoms are a result of the metastases to bone and the attendant pain rather than the primary tumor.

Widespread disease is present in more than half of the patients. They show irritability, loss of appetite, weight loss, and pallor because of anemia. Unexplained fever may be a presenting complaint. Bone pain is common. As this tumor has a predilection for metastasizing to the bones of the skull, it typically may produce the appearance of "black eyes." Some children, especially babies, may have nodules within the skin that have the appearance of bluish discoloration likened to a blueberry muffin.

These tumors may, at times, secrete a hormone that can cause skin flushing, increased perspiration, rapid heartbeat, elevated blood pressure, and headaches. Rarely, patients will experience chronic diarrhea, which is unresponsive to medical therapy, or rapid side-to-side eye movements.

Treatment. Treatment and prognosis depend upon the extent and/or stage of the disease. While the outlook in early stage disease is excellent, children with disease that has spread to the bone cannot, at the present time, be cured.

Approaches to treatment of neuroblastoma are similar to those of other solid tumors and include surgery, x-irradiation, and chemotherapy. The most effective therapy is complete surgical removal, but unfortunately, this can only be accomplished when the disease is localized, as it is in the minority of children. It is usually widespread at the time of presentation. A surgeon may be called upon to remove the tumor when possible, to reduce its mass when complete removal is not possible, and to provide biopsy specimens to make proper diagnosis. Some tumors can be removed after reduction in size by chemotherapy and radiation therapy, a so-called "second-look" procedure. New approaches to therapy for neuroblastoma are continually being investigated, especially for those children whose outlooks remain dismal.

Wilms' Tumor

Wilms' tumor is a tumor of embryonal kidney cells. The average age of onset is three years, and 90 percent of cases are recognized in children under seven years of age.[19] As has been noted earlier, certain congenital anomalies show an increased association with Wilms' tumor. Under optimal clinical circumstances and with coordinated multidisciplinary management, long-term disease-free survival can be expected in more than 90 percent of these patients.[20] Evidence suggests that the declining mortality in this tumor is correlated with therapeutic advances rather than early diagnosis.

Clinical Manifestations. In most cases, the presence of an abdominal mass or an enlarged abdomen is the initial complaint. Abdominal pain occurs in more than a third of patients.[21] Other general symptoms may include malaise, loss of appetite, and fever. Bloody urine has been reported in less than a quarter of the children with Wilms' tumor.[22]

Diagnosis and Treatment. The diagnosis is made by an x-ray of the kidney, using an intravenously administered contrast (IVP) or by an ultrasound study, wherein the sound waves are reflected within the abdominal structures. These studies help to determine whether there is a mass present, where it is, and what is the appearance of the second kidney. Computer-assisted x-rays are also of some value in defining the extent of the mass in the kidney, expecially if there is a remote possibility that only part of the kidney need be removed with the tumor. Most children will require removal of the entire kidney.

Analogous to the situation with neuroblastoma, the extent of the tumor is "staged" to tailor a therapeutic approach and arrive at a prognosis. For this reason, a chest x-ray is an important study, as these tumors tend to spread to the lungs. After surgery, radiation is used at the site of the original tumor if any residual cells are thought to be present in the abdomen. Chemotherapy is always given to patients with Wilms' tumor, even when there is no apparent disease, since this approach has been found to reduce the recurrence rate and greatly improve the probability of a cure. Both chemotherapy and irradiation are used to treat lung involvement. Currently a combination of two or three chemotherapeutic agents has been found to be significantly superior to any of these same drugs used alone.

Soft Tissue Sarcoma

The soft tissue sarcomas originate from cells present in muscle, tendons, fascia, and fibrous and connective tissue. Rhabdomyosarcoma is the most common of these in childhood. It occurs with approximately the same frequency as neuroblastoma and Wilms' tumor but more frequently in school-aged children and less often in babies. Rhabdomyosarcoma can occur anywhere in the body where there are skeletal muscles, but approximately two-thirds of these tumors occur in the head and neck regions. Metastases may be present in 20 to 40 percent of patients at the time of diagnosis.[23] The most common sites of spread are the lungs, lymph nodes, bone, bone marrow, and liver.

As with Wilms' tumor, there may be metastases even when all of the tumor has been removed; therefore, adjuvant chemotherapy is always used. Irradiation is reserved for incompletely removed tumors. The outcome is influenced by the extent of disease at the time of presentation, the initial site of disease, the histology of the tumor, and the age of the patient. When disease is controlled locally, the outlook is excellent. Newer and more aggressive therapies are now being used in children with advanced disease to improve the present cure rate for these children.

Primary Malignant Tumor of Bone

Primary bone malignancies are sixth in frequency of cancers diagnosed in children under 15 years of age, but in adolescence, they rank third below leukemia and lymphoma.[24] Osteosarcoma, a tumor found primarily in the second and third decades, is the most common primary malignancy of bone in the young.[25]

Osteosarcoma arises from bone-forming tissue and most commonly involves bones of the extremities, especially of the lower extremities. It occurs frequently during the period of rapid bone growth in adolescence and shows a definite male preponderance after the age of 15. The most frequent initial symptoms are pain and swelling at the site. These symptoms are often present for a few months before diagnosis. Redness, tenderness, warmth, or limitation of motion in the joint are also occasionally found. Diagnosis begins with suggestive radiographic studies followed by a biopsy.

The management of patients with bone tumors is currently controversial. Previously, all patients were treated with amputation of the affected extremity. Changes in surgical management have occurred, with some patients being amenable to removal of the affected bone without amputation and its replacement with a prothesis. Also, as spread to the lungs occurs in three-quarters of patients before one year from diagnosis, many centers begin to administer chemotherapy as an adjuvant. The drugs used are those found effective in destroying metastatic deposits in the lungs or in reducing their growth rate. At present, it is not clear what role chemotherapy will play in improving survival of these children. Because this disease spreads primarily to the lungs, repeated chest x-rays are necessary to follow the progress of these patients. Chemotherapy and surgery are recommended for control of pulmonary metastases. Some patients may be rendered free of disease for long periods using this approach.

CONCLUSION

Modern treatment has enabled us to cure more than half of children with cancer. Sometimes the price of the cure is high, in that these children are confronted by both short-term and long-term effects of treatment. Some of the latter result in growth failure, learning problems, and failure to mature and reproduce normally. We are working toward ways to make children more comfortable during treatment and to decrease the negative lasting effects that some children experience from the treatment of cancer.

REFERENCES

1. J. L. Young, Jr. and R. W. Miller, "Incidence of Malignant Tumors in U.S. Children," *The Journal of Pediatrics* 86 (1975): 254–58.
2. S. Kramer, A. T. Meadows, P. Jarrett, and A. E. Evans, "Incidence of Childhood Cancer: Experience of a Decade in a Population-Based Registry," *Journal of the National Cancer Institute* 70 (1983): 49–55.
3. Young and Miller, "Incidence of Malignant Tumors in U.S. Children," pp. 254–58.
4. Kramer, Meadows, Jarrett, and Evans, "Incidence of Childhood Cancer," pp. 49–55.
5. Young and Miller, "Incidence of Malignant Tumors in U.S. Children," pp. 254–58.
6. Ibid.
7. Ibid.

8. A. L. Herbst, H. Ulfelder, and D. C. Poskanzer, "Age-Incidence and Risk of Diethylstilbestrol-Related Adenocarinoma in the Vagina and Cervix," *American Obstetrics & Gynecology* 128 (1977): 43–50.
9. R. W. Miller, "Persons with Exceptionally High Risk of Leukemia," *Cancer Research* 27 (1967): 2,420.
10. Ibid.
11. D. J. Fernbach, "Natural History of Acute Leukemia," in *Clinical Pediatric Oncology,* 3d ed., ed. W. W. Sutow, D. J. Fernbach, and T. J. Vieth (St. Louis, MO: C. V. Mosby Co., 1984).
12. Kramer, Meadows, Jarrett, and Evans, "Incidence of Childhood Cancer," pp. 49–55.
13. J. V. Simone and G. Rivera, "Management of Acute Leukemia," in *Clinical Pediatric Oncology,* 3d ed., ed. W. W. Sutow, D. J. Fernbach, and T. J. Vieth (St. Louis, MO: C. V. Mosby Co., 1984).
14. M. D. Walker, "Tumors of the Central Nervous System," in *Cancer in the Young,* ed. A. S. Levine (New York: Masson Publishing Co., 1982).
15. Ibid.
16. M. P. Sullivan, L. M. Fuller, and J. J. Butler, "Hodgkin's Disease," in *Clincial Pediatric Oncology,* 3d ed., ed. W. W. Sutow, D. J. Fernbach, and T. J. Vieth (St. Louis, MO: C. V. Mosby Co., 1984).
17. J. R. Anderson, J. F. Wilson, R. D. T. Jenkin, A. T. Meadows, et al., "Childhood Non-Hodgkin's Lymphoma. The Results of a Randomized Therapeutic Trial Comparing a 4-Drug Regimen (COMP) with a 10-Drug Regimen (LSA2-L_2), *New England Journal of Medicine* 308 (1983): 559.
18. P. A. Voutе́, "Neuroblastoma," in *Clinical Pediatric Oncology,* 3d ed., ed. W. W. Sutow, D. J. Fernbach, and T. J. Vieth (St. Louis, MO: C. V. Mosby Co., 1984).
19. J. B. Belasco, J. Chatten, and G. J. D'Angio," Wilms' Tumor," in *Clinical Pediatric Oncology,* 3d ed., ed. W. W. Sutow, D. J. Fernbach, and T. J. Vieth (St. Louis, MO: C. V. Mosby Co., 1984).
20. Ibid.
21. Ibid.
22. Ibid.
23. H. M. Mauer and A. H. Ragab, "Rhabdomyosarcoma," in *Clinical Pediatric Oncology,* 3d ed., ed. W. W. Sutow, D. J. Fernbach, and T. J. Vieth (St. Louis, MO: C. V. Mosby Co., 1984).
24. P. A. Pizzo, "Rhabdomyosarcoma and the Soft Tissue Sarcomas," in *Cancer in the Young,* ed. A. S. Levine (New York: Masson Publishing Co, 1982).
25. U. Bode and A. S. Levine, "The Biology and Management of Osteosarcoma," in *Cancer in the Young*, ed. A. S. Levine (New York: Masson Publishing Co., 1982).

The Child with Cancer in School

by Judith W. Ross, M.S.W., A.C.S.W.

OVERVIEW

School is a focal point of achievement for all children, but for the child experiencing a life-threatening illness, school symbolizes the possibility of a future. Although he or she may struggle to keep up with class assignments and extracurricular activities and may feel emotional distance from age peers, it is vital that the child with cancer attend school. At school, expectations are placed and connections are maintained with regard to aspects of life that are separate from the illness. This is important to the child's emotional well-being.

Because cancer is so many diseases with such a variety of therapies, side effects, and outcomes, it is impossible to provide a complete list of prescriptions and prohibitions for educators. The best advice is quite simple: be informed and communicate thoroughly and often with parents, patients, and the child's treatment center. Above all, don't hesitate to ask questions or for help. In the following sections, guidance is offered to educators who come in contact with students at various points in their experience with cancer. Special problems related to childhood cancer are also addressed.

RETURN TO SCHOOL AFTER INITIAL TREATMENT

Many pediatric cancer centers now have an educational specialist or designated person whose role is to facilitate school reentry or assist with school-related problems. When this is not the case, the social worker or nurse specialist will be in contact with schools attended by his or her patients. In some situations, particularly with older patients, it is advisable for the school to appoint a specific person to work with the center and keep other personnel at school informed and up-to-date. Some treatment centers present seminars for educators to improve their understanding of childhood cancer, its treatment, and the psychological and social effects on the patient and family.[1,2]

What the Child Knows

When a youngster first returns to school after a diagnosis of cancer, he or she usually has some knowledge of the disease and its therapy. Most treatment centers provide information and reading material to the patient and the parents. The younger child, of course, will receive a more simplified version than the older child, but the seriousness of the illness is not concealed. Often the child can be reassured that treatments will help to make him or her well. The child's reactions and ability to articulate questions will also have an effect on what he or she is told. Many of the medical procedures that the child must undergo are painful, and the side effects of the treatment are unpleasant and distressing, so the young patient deserves an explanation of why these must be endured. Parents are encouraged to initiate and participate in discussions with the child. Whenever possible, the word *cancer* is used to describe the illness, and the names of specific diseases such as leukemia, Hodgkin's disease, and lymphoma also are commonly used. Such an open approach fosters communication between patient and parents and with other members of the family and helps to prepare children to talk about the illness with others who are concerned and/or curious.

The Child's Reactions

Educators should be aware that when the child returns to school he or she is attempting to cope with much more than the physical aspects of the illness. The patient cannot be shielded completely from parents' feelings of being overwhelmed and distressed. He or she is aware, without being told, that they are worried and afraid. If they cannot talk with their child about the illness, provide a reasonable explanation for their own reactions, and encourage their son or daughter to express apprehensions, the child fears the worst and is left to manage these fears and uncertainties alone. The parents' role as trusted protectors can thus be jeopardized.

The hospitalization at the time of diagnosis also has its effect on the child. The new surroundings and routine, the lack of privacy, and the succession of strangers who examine and handle him or her tax self-control and contribute to stress. As children develop, they become increasingly aware of their own mortality and the possibility of permanent physical disability and death. While most children with cancer do not dwell on fears of mutilation and death, such thoughts are difficult to suppress when in the hospital because of the intensity of medical intervention and the presence of other very ill or dying children.

Both the illness itself and the treatment, though in many cases only temporarily, affect appearance, stamina, and sense of well-being and make these children aware of being different from school peers. Their attention is drawn to aspects of life and daily function that before were taken for granted. Thus, the way these children perceive themselves and the way they are perceived by others is altered.

Timing the Return to School

Some young cancer patients can return to school quite soon after the initiation of therapy. Others may be absent for weeks or months. The time away from school, the child's physical condition, and the intensity of the treatment will affect the resumption of academic and extracurricular activities. The parents' attitudes will also play an important part in the timing and the manner in which the child returns to school. Most parents recognize the importance of maintaining educational continuity, but after cancer is diagnosed, they regard their children as vulnerable and fear that at school they will be unprotected. Parents' feelings of insecurity multiply when the children are away from their watchful eyes, and consequently, they may delay taking the appropriate steps for reenrollment. Patients also may express reluctance to return to school because they doubt their ability to make up lost work and compete with schoolmates, or because they anticipate negative reactions, rejection, and social isolation. Children take cues from their parents who, because of pessimism about their child's future, can no longer invest themselves in the child's school career. A small percentage of children exhibit school phobias or physical insecurity at school. These problems usually are amenable to the counseling provided at most cancer centers.

Returning to School

Despite these obstacles, most children with cancer do return to school and can be assumed to be well enough to participate in all activities unless otherwise specified. Educators can do much to ease the child's reentry. One of the most important first steps is to arrange a meeting with the parents. Ideally, this meeting will take place prior to the return to school and will include a representative from the treatment center. A thorough discussion of the child's medical condition is warranted, including the treatment and possible side effects. Subject matter should also include changes in the child's appearance, activity level, mood, and ability to concentrate. Special requirements and parents' preferences for care and handling of the child at school should be explored. Parents should be requested to share reading materials that will assist those at school in understanding the child's condition.

Some parents are initially reluctant to discuss the illness with school personnel because it means confronting the possibility of a negative outcome or disclosing their emotions. Parents who attempt to conceal the illness may expect educators to discriminate against their child or be overprotective or pitying. If parents do not request a meeting, those at school should, stressing that they share responsibility for the child and must therefore be adequately informed. Talking about the illness can be stressful for the parents, but educators must not assume that by asking questions they will be adding to parental distress. Most parents want their son or daughter to make a happy adjustment to school, and they feel reassured when school personnel are knowledgeable and prepared. By initiating or participating in such discussions, educators demonstrate their concern for the child's well-being and their commitment to his or her education, which is synonymous with his or her future. Moreover, by focusing on the positive aspects, they can help to improve the quality of the child's life.

Educators should not hesitate to ask the patient, in private, about his or her medical problem. This will provide an excellent opportunity to appreciate the student's understanding of the condition and his or her expectations. Of course, some youngsters will choose not to respond, but educators are often surprised to learn that their students like to talk about their experiences; after all, the illness has become an important part of their lives. Another factor contributing to the willingness, even enthusiasm, of patients to talk about their illness relates to their pride in mastering the many difficult physical and emotional challenges that have been posed. Moreover, chronically ill children are in closer contact and participate in more discussions with adults than do well children. This makes them more at ease with the questions of adults than most of their age peers would be.

Educators can facilitate the child's successful return to school and help to maintain academic continuity by discussing with the patient (and, if appropriate, the parents) expectations for home and classroom work and missed assignments. To a certain degree, missed work can be anticipated and a plan established so that the student can finish work that is required. The ill student does not want to be rewarded for work not completed, but expectations probably cannot be the same as for other students. One teenager expressed exasperation with a teacher who insisted he hand in every missed assignment, which was impossible because of time constraints. Although the student felt he knew the material and could fulfill major assignments and take exams, the teacher thought the boy wanted to be treated the same as the other students. The student replied, "I want to be treated fairly."

To be fair may not be any easy task; often the teacher must perform a delicate juggling act. On the one hand, the student must not be overindulged with unearned credit; on the other hand, the overall learning goals must be kept in perspective. The teacher should take into account the fact that the patient is struggling with reduced stamina, emotional preoccupation, and uncertainty about physical capacity and social status.

MAINTAINING EDUCATIONAL CONTINUITY

The first days and weeks after returning to school are the most significant, but subsequent contacts with educators and fellow students crucially influence the patient's educational career. For the youngster and his or her family, the diagnosis of cancer soon becomes a familiar, if unwelcome, fact, but each school year, he or she will encounter teachers, students, and others who learn about the illness for the first time. Even though he or she may be well and feel optimistic about the future, there are those who will behave as if he or she is near death.

Teachers who discover that one of their students now is being or has been treated for cancer should obtain information so that they will be prepared to handle situations likely to occur during the course of their work with that student. Usually, this entails meeting with the student and parents to review the current medical status, frequency of contacts with the medical center, and whether or not medication is being taken. The student's attitude toward the condition, expectations for the coming school year, and anticipated problems should be explored. Particular attention should be paid as to how the student and parents want to handle questions that arise among the other students. Youngsters who are off treatment and years from the time of diagnosis may no longer regard themselves as cancer patients but can still benefit from this kind of discussion.

EDUCATORS' FEELINGS

Uncomfortable feelings may be evoked when interacting with young cancer patients or with their parents. Educators may feel the need to protect themselves from intense emotional involvement with these ill students, from negative reactions aroused by the student's appearance, or from the fact that he or she has a life-threatening illness. Lack of knowledge about childhood cancer or its treatment or unhappy experiences with relatives or friends who have had cancer may negatively affect the educator's ability to initiate or participate in discussions with the patient and the parents and may result in an inability to work effectively with the student and classmates. The common association of cancer with death may lead an educator to assume, wrongly, that the patient will become gravely ill at school or that he or she cannot participate fully in academic or extracurricular activities.

Educators who are not sure of their feelings about the student or the illness and feel that they might avoid, overprotect, or not accept the patient may need help. Colleagues, friends, or the treatment center staff can provide understanding, emotional support, and advice. Just as the parents provide the general framework for the child's acceptance of himself or herself and the illness, the teacher sets the guidelines for the way the child will be seen and how he or she feels about himself or herself while at school. The patient and the other students will be aware of and adversely affected by the teacher's inability to respond appropriately or to manage his or her feelings.

ATTITUDES OF CLASSMATES

The illness of a child can cause fear and worry among classmates. When the child first becomes ill, the other children must be given some explanation for their classmate's absence. Later, they should be prepared for physical manifestations of the cancer and its treatment and for periodic absences from school. What the other children and, in some cases, their parents are to be told will depend on many factors, including the age of the patient and classmates and how they are grouped. Young schoolchildren are usually together in one class for an entire day, and relationships among them are intense, while children in middle or high schools often are in shifting groups and, therefore, know only some of their classmates very well. Discussions about the patient with younger children should probably take place after parents have been notified so that they can be prepared for further questions at home. Even if quite young, the patient should be involved in planning and decision making in this matter.

Since children often are cruel to a child who is different—their way of making the sick child less like themselves—they may need help in understanding that, despite the illness, the patient is still the same person as before. Long absences or changes in a patient's appearance may frighten elementary school classmates. Young teens may be especially susceptible to signs of illness or altered physical appearance because they are struggling with changes occurring in their own bodies. Older teenagers may be sympathetic, but many factors will contribute to the way peers respond. The teacher's attitude will also affect acceptance of the patient. Youngsters resent and react strongly against children who are favored or pampered by teachers. Classmates will benefit from an opportunity to express their concerns about the patient, to share their reactions to the illness, and to ask questions.

SPECIAL PROBLEMS

Some children treated for cancer will return to school with noticeable handicaps. Those who have experienced amputations or limb replacement may require special attention and help in readjusting to school life. Teenagers who have been very active in sports prior to amputation often want to continue to participate, and probably they can. These youngsters have a tremendous will to achieve and to compete. There are, however, some patients who will not be able to resume previous activities and, therefore, face loss of status and identity associated with prowess. It is important for adults to understand the need to overcome limitations and to offer encouragement.

Brain Tumors

Youngsters with impairments resulting from a brain tumor or its treatment may develop subtle alterations, or they may be severely handicapped. Assistance with academic work will be needed for some, while others may require a reduced program of physical activity because of weakness, unsteadiness, or lack of coordination. Speech and eyesight can also be affected. The child with a brain tumor can suffer a marked change in appearance. Obesity because of high doses of steroids, partial baldness, a large scar, crossed eyes, facial palsy, and other anomalies, although they may be temporary, can make reintegration to school quite difficult. Behavior at school can be affected by a voracious appetite and moodiness, which are also temporary side effects of steroids. Intellectual deficits, if present, retard learning but also create social handicaps because of inability to manage social cues. Hormonal irregularities affect growth and stature, personality, impulse control, and sexual maturation. A high proportion of children with brain tumors experience compound problems which create social barriers with peers. Often these barriers are insurmountable. These children need increased understanding and assistance from all levels of school personnel, and care must be taken not to underestimate their capacities.

Learning Problems

Tremendous strides have been made in treatment, resulting in prolonged life and often in cure for some young cancer patients, but the cost has been high. Learning problems have been observed not only in those with brain tumors but also in children who received radiation treatments to the brain to prevent central nervous system leukemia. Memory loss, sequencing difficulties, inattentiveness, and trouble concentrating are among the observed problems affecting academic achievement in this group.[3] Although patients are now treated with lower doses of radiation, it is still too soon to know whether the adverse late effects will be avoided. Investigations attempting to provide answers are under way.

Since there are variations in intellectual potential and sensitivity to treatment, it cannot be predicted whether or not a particular child will be affected, in what ways, and to what extent. Many will require help with certain subjects; some will need special classes or special schools. Neuropsychological testing designed to measure cognitive, motor, and integrative functions has been helpful in evaluating the strengths and specific deficits that contribute to a youngster's learning experience. Many pediatric cancer centers are able to refer to a neuropsychologist for this kind of testing.

Absence from School

Several recent studies of school attendance among cancer patients indicate that even two or three years postdiagnosis, most children with cancer miss a critical amount of school—more than 20 days per year.[4–6] In one study, boys missed less time than girls, and children from small communities missed less time than those from large cities (populations greater than 100,000). This may suggest that absences can be prevented through encouraging the patient and parents and establishing a close relationship between family and school.[7] Home instruction is advised when regular school attendance is not possible.

Responsible school personnel should not assume that because a child has cancer, he or she cannot be in class. They should explore thoroughly the reasons for frequent or extended absences. Excessive absenteeism can be indicative of the parents' lack of expectations now that their child is seriously ill, of their need to keep the child close, or of family dysfunction. In some cases, the assistance of the treatment center may be needed to identify or treat the problem.

It should be stressed that most children seem to want to attend school. At school, the child with cancer is one among many children, reassured of normalcy. The serious attitude toward schoolwork exhibited by many children with cancer may result from a lack of confidence regarding their capabilities and the need to allay anxiety.

Social Adjustment

A current report found that children with cancer were less likely than their healthy classmates to initiate or try new activities.[8] They were less verbal, more passive, self-conscious, and easily embarrassed. They cried, complained, worried more, had fewer friends, and were less active participants in both formal and unstructured activities. Children with cancer did not express emotions freely and maintained a self-protective posture.

Denial is one of the coping mechanisms commonly employed by adolescents with cancer. Even though these adolescents understand that they have cancer and are aware of the need for treatment, they selectively ignore the seriousness or negative consequences of the illness. This allows for continued social and emotional growth. But healthy denial, in addition to the dependent posture forced upon them at a time when they are striving to loosen ties to home and parents, can result in such maladaptive behavior as regression, increased anxiety, withdrawal from peers, noncompliance with medical therapy, and even high-risk-taking behaviors.[9] When these problematic behaviors are manifested at school, they should not be overlooked.

Youngsters who have confronted cancer and its treatment and have struggled with their own and their family's reactions have become, to some degree, different people. Often patients appear older and are more mature and serious-minded than peers. They may find that previous interests and companions are less attractive or seem too frivolous. Although friends may not be rejecting, these youngsters may be unable to resume their place socially because of their own changed priorities and altered focus. They can benefit from encouragement and from understanding educators who can guide them to endeavors that may be more satisfying and productive and that will permit more appropriate social contacts.

RELAPSE

A relapse, or recurrence of the disease, usually means that the child will not be cured, although after a first relapse, years of life may still be ahead. Members of the health care team tread a fine line when they interpret relapse to the family. They must explain the gravity of the situation while fostering hope. A relapse is extremely stressful, especially after a long period of remission when the patient has felt well and family members have been optimistic about the future. New therapies, sometimes experimental, are called for, with frequent visits to the treatment center. Feelings of despair abound, and parents draw closer to the child, who may now feel ill and be debilitated from the cancer or the intensive treatment.

A patient must be given some understanding of the new circumstances, but what he or she is told at this juncture will depend upon many factors, among them age and ability to comprehend and to verbalize questions. The family and its belief system will also dictate the amount and type of information given to the youngster. At the very least, he or she will be told that the medicines he or she has been taking are not working and that new medicines now are needed. Some children will request and receive more details, but hopes are never dashed.

The child who has suffered a recurrence will probably continue to attend school, although there will be periods of nonattendance and possibly diminished energy. Once again, physical appearance may alter drastically. This is a difficult period for the family, but meetings should be arranged between school staff, the parents, and the patient so that the child can be managed appropriately at school. A reduced schedule may help the child to maintain contact, as will letters, pictures, cards, and visits from classmates who want to express their concern for the patient.

TERMINAL ILLNESS AND DEATH

It is always hoped that the new treatments will once again produce a remission and return the child to previous levels of activity, but some children will experience repeated relapses and will die.

Even during late phases of the disease, some patients can, and very much want to, attend school for part of the day or week. To continue as a member of the class means a great deal to the dying child. Close communication and careful planning are extremely important during this time. Children who are too ill to attend school still benefit from learning and usually look forward to working with a homebound instructor. They appreciate hearing from classmates and may be able to participate in special events at school, such as class parties.

The patient's condition is bound to arouse painful feelings and questions among classmates. Care should be taken to maintain contact with the child who is at home dying, not only because of the meaning to the patient, but to help prepare the other young students. All children have fears of death at some time, and death of an age peer is especially disturbing. Children need to know that the dying child is not abandoned, that everything is being done to make him or her well and free of pain or discomfort. They also should be reassured that death from illness is uncommon in children. Finally, their own contributions toward making their classmate's life special should be acknowledged. It is best if they can be told ahead of time about the nearness of death so that they can prepare themselves.

Some children may wish to participate in the funeral service, while others will not. Individual choices and preferences should be respected, but classmates can be helped to share feelings and ask the many questions that their friend's illness and death have provoked. Planning or participating in a class or school memorial may help classmates remember their former friend and teach them that loved ones who have died need not be forgotten.

LONG-TERM SURVIVAL

Despite the death of many children from cancer, as many as 60 percent now are expected to be cured.[10] These particular patients cannot always be identified at diagnosis, so unless relapse occurs, all children are treated as if they will grow up. To assume that a child does have a future helps to make life worth living.

With prolonged remission, visits to the center for treatment or for checkups become routine, and the child's pattern of response to these visits and treatment is predictable. After a period of uninterrupted remission, usually lasting several years, treatment is discontinued. Although he or she is still not considered cured, the child and family experience a sense of accomplishment, even triumph. However, feelings of vulnerability and uneasiness may also surface, as do fears that the cancer might return without the protection of treatment. Older children may respond temporarily with diminished self-confidence, sadness, lack of energy and motivation, and an inability to concentrate. These reactions are disturbing and can interfere with schoolwork. Help may be needed in the form of reassurance and support and sometimes counseling.

As time off treatment lengthens into years, patients are considered long-term survivors, but new concerns may arise. The child who was overprotected may find it difficult to make decisions or take steps toward independence. Such youngsters can benefit from assignment of special responsibilities at school or participation in extracurricular activities.

More than other youngsters, one who has survived a life-threatening illness needs guidance in planning for the future. Vocational or career preparation is extremely important. Filling out a job application, applying for a scholarship or financial aid, or writing a biography as part of admission to a university can be extraordinarily difficult. Thoughts of the illness and unanswered questions are brought to the foreground, and dilemmas about how much information to share with prospective employers or educational institutions must be resolved. Educators play a critical role in helping these youngsters plan for the future.

REFERENCES

1. J. W. Ross and S. A. Scarvalone, "Facilitating the Pediatric Cancer Patient's Return to School," *Social Work* 27 (1982): 256–61.
2. J. W. Ross, "Resolving Non-Medical Obstacles to Successful School Re-entry for Children with Cancer," *Journal of School Health* 54 (1984): 84–86.
3. A. T. Meadows, J. Gordon, D. S. Massari, P. Littman, J. Ferguson, and K. Moss, "Declines in IQ Scores and Cognitive Dysfunction in Children with Acute Lymphocytic Leukemia Treated with Cranial Irradiation," *Lancet* 2 (1981): 1015–18.
4. P. Deasy-Spinetta, "The School and the Child with Cancer," in *Living with Childhood Cancer,* ed. J. J. Spinetta and P. Deasy-Spinetta, (St. Louis, MO: C. V. Mosby Co., 1981).
5. N. U. Cairns, P. Klopovich, E. Hearne, and S. B. Lansky, "School Attendance of Children with Cancer," *Journal of School Health* 52 (1982): 152–55.
6. S. B. Lansky and N. U. Cairns, "Poor School Attendance in Children with Malignancies," *Proceedings of the American Association of Cancer Research* 20 (1979): 390.
7. Cairns, Klopovich, Hearne, and Lansky, "School Attendance of Children with Cancer," pp. 152–55.
8. Deasy-Spinetta, "The School and the Child with Cancer."
9. L. K. Zeltzer, "The Adolescent with Cancer," in *Psychological Aspects of Childhood Cancer,* ed. J. Kellerman (Springfield, IL: Charles C. Thomas, 1980).
10. A. T. Meadows, M. Krejmas, and J. B. Belasco, "The Medical Cost of Cure: Sequelae in the Survivors of Childhood Cancer," in *Status of the Curability of Childhood Cancers,* ed. J. Van Eycs and M. P. Sullivan, (New York: Raven Press, 1980).

RESOURCES

Suggested Reading

"Cancer in School-Age Children: A Special Issue." *The Journal of School Health*. March 1977.

Kellerman, J., ed. *Psychological Aspects of Childhood Cancer*. Springfield, IL: Charles C. Thomas, 1980.

Mills, G.; Reister, R.; Robinson, A.; and Vermlye, G. *Discussing Death*. Homewood, IL: ETC Publications, 1976.

Spinetta, J. J., and Deasy-Spinetta, P., eds. *Living with Childhood Cancer*. St. Louis, MO: C. V. Mosby Co., 1981.

Students with Cancer, A Resource for the Educator. U.S. Dept. of Health, Education and Welfare, Public Health Service, National Institutes of Health, National Cancer Institute, Bethesda, MD 20205. NIH Publication #80-2086, January 1980 (no charge).

Useful Addresses

American Cancer Society, Inc., 777 Third Ave., New York, NY 10017.

Cancer Information Clearinghouse, National Cancer Institute, Bldg. 31, Room 10A18, Bethesda, MD 20205.

Candlelighters Foundation, 223 C St., SE, Washington, DC 20003.

Telephone Number:

Cancer Information Service: 800-638-6694.

Hemophilia

by Frances M. Gill, M.D. and
Regina B. Butler, R.N.

OVERVIEW

Hemophilia is an inherited disorder in which a protein involved in the coagulation of blood is either deficient or absent. These proteins, of which there are 10, are called clotting factors. Persons with hemophilia do not bleed faster than normal persons, but they may bleed longer unless they receive appropriate treatment. Sometimes even if the bleeding initially stops, a good clot can't be maintained long enough to allow healing. Although the bleeding episodes can be treated, there is no cure for hemophilia.

The term "hemophilia," when strictly applied, refers only to the absence or deficiency of factor VIII (hemophilia A) or factor IX (hemophilia B). In this chapter, the discussion will center on these classic disorders since they are among the most common, and certainly the most severe, of the inherited bleeding disorders. When used, the term "hemophilia" will refer to these conditions. There are less severe coagulation factor deficiencies, such as von Willebrand's disease, which occurs equally in males and females. It is a combined deficiency of factor VIII and of von Willebrand's factor, which is necessary for platelets to work properly. Platelets are small particles in the blood that aid clotting. Most children and adults with von Willebrand's have very few bleeding problems. In those few who do, the bleeding is generally different from that in hemophilia. The common problems are nose bleeding, gastrointestinal bleeding, heavy menstrual flow, bruising, and bleeding after childbirth. Children with very severe von Willebrand's disease can have joint bleeding, but it is uncommon. Spontaneous intracranial bleeding does not occur. Although spontaneous bleeding is uncommon in most patients, major bleeding can occur after surgery or after teeth are pulled.

People with von Willebrand's disease should not take aspirin. Few restrictions are needed for most patients. Those with the severe form will have activity limitations like those observed for hemophiliacs.

Inherited deficiencies of prothrombin, fibrinogen, or of factors V, VII, XI, or XIII occur equally among males and females and are rarer than hemophilia and von Willebrand's disease. Most patients with these deficiencies will have only mild bleeding problems. Severely affected patients may need precautions similar to those for hemophilia. Since these diseases vary so much in severity, it is important to check with the child's doctor to see if limitations are needed. Appropriate factor replacement products are available for all these disorders.

Incidence and Population Affected

Hemophilia occurs in one out of 10,000 males, and it is estimated that in the United States there are 20,000 males with hemophilia.[1,2] Only very rarely is a female affected.* Deficiencies of factors VIII and IX occur in all racial and ethnic groups. There are approximately seven times as many persons with factor VIII deficiency as with factor IX deficiency.[3,4]

Inheritance

Factor VIII and factor IX deficiencies are sex-linked disorders. The genes for production of these factors are carried only on the X chromosome, which is one of the two chromosomes each person has that determines sex. Females have two X chromosomes (XX), and males have an X and a Y chromosome (XY). To be a male, the child must receive a Y chromosome from the father and an X chromosome from the mother. The child who receives an X chromosome from both the father and mother will be female. A woman who carries the gene for hemophilia on only one of her X chromosomes (a carrier) will not have hemophilia. The normal gene on the other chromosome will produce sufficient amounts of clotting factor. Very rarely, a carrier will have very low levels of factor VIII or IX and, consequently, will have bleeding problems. If a carrier passes her abnormal X chromosome to a son, the boy will have hemophilia, as there is no genetic material on the Y chromosome for the production of factors VIII or IX. If a daughter gets the defective X chromosome, she will be a carrier, like her mother. Most girls who have factor VIII or factor IX deficiency have two abnormal X chromosomes, one from a hemophilic father and another from a carrier mother. This is why hemophilia almost always occurs in boys.

---

*Editor's Note: The term ''he'' as opposed to ''he or she'' is used in this chapter to represent all hemophiliac patients because this disease is confined almost exclusively to males.

Is hemophilia ever acquired or must it always be inherited? In a significant number of families (about 40 percent of severely affected hemophilia A families) there is no known family history. No one knows whether these cases result from truly spontaneous mutations—that is, the defect arises for the first time in the mother's or child's genetic makeup—or whether by chance no male child within recent family history received the defective X chromosome.

It is possible to acquire an inhibitor to a specific clotting protein. This inhibitor blocks the action of the clotting factor. Inhibitors to factor VIII are the most common, and even they are very rare. They tend to occur in people who have some underlying disease, in the elderly, or in postpartum women.

Medical Problems in Hemophilia

The amount of bleeding that can be expected in a child with an inherited bleeding disorder depends on the severity of the deficiency. With factor VIII and IX deficiencies, those children who have less than 1 percent of the normal amount of factor (normal people have 50 to 100 percent) are considered to have severe hemophilia and will have frequent bleeding problems. In many cases, bleeding, particularly in the joints, will occur spontaneously without the child's recalling any injury. If the child has 1 percent to 5 percent of the factor (moderate hemophilia), spontaneous bleeding occurs but is less common. Persons with 5 percent or more, and particularly those with more than 20 percent of normal factor (mild hemophilia) usually have bleeding only after experiencing a specific insult, such as a major cut, surgery, or extraction of a tooth. They generally have few problems that arise from daily activities.

Bleeding can occur almost anywhere in the body. The consequences of the hemorrhage depend on the site of the bleeding. Obviously, the most worrisome hemorrhages are those that might cause death or significant loss of some necessary function. Bleeding is treated by replacing the deficient factor. This is derived from human blood and infused through the veins.

Soft Tissue and Muscle Bleeding

The most common type of bleeding is that into the soft tissue beneath the skin. These hemorrhages look like large bruises, and many children with hemophilia, particularly when just learning to walk, look like battered children. Such bruises rarely cause problems. Bleeding into the muscles may be troublesome if it threatens the function of a muscle nerve, but it usually can be treated easily.

Joint Bleeding

Joint bleeding (hemarthrosis), which occurs frequently in children with severe factor VIII or IX deficiency, is the most common type of bleeding requiring treatment. The most frequent sites are the knees, elbows, and ankles. Bleeding can occur in the shoulder or hip and very rarely in the wrist and small joints in the fingers and hands. The child may remember some trauma, such as falling on the knee or twisting the ankle, but many times the bleeding seems to begin without cause. The stresses of normal walking or running can lead to spontaneous joint bleeding.

These hemorrhages are important for many reasons. The pain is greater when the joint is moved and the muscles act to prevent movement. The child cannot bend or bear weight on that joint. Repeated hemorrhages in the same joint can lead to chronic damage to the bone and cartilage of the joints. Arthritis similar to the osteoarthritis seen in older people develops. Treatment should begin early in a hemorrhage in order to reduce joint damage and to prevent severe pain.

Other Sites of Serious Bleeding

Bleeding in or around the brain is a major threat to normal function and is the most frequent cause of bleeding death in hemophilia. Intracranial hemorrhages can result from trauma, minor falls, or can occur spontaneously. Bleeding into the tissue beneath the lining of the abdominal cavity, called the retroperitoneal space, is very dangerous. Hemorrhage in the gastrointestinal tract, resulting in vomiting blood or passing blood in the stools, can cause the loss of large amounts of blood. Bleeding around the trachea (windpipe) can close off the airway.

Other Common Sites of Bleeding

There may be bleeding into the urinary tract, with blood in the urine being quite common. This usually does not cause any problems. Nosebleeds occasionally require treatment. The child may bleed from a loose tooth, after a tooth is pulled, or if he gets a cut in the mouth. Bleeding from the tonsils may also occur, particularly during tonsillitis.

Course

The lifespan of the person with hemophilia has increased markedly with the availability of factor replacement. Although the median age of severely affected patients is still younger than that of the total U.S. male population, most patients can look forward to a long and productive life. However, bleeding is still a significant cause of death.

The disease itself does not worsen with age. The level of factor present is genetically determined and does not vary with age. The pattern of the bleeding varies somewhat throughout life. Young children tend to have more mouth and subcutaneous hemorrhages because they are likely to fall when learning to walk or climb. During school age, the most frequent problems are muscle and joint bleeding. Adolescents, older teenagers, and adults generally have fewer hemorrhages than younger children. As hemophiliacs grow up, they become more responsible for their own activities. They learn to avoid situations that are sure to cause bleeding problems. Joint damage and arthritis worsen with age. The accompanying arthritis does not cause pain until the third decade of life or later.

Psychological Aspects

Some people feel that psychological stresses may cause an increased number of hemorrhages. Many patients feel that they can decrease the frequency and severity of their bleeding by such methods as biofeedback and self-hypnosis. Some patients report that they bleed more when excited about holidays or nervous about a test at school. These factors, however, are not clearly defined.

Certainly, hemophilia can produce guilt and conflict within a family which in turn can cause behavioral and psychological problems in the child and even in siblings. As with other inherited disorders, there is frequently guilt on the part of the carrier(s), who may feel at fault for having caused the child's suffering. Also, parents feel badly that the child is restricted from activities that are enjoyable but potentially dangerous. These attitudes prompt many parents to "make up" for the child's restrictions in ways that could result in behavioral problems. The mother and father may disagree on the approach to the child, and this may cause a major conflict between the parents.

Depending upon its severity, hemophilia can impinge in a major way on the child's and the family's routine. The young child with severe factor VIII or IX deficiency typically requires one to two treatments a week. The necessity of trips to the hospital at unplanned and often inconvenient times limits the family's ability to plan activities. The parents' work schedule may also be disrupted. The financial cost is also burdensome. Although state and federal programs and improved insurance coverage have helped, family budgets are often stressed. Even when medical costs are covered, transportation costs and lost hourly income can decrease money available for other family needs and pleasures. It is easy to imagine how badly the child must occasionally feel for being the center of so many family problems.

THERAPY

Factor Replacement

The keystone to treatment of bleeding in any inherited bleeding disorder is the replacement of the missing or deficient factor. This factor is isolated from plasma obtained from blood donors, either paid or volunteer. Hemophiliacs are the biggest single consumer group of blood products in this country. In some centers, hemophiliacs receive factor replacement only during periods of bleeding. This is called "on demand" therapy. At the first sign of bleeding or in preparation for surgery or dental work, the specific factor is administered intravenously to raise the level of that factor so that clotting can take place. Some centers use "prophylactic infusions," that is, infusions of the specific factor given every two to three days to try to prevent bleeding. The cost of this type of therapy is immense, and there is not presently enough blood collected in this country to offer prophylactic therapy to all hemophiliacs. However, regularly scheduled treatments can be given to children who are having recurrent bleeding in one joint or who are receiving physical therapy for problems in a joint.

Time Involved in Treatment

Treatment given at a hemophilia center or hospital requires a large part of both the parents' and the child's day. A parent must take the child to the hospital, wait in the emergency room or treatment area, wait for the factor to be prepared and given, and then sometimes wait for a final evaluation of the child's condition. Home care, as described below, reduces the disruption in the family.

The number of treatments required depends upon the site of the bleeding. Most joint hemorrhages can be treated effectively with one dose of the replacement factor, but if the child has had a lot of trouble with the joint, two or three treatments over a 24-hour period may be needed. In muscle hemorrhages, only one treatment is usually needed unless there is pressure on a nerve. Hospitalization is usually necessary for more serious bleeding episodes. Duration of hospitalization can be from three days for muscle or gastrointestional bleeding to three weeks or more for bleeding in the brain.

Home Care

"Home care" refers to the administration of the factor replacement at home or in a nonhospital setting by the child or, when the child is young, by a family member with the child's cooperation. The goals of home care are to make the child and family more independent of medical personnel, to initiate treatment in the early stage of bleeding, and to minimize complications. Home care saves the time and some of the cost involved in emergency room visits, decreases disruption in family life, and allows the child to attend school with fewer interruptions.

At the time of diagnosis, home care should be mentioned to the parents as a possibility for the future. Although home care is not appropriate for every family, it is a goal that can be worked toward by most severely affected families. Children can begin home care when they are three or four years old. Their veins are then large enough for their parents to treat them, and the children are old enough to cooperate and understand why the family must hurt them to help them. Parents are taught about the disease, what the treatment is, when to treat, and how much factor to give. They are taught the techniques of administering factor intravenously. Children are encouraged to participate in their own care from a very early age, and gradually they take over the treatment, thus taking a large step toward independence. Often, older children store some factor material at their school so that they may treat themselves if an injury occurs. This results in only a 15- to 20-minute interruption in their school day rather than a trip home or to the hopsital.

Problems of Treatment

Allergic reactions to the blood product after a treatment can occur. This usually happens immediately after administration of factor and is usually a minor allergic reaction, such as hives. Rarely is there a major allergic reaction.

The risk of acquiring hepatitis is high for children with the severe form of hemophilia who get frequent, multiple treatments. About 95 percent of those who have received multiple treatments have the markers showing that they have had hepatitis B. There is also a risk of acquiring non-A, non-B hepatitis. About 30 percent of hemophiliacs have had symptomatic hepatitis with jaundice.[5,6] Hepatitis B vaccine is now available.

Acquired immunodeficiency syndrome (AIDS), a serious disease, can be acquired from blood products and has occurred in heavily treated hemophiliacs.

There may be some minor long-term liver problems, but this is not clearly defined at this time.

Treatment of Orthopedic Problems

Often, when a child has bled into a joint, a splint is used for several days to rest the joint and allow healing. If the bleeding occurs in the leg, the child will use crutches to take the pressure off the joints. Unlike the child with a broken leg who must be continuously on crutches for a certain number of days, then off for good, the hemophiliac may come to school on crutches for a few days, then be off them, and in another few days use them again. Occasionally, a child will require orthopedic surgery for a joint that has sustained chronic bleeding and damage. This will require an absence from school of several weeks. A lengthy period of physical therapy may be necessary after the surgery. Physical therapy also may be needed for chronic joint or muscle problems.

SCHOOL LIFE

There are no academic deficits associated with hemophilia unless bleeding in the brain has affected the child's mental ability. By and large, hemophiliacs do well in school if they have not missed much time. This has been ascribed to their desire to excel in some area. These children should be motivated to achieve their best, for there are only a few vocations that are closed to them. Very heavy physical labor and high-risk jobs, such as riveting girders, are obviously restricted. But the majority of white- and blue-collar jobs are open to hemophiliacs.

Time Lost from School

It is difficult to generalize about how much time a child with hemophilia is typically absent. The number of days missed will depend on the severity of the factor deficiency and the method of treating bleeds. Absences are usually unpredictable, but most children do not miss enough school days consecutively to affect their performances. In Pennsylvania, the average number of school or work days lost in 1977–78 was 5.5 days per year for patients with hemophilia A who required treatment.[7] In 1982–83, the figure fell to 3.1 days (unpublished data).

Children who are on home care, who have a good understanding of their disease, and who know how and when to treat problems may miss very little school. They can treat a hemorrhage in the morning and still go to school. Many children keep their factor at school and, when necessary, either administer it themselves and go back to class or summon a parent to give the factor. Treatment takes only a half hour or so. When a child must go to a hospital emergency room, a whole school day may be lost.

These children should be required to make up work after being absent. If a child needs surgery or is having a major problem with a joint, arrangements should be made for him to keep up with the work at home. When a child with hemophilia begins to miss much time, either individual days or several days in a row, the teacher should obtain permission from the parents to speak with the doctor or nurse. An organized plan for dealing with these absences can be made. Rarely do these children need homebound teaching, and it should only be used as a last resort. It is helpful if the child is given two sets of books, one to keep at home and one at school. Then, when he must stay out of school unexpectedly, he can get his work by telephone and use the books at home to keep up with the class.

Peer Relationships

Whether the child with hemophilia will attract the positive attention of his peers will depend upon his own attitude. Being comfortable with himself, having a good self-image, and not perceiving himself as being ill are attitudes that are almost essential in forming good peer relationships. Children from supportive families that have learned to live with the disorder and cope with its problems and are able to help the child with problems usually do very well. Often a child's peers know he has hemophilia, and they usually recognize and understand that the disease limits participation in certain sports and activities. Home care, which cuts down on time spent in the hospital and interruption in normal activities, is helpful in permitting normal peer relationships.

Physical Activities

Participation in regular physical education classes can be a problem, particularly in junior and senior high school. Often, the physical education given at these levels consists mainly of rough contact sports, which are dangerous to children with hemophilia. Many schools now have adaptive physical education, which means that children with hemophilia can participate in activities that are safe for them. If such classes are not available, the level of participation in a regular class depends on the individual. To exclude children with hemophilia from physical education completely is inappropriate. These children have the ability to participate in many activities and should engage in appropriate physical education at all grade levels. Most children can be believed regarding whether or not they can participate in a certain activity. They know what their limits are and usually abide by them. School personnel should also seek the advice of the children's parents and health care teams. Children with hemophilia do not need more rest than other children.

It is difficult for hemophiliac children when too many limitations are put on activities, so only those activities that carry the highest risk of injury to the head or abdomen should be off limits. Severely affected hemophiliacs are not allowed to engage in contact sports, such as football. Not so clearly defined are participation in baseball, softball, and basketball. Much depends on how well the games are supervised and how rough they are. Generally, varsity sports are prohibited, but some children can play Little League baseball if they are not pitching or catching. Neighborhood basketball games are also permitted.

Children should not ride motorcycles but they can ride bicycles. It is recommended that they not begin until they are six or seven years old, when coordination has improved and learning is accompanied by fewer falls. Skateboards are forbidden.

Golf, tennis, running, and swimming are allowed and can even be performed on a competitive basis if the child wishes. Swimming is an excellent activity because it strengthens muscles and exercises the joints without weightbearing. Swimming is advised as therapy and as a means to prevent hemorrhages. Strong muscles are actually protection for the joints and can reduce the amount and severity of joint bleeding. Calisthenics are also allowed.

APPROACH TO THE CHILD WITH HEMOPHILIA

The best way to learn how to treat the child appropriately is to request a member of the hemophilia center to visit the school. He or she will discuss the individual child and his specific problems, what hemophilia is and is not, and what to expect and what not to expect.

It is important that school personnel respect the child's knowledge of hemophilia. If a child tells a teacher or nurse that he is bleeding, he should be believed even if there are no outward signs of bleeding. It is at that point—when there is not yet outward evidence—that treatment should begin. Educators should remember that the majority of hemorrhages occur in the muscles and joints and not out through the skin. The child should also be relied on to report what can and cannot be done on a given day. Limitations can vary according to the child's condition.

There are times when the child's mobility will be affected, and allowances should be made. When it is necessary for the child to use crutches, it would be helpful for him to be allowed to leave class three or four minutes early. It also would be helpful to have books available for use in each classroom or to have a friend carry the books. Children with elbow hemorrhages also find it difficult to carry books.

Sometimes, an elbow hemorrhage keeps a child from writing. However, it is still appropriate for him to be in school and learn by listening and taking part in discussions. Even though the ability to do all the schoolwork is impaired, having the child attend under these conditions forms the pattern for good attendance under adverse conditions.

It is appropriate for teachers and other advisers to try to channel the interests of the child away from athletics to other interests such as drama club, reading, chess, band, chorus, debating, acting as a library or audiovisual aide, and hobbies. It is sometimes forgotten that many children without hemophilia have little inclination toward sports and are perfectly happy without a strong involvement in athletics. Furthermore, it is only a small minority of high school students who are on varsity sports teams.

Excusing the child because of the illness is a big mistake many people make. Parents do it by not disciplining the child as consistently or as strictly as their other children, and teachers do it by saying, "He acts that way because he has hemophilia." When teachers and parents perceive a shortened lifespan for the child, this attitude is further intensified. The child may develop a pattern of blaming the disorder for all failures and may use the disease to get out of unpleasant or difficult situations and duties. As a result, the child will grow up unprepared for adult responsibilities and relationships. Although the lifespan is probably shortened somewhat by severe hemophilia, this is not predictable in individual patients. All these children should be encouraged to achieve and to develop acceptable personality traits.

Another common mistake is to put more restrictions on the child at school than are necessary. There is nothing inside the ordinary classroom that he cannot do. In gym and on the playground, limits should not be placed beyond those which the family and physician have set. Excessive caution can be minimized by teachers facing their own fears about hemophilia and recognizing that the restrictions may be more for their own emotional well-being than for the child's safety. Communication with the child's medical team can help alleviate such fears.

It is inappropriate to draw attention to the child's condition. For example, an extreme case occurred when a teacher announced to the entire class that the children should not bump Joe (not his real name) because he had hemophilia and should not touch him or he could bleed to death. Of course, this was an unusually insensitive way to treat any child, but more subtle ways of drawing attention to the child's disorder can also be psychologically damaging. When classmates have questions about the child's hemophilia, they should be answered individually. When a child cannot participate in a given activity, no general explanation is necessary. Generally, the child can answer classmates' questions.

Sometimes a situation is unwittingly created in which the child feels punished for not being able to participate. If a student cannot attend physical education classes, it is not a good idea to send him to the library or give written work to compensate. Children usually perceive written work in place of physical education as punishment. If there is no appropriate physical education program for the child at a given time, a class of the child's choosing or study hall should be scheduled.

MEDICAL PROBLEMS THAT MAY OCCUR IN THE CLASSROOM

The first thing to remember when a child with hemophilia is hurt or begins to bleed is that he does not bleed any faster than other children—only longer. Even with a major injury, there will be the same amount of time to get to the hospital and receive treatment as if the injury occurred in another classmate. Minor bumps will cause bruises but certainly not death. If a child with hemophilia sustains trauma (such as a fall down steps or from playground equipment), it is more of a problem than for a child without hemophilia, but none of these situations is untreatable. The attitude should be "What do we do about it now that it has happened?" Knowing what to do in case of an emergency will help everyone feel more comfortable with the hemophilic child. Again, discussions with the child's physician or a hemophilia nurse-specialist are helpful. The following are general guidelines for situations that may arise.

Cuts

Cuts are not a problem unless there is extreme pain or the cut is deep, in which case the parents should be notified. If the cut would not be disturbing in an ordinary child, it should not be disturbing in a child with hemophilia. Use normal first aid procedures, cleaning the wound and applying pressure. If the cut is deep enough to require suturing, treatment with factor will be needed to stop the bleeding and keep it from recurring at the sites of suture placement. Cuts in the mouth often require treatment with factor.

Bumps, Falls, and Bruises

The child will probably always have a lot of bruises under the skin. As long as they are superficial, no treatment is required. However, after a fall or other injury, swelling may result from bleeding into the muscle, and treatment should be given. Sometimes, a child will say that he needs treatment even if there isn't outward evidence, such as swelling or redness. The child should be believed in such instances, since he can recognize the earliest symptoms of bleeding into the joints and muscles. This is often reported as a "funny feeling" or tingling sensation in the joint, which the child associates with bleeding.

Head Injuries

It is essential that every head trauma sustained by the child be reported to the parents immediately so that treatment can be sought right away. Head injuries are potentially life-threatening, as there can be bleeding into or around the brain. The appearance of the head gives no clue as to the seriousness of the problem. Bumps and lumps, or their absence, do not indicate what is going on inside the brain.

Headache and Other Serious Bleeding Problems

Parents should be notified if the child complains of a headache, seems drowsy, does not act like himself, or begins to vomit. These are possible signs of bleeding in the brain.

If the child reports nosebleeds or blood in the urine or stools, his parents should be notified. Injuries to the neck, back, and abdomen can also lead to serious problems.

Aspirin

Hemophilacs should not be taken aspirin. Aspirin interferes with platelet function and can therefore aggravate bleeding. Aspirin substitutes containing acetominophen (such as Tylenol or Datril) can be given for pain and fever.

Observance by School Personnel

Teacher observation is important, particularly in a young child. If a child falls or gets a bad knock on the playground, the parents should be notified at the end of the day so that they can be on the watch for symptoms of bleeding later that evening. If the bump or injury has been to the head, they should be notified immediately. If the teacher notices that a child is not moving a particular joint or that it appears swollen and warm, he or she should determine whether the parent knows about the swelling. If treatment has not been given for the hemorrhage, it should be started as quickly as possible.

Teachers can be alert to signs and symptoms of bleeding in the brain, such as drowsiness, irritability, severe headache, pupils that are unequal, and projectile vomiting. This is an emergency situation, and an ambulance should be called.

FOSTERING CLASSMATES' UNDERSTANDING

When the child with hemophilia has a good self-image, and parents and teachers have positive feelings about his abilities and treat him as a person rather than as a "sick person" or "hemophiliac," classmates will tend to be more understanding of the situation. Ideally, classmates should understand that hemophilia is a problem but that it is not the child's whole life. He has many concerns in common with other children, and on most occasions, these will take precedence over the health problem as a focus for his life. Teachers can influence classmates' feelings toward the child by allowing him to compete with healthy children in a healthy way and by expecting him to follow the same rules as other children.

It is also important to clear up misconceptions that might cause others to shun the child. If the teacher understands and really believes that the child will not bleed to death from some minor injury, he or she can pass on a sense of comfortableness with the child to other children. When children perceive that the teacher is nervous around the child, they will tend to stay away or treat him differently.

Questions will come up about the child's condition, especially if the disorder is serious. Although it is not appropriate for teachers to explain hemophilia formally to the entire class, teachers can help the child when he is trying to explain to his friends what hemophilia is. Here again, when school personnel have a good knowledge of hemophilia, accurate information can be given in informal situations as the need arises.

REFERENCES

1. C. R. Petit and H. G. Klein, "Hemophilia, Hemophiliacs, and the Health Care Delivery System," DHEW Publication No. (NIH) 76-871, 1976.
2. "National Heart, Lung, and Blood Institute Study to Evaluate the Supply-Demand Relationship of AHF and PTC through 1980." DHEW Publication No. (NIH) 77-1274, 1977.

3. Petit and Klein, "Hemophilia, Hemophiliacs, and the Health Care Delivery System."
4. "National Heart, Lung, and Blood Institute Study."
5. R. Biggs, "Jaundice and Antibodies Directed against Factors VIII and IX in Patients Treated for Haemophilia or Christmas Disease in the United Kingdom," *British Journal of Haematology* 26 (1974): 313.
6. A. I. Cederbaum, P. M. Blatt, and P. H. Levine, "Abnormal Serum Transaminase Levels in Patients with Hemophilia A," *Archives of Internal Medicine* 142 (1982): 481.
7. M. E. Eyster, J. H. Lewis, S. S. Shapiro, F. M. Gill, et al., "The Pennsylvania Hemophilia Program 1973–1978," *American Journal of Hematology* 9 (1980): 277.

RESOURCES

Suggested Reading

The Hemophilia Patient/Family Model. The Hemophilia Educational Resources Project, National Hemophilia Foundation, 19 W. 34th St., New York, NY 10001.

Hilgartner, Margaret W., M.D., *Hemophilia in Children*. Littleton, MA: PSG Publishing Company, 1976.

Jones, Peter. *Living with Hemophilia*. Philadelphia, PA: F. A. Davis, 1974.

The Student with Hemophilia, A Resource for the Educator. The National Hemophilia Foundation, 19 W. 34th St., New York, NY 10001.

Understanding Hemophilia. A Guide for Parents. Hemophilia Foundation of Illinois, 327 S. LaSalle St., Room 1648, Chicago, IL 60604.

Useful Address

National Hemophilia Foundation, 19 W. 34th St., New York, NY 10001.

Sickle Cell Anemia

**by Haewon C. Kim, M.D.,
Grace Gaston, M.S.W., and Janet Fithian**

OVERVIEW

Sickle cell anemia is a hereditary blood disorder that affects one in 650 black Americans.[1] The red blood cells of persons with this disorder survive in the circulation for only 15 to 20 days in contrast with the normal 120 days, resulting in a chronic anemia. These red blood cells also have a tendency to lose their normal discoidal shape and become rigid and deformed, sometimes taking on a "sickle" shape. Such pointy, elongated cells are not always pliable enough to squeeze through small blood vessels as do normal cells. As a result, vessels can become blocked and surrounding areas deprived of the circulation of blood, causing tissue damage (infarction). Manifestations of tissue damage include painful episodes and a susceptibility to infection. The course of the disease is variable. Some children have frequent, severe problems and others have only sporadic health problems related to sickle cell anemia.

Cause

Sickle cell anemia is caused by an abnormality of hemoglobin, the red protein in red blood cells that carries oxygen from the lungs to the tissues. The hemoglobin molecule is made up of two pairs of globin chains, two alpha (α) chains and two nonalpha chains, examples of which are beta (β) and delta (δ) chains. The globin chains are composed of amino acids, and each chain contains iron-protoporphyrin IX, which binds with the oxygen that is transported by the red blood cells. Normal adult hemoglobin (Hb A) is made up of two α chains and β chains and accounts for 95 percent of the total hemoglobin in red blood cells.[2] The remainder consists of minor hemoglobins which are not relevant to this discussion. In persons with sickle cell anemia, the major hemoglobin is not Hb A but is called sickle hemoglobin, or Hb S. It differs in that there is a substitution of one amino acid, valine, for glutamic acid in one position out of 146 on each of the chains. When the substitution is only on one chain, the person will have sickle cell trait. This subtle alteration makes it easy for Hb S to associate into long fibers within the cell, causing these cells to deform.

Pattern of Inheritance

Sickle cell anemia (Hb SS) results when a child inherits two genes for Hb S, one from the mother and one from the father. Each parent must have at least one sickle gene in order for the child to have sickle cell anemia. Most commonly, the parents have sickle cell trait, which means that they each carry one gene for Hb A and one gene for Hb S. Because sickle cell trait is a benign condition, many people are not aware of having it. In the case of two people with sickle cell trait, there is a one in four chance for each pregnancy that the child will have sickle cell disease, a one in two chance that the child will have sickle cell trait as do his or her parents, and a one in four chance that the child will have normal hemoglobin. Prenatal diagnosis is available to couples who risk having a child with sickle cell anemia.

It is also possible for a child to inherit another abnormal hemoglobin that will act in combination with Hb S. The disorders that result are called "variants of sickle cell disease," and usually have a milder course than sickle cell anemia. The most common is Hb SC disease, which is a combination of Hb S and Hb C. The terms "homozygous sickle cell disease," or "sickle cell anemia," is used to distinguish Hb SS from these variants. The information in this chapter will pertain to sickle cell anemia.

Population Affected

In the United States, sickle cell anemia and trait are found primarily in people of African ancestry. However, some Caucasians, especially those coming from Mediterranean areas, the Middle East, and some parts of India, have this disorder. Males and females are affected equally.

Onset and Course

Unless a child has had a blood test to detect sickle cell anemia at birth or as part of well-baby care, families are usually unaware that the child is affected until the first signs and symptoms appear, usually during the second half of the first year of life. By this time most of the fetal hemoglobin (Hb F), which is the major hemoglobin in fetal life, has been gradually replaced by adult hemoglobin. Normally Hb F is replaced by Hb A. In the case of a baby with sickle cell anemia, it is replaced by the abnormal Hb S. When enough Hb S is present, symptoms can develop. Often, the first symptom is a painful swelling of the hands and feet called "hand-foot syndrome." Another early manifestation is a sudden, severe infection. It is very unusual for a child with homozygous sickle cell disease to reach school age without the disorder's having become apparent.

It was once thought that the lifespan of the person with sickle cell anemia was about 20 years. However, comprehensive medical care, the availability of antibiotics, prompt treatment of infections early in childhood, and improved living conditions have greatly reduced mortality in these patients. It is also possible that in the past only those most seriously ill sought out medical care, thus producing the impression that nearly all persons with sickle cell anemia had a very complicated course and a greatly shortened lifespan. Although accurate statistics with respect to lifespan are not yet available, many persons with sickle cell anemia live beyond middle age, hold jobs, and carry out family responsibilities.

Sickle Cell Trait

Sickle cell anemia and sickle cell trait are often confused. As mentioned above, those with sickle cell trait have inherited one gene for Hb S, while those with sickle cell anemia have inherited two, one from each parent. In the red cells of persons with sickle cell trait (Hb AS), there is not enough Hb S to cause sickling, except in situations where the oxygen level is extremely low, such as on high mountains. Sickle cell trait is not an illness and persons with it should not be denied employment or life insurance, nor should their activities be restricted. The frequency of sickle cell trait in professional football players and track athletes is the same as that in the general black population.[3]

Sickle cell trait is common in American blacks, occurring in 8 percent of this population.[4] The incidence is much higher in certain regions of Africa. It appears that having sickle cell trait is an advantage where parasites causing malaria flourish. Apparently these parasites have difficulty surviving in red cells containing Hb S. Throughout history the incidence and severity of malaria was reduced in persons carrying one Hb S gene, allowing them an increased chance of survival compared with those not having sickle cell trait or those having sickle cell anemia. The importance of identifying persons with sickle cell trait is for family planning.

CLINICAL MANIFESTATIONS

The term "sickle cell anemia" indicates that the main feature of the disorder is anemia. Although it is true that children with sickle cell anemia are always anemic, with hemoglobin levels (blood counts) usually between 6.5 and 8.5 g/dl, the body adjusts to this state. A normal hemoglobin level in children is not less than 11 g/dl. This anemia rarely causes problems in carrying out routine activities, but trouble can develop quickly under circumstances that further reduce the hemoglobin level, such as bleeding, increased destruction of red blood cells, or an interruption in their normal production. The most common and pervasive problems from sickle cell anemia result in the clogging of the blood vessels by sickled cells.

Complications in sickle cell anemia that come on suddenly are called "crises." There are four kinds of crises: painful, splenic sequestration, aplastic, and hyperhemolytic. These will be discussed, as will be other manifestations, such as increased susceptibility to infection, stroke, and organ damage.

Painful Crisis

Painful, or vaso-occlusive, crisis, the most common of the crises, is experienced by almost all patients. This is an attack of pain mainly involving the bones and joints of the hands and feet (mostly in younger children), arms and legs, back and chest (mostly in older children), or abdomen. When small blood vessels are blocked by sickled cells, the surrounding areas become starved for oxygen, and pain results. The pain may be so mild that the child can continue his or her activities, or it can be so severe that drugs or even hospitalization is required. This is not a life-threatening complication, even when severe, but it can be very incapacitating. Some patients have frequent painful episodes, requiring multiple hospitalizations within a year, while others have long crisis-free periods. Sometimes a particular child will experience a series of crises within a short time, then not be bothered by this problem for months or even years. Because they occur unexpectedly and differ in severity and length, painful crises often have a very negative psychological impact on patients and their families.

Splenic Sequestration Crisis

This is the most immediately life-threatening complication in sickle cell anemia and requires prompt emergency treatment. Large amounts of blood become trapped in the spleen, which becomes grossly enlarged. It may be likened to a hemorrhage, with the blood going into the spleen. A child undergoing splenic sequestration becomes pale, weak, and listless; has a swollen and painful abdomen; and perspires. The hemoglobin level drops drastically, and the child can go into shock and die. The treatment is blood transfusion, which gives the body the blood needed to function. Fortunately, splenic sequestration seldom occurs in children over five years of age, as by that time, the spleen usually has been destroyed by sickling. However, splenic sequestration does occur in older children with variants of sickle cell disease.

Aplastic Crisis

The aplastic crisis is a result of a temporary cessation of the production of red blood cells by the bone marrow. This interruption often happens in the case of a viral infection and can happen to people with normal hemoglobin as well as people with sickle cell anemia. It has serious consequences in the latter because their hemoglobin level is low to begin with, and the lifespan of their red blood cells is greatly shortened. If the bone marrow does not constantly produce red blood cells, their usual anemia can worsen quickly. In an aplastic crisis, the hemoglobin level can drop even lower than 3 to 4 g/dl before it is recognized. A sign of an aplastic crisis is pallor and lethargy, but since it is usually accompanied by a viral infection, families very often attribute this change in their child to a cold or other illness. Inexperienced persons may not easily identify pallor in black children. However, it may be determined if the conjunctivae and fingernail-beds are pale. Usually normal bone marrow activity resumes in a week or two.

Hyperhemolytic Crisis

The hyperhemolytic crisis results from a massive destruction of red blood cells and often occurs with infections. It has been suggested that it may be particularly sudden and severe in persons with sickle cell anemia who also have glucose-6-phosphate dehydrogenase (G6PD) deficiency and have been exposed to certain toxins or drugs. Information that a child has G6PD deficiency in addition to sickle cell anemia should be in the school records. Also, the child's physician should be consulted before the child is given any medicine, even aspirin.

The symptoms of a hyperhemolytic crisis are the same as those of an aplastic crisis, except that there will also be jaundice and dark urine from the products of the broken-down red blood cells. The treatment is the same as that for the aplastic crisis.

OTHER MANIFESTATIONS

Infection

Children with sickle cell anemia have a high incidence of infection, particularly pneumonia, sepsis (acute illness caused by bacteria in the bloodstream), meningitis, and osteomyelitis. Infection used to be the primary cause of death in young children with sickle cell anemia and still accounts for much of the morbidity and mortality related to it. All of the reasons for this susceptibility to infection are not completely understood, but the major reason is that repeated sickling within the spleen is damaging and causes the spleen to lose the ability to remove bacteria from the bloodstream. This occurs even in infants less than one year old. Because of the loss of splenic function and because immune functions are not yet fully developed, children under three years of age are at risk for serious infections. Most infections respond to prompt treatment with antibiotics.

Stroke

Approximately 6 percent of children with sickle cell anemia experience a stroke.[5] Once a child has had a stroke, there is a tendency for stroke to recur. Cerebral arteriograms on patients with stroke have shown narrowing or occlusion of the major cerebral arteries, suggesting damage to blood vessels from red cell sickling within these vessels.[6,7] Studies have shown cerebral infarction—the obstruction of circulation to an area in the brain resulting in death of tissue—to be the most frequent cause of stroke in these children. Much less common causes are ruptured aneurysms and hemorrhage.[8] Most commonly, children with stroke present with weakness or paralysis affecting a limb or limbs on one side, facial weakness on one side, or complete loss of speech or speech disturbance. Less frequently there may be seizures, coma, or even death. Stroke in children differs from that in adults in that it is more apt to occur as a transient event (transient ischemic attack), with symptoms lasting from a few hours to a day or so. The patient usually makes a good recovery from the initial event, but varying degrees of neurologic deficits persist in some children. With the treatment program described in the section on therapy, patients have had good neurologic recovery. Most of them function at a satisfactory or even better than average level in school.[9]

Other Complications of Red Cell Sickling

Vaso-occlusion by sickled cells silently causes organ damage, which may not be apparent for several years. Loss of splenic function has already been mentioned. Although chronic kidney disease is not common in children with sickle cell anemia, continuous sickling causes the kidneys to lose the ability to concentrate urine. The output of urine is increased, resulting in frequent urination, enuresis (bed-wetting) in some, and dehydration during hot weather or with increased activity. Occasionally, there is a sudden onset of painless bloody urine, usually in adolescents or adults.

Most persons with sickle cell anemia have an enlarged liver and some liver dysfunction. Jaundice is present in varying degrees, although symptomatic liver disease is unusual. Aseptic necrosis (death of tissue not related to infection) of bone from damage caused by infarction can occur in any bone but mostly readily occurs in the head of the thigh bone. This can begin in children over five years of age but is more common later in life. It is a disabling complication; however, if diagnosed before serious damage, it can be treated by a program of nonweightbearing and/or bracing and physical therapy. Occasionally, an adolescent or young adult will develop ulcerations in the lower leg, especially around the ankles, either spontaneously or following trauma. Another infrequent complication of vaso-occlusion is priapism, which is the painful swelling of the penis due to trapping of blood. This usually occurs without relation to sexual excitement and is managed by blood transfusion. Serious visual deficits can occur as a result of sickling in the retinal vessels.

Some children with sickle cell anemia are developmentally delayed physically and sexually. In a few of these children, the delay is extreme, so that the child may look a few years younger than others in the class or be the smallest child in the class. A late catch-up usually occurs, and adults with sickle cell anemia are generally as tall as others. The exact cause of this delay is not known, but in some cases a disturbance in the hypothalamus is responsible.[10]

THERAPY

Children with a sickle cell disease should be cared for by a pediatric hematologist (specialist in blood disorders of children) in a sickle cell center. The National Institutes of Health publishes a directory of national, federal, and local sickle cell disease programs (see Resources). In addition to providing medical care, these programs provide nursing and social worker services by personnel who are knowledgeable about the specific medical and social problems related to sickle cell anemia. Screening for sickle cell trait, genetic counseling, and education about sickle cell anemia and trait are usually available through these centers. When this more specialized care is not available, pediatricians who consult with hematologists may be called upon to care for these children.

There is no cure for sickle cell anemia or any sickle cell disease. Although many substances have been tried to prevent red cell sickling, none has been proven both safe and effective. Treatment primarily involves preventive and supportive care, with prompt, specific treatment of complications as they arise. Children should be seen once every three months unless there are special medical problems requiring more frequent visits. Yearly retinal examinations are recommended with indirect ophthalmoscopy from the age of 10. Various therapies for specific complications are discussed below.

Control and Prevention of Infections

The prompt use of antibiotics has greatly reduced mortality and morbidity from infections. If a child has a fever over 101°F for 24 hours or more, a doctor should be consulted. If the child is given an antibiotic, he or she must complete the entire course of treatment, which is usually about 10 days. Some children, primarily preschool-aged children, will be given penicillin twice daily to prevent infections.

Because children with sickle cell anemia are susceptible to bacterial infection, they should be given Pneumovax, which is a vaccination that offers protection against the majority of infections caused by Streptococcus pneumoniae. It is given twice to children under the age of two and once to children over two years of age. This vaccination may have to be repeated in five years.

Treatment of Painful Crisis

Painful crises are frequently managed at home or even at school by increasing fluid intake and using drugs such as aspirin and acetaminophen (Tylenol or Datril). These drugs are sometimes given in combination with codeine for use at home. If pain is not relieved by this conventional therapy, the child should be brought to the hospital emergency room for stronger drugs to relieve pain, such as Demerol or morphine, and/or intravenous fluids. If the child isn't relieved within a few hours, he or she will be hospitalized, usually for several days.

When pain is severe, every effort is made to relieve the pain, including the use of narcotic drugs. But since such drugs are addictive, they must be used under the guidance of a physician who is familiar with the patient's care. Those associated with the child should be alert to changes in patterns of performance, school absences for other than documented medical reasons, and changes in personality and motivation. If these occur, the student's parents and physician should be contacted to evaluate the cause of these changes. Narcotics are definitely not needed between severe painful episodes or to prevent painful episodes. If it comes to the attention of school personnel that the student is using such drugs in this way, parents and physicians should be contacted.

Transfusion Therapy

Blood transfusions are used only when absolutely necessary, such as for splenic sequestration crises, severe aplastic or hyperhemolytic crises, intractable painful crises, and on a long-term basis to prevent the recurrence of stroke. At The Children's Hospital of Philadelphia, patients who have had stroke and whose arteriograms show abnormalities are enrolled in a program of frequent and long-term transfusions to keep their level of sickle hemoglobin below 30 percent of the total hemoglobin concentration. We have found that this program either prevents or slows the progression of arterial abnormalities and greatly reduces the incidence of recurrence while the child is on transfusions.[11] A child on a chronic transfusion program will miss one day of school every three or four weeks.

Blood transfusion should not be given unless absolutely necessary, as there is a risk of transmission of hepatitis and other infectious diseases. Also, transfused blood contributes to the accumulation of excess iron that ultimately causes organ damage. In children who have large accumulations of iron, a treatment program using Desferol, a drug that removes iron from the body, is required. This is a cumbersome and expensive procedure which necessitates a major commitment from the patient and the family.

Increased Fluid Intake

Children with sickle cell anemia should always drink large amounts of fluid, even when well, to make up for the copious amounts of urine that are excreted because of the kidney's inability to concentrate urine. Another reason is to keep the blood diluted so that red cells do not become so concentrated in the bloodstream and are therefore less likely to restrict circulation in small vessels. When children are too ill to drink, fluids must be supplied intravenously.

Good Nutrition and Folic Acid

As in all children, good nutrition is important in children with sickle cell anemia. There are no foods that are used for treatment, nor are any foods restricted. All children with sickle cell anemia should take folic acid (one of the vitamins) supplements daily. Because the bone marrow must produce many more red cells than normal, requirements for folic acid are increased. Folic acid contributes to the nuclear material in growing cells. Iron should be given only if iron deficiency has been confirmed by laboratory tests, never on the basis of the anemia alone.

SCHOOL LIFE

Because sickle cell anemia is so variable, it is difficult to generalize about its impact on a child's school life. In many children individual characteristics, capabilities, and circumstances may be more relevant to school life than their sickle cell anemia.

Academic Performance

Except for some children who have had strokes with neurologic after-effects, children with sickle cell anemia are not different intellectually from the normal population. According to a study done in 1977 to assess the vocational potential of such children, it was reported that, while the range of scores was from borderline mentally retarded to "bright normal" under Bernet-Wexler, the mean scores for both males and females fell within the average range of intelligence.[12] However, many children with sickle cell anemia do not do well in school. The most obvious reason is time lost from school because of illness.

Absenteeism

Absenteeism will vary from child to child and in individual children from year to year. In a recent study of 49 children with sickle cell anemia done at The Children's Hospital of Philadelphia, 70 percent had only two or fewer crises per year.[13] Only 25 percent had four or more. A child can have a year of good health, followed by a year plagued by infections and painful crises, leading to the loss of many school days. Some patients lose as many as 40 to 50 days of school in one year. Although these absences may be frequent, they are seldom of such duration as to allow the child to take advantage of homebound tutoring programs.

Because elementary education is dependent upon a cumulative input of information, frequent absences usually result in low academic skill levels despite normal intelligence. Children forced to compete with peers without equal access to information are sometimes humiliated when called on in class. To escape this unpleasantness, some children appear to manifest more frequent symptoms of the disease to avoid school, act out in class, refuse to participate in appropriate activities, and/or fight with peers. They may also convince parents that the teacher is not sensitive to their needs, thus creating tension between the school and the home. Often these behaviors temporarily benefit the child in that they distract attention from academic deficits and focus attention by both parents and teachers on other areas. However, the child's low academic skill level is eventually discovered and even lower self-esteem results, which decreases motivation further.

Physical Activities

Children with sickle cell anemia—indeed, all children with chronic illness—should be encouraged to participate in as many school activities as possible, as this is important to their healthy psychological development. They can participate in routine physical education classes and playground games, but participation in varsity sports is discouraged because the pressure of competition may drive these children to exceed their limits. The general rule is that the child should not be pushed to the point of becoming tired and should be urged to drink plenty of fluids while exercising, especially in hot weather.

These children should avoid extremely cold temperatures but can undertake outdoor activities in winter unless the weather is bitterly cold. Of course, they must be dressed appropriately.

Psychosocial Aspects

A study of personality development of persons with sickle cell anemia revealed no gross psychopathology. However, verbal histories revealed a developmental "lag in personal development, inexperience, and an element of social distress."[14] Just as absences from school cause academic deficits, being away from peers sporadically causes social problems. It was noted that some parents and family members restricted social activities which they felt could cause painful crises though physical exertion. Such overprotectiveness can cause a division between children and their peers. Also, the painful crises themselves disrupt social activities, with a negative psychological impact. Children with frequent painful crises often find that their plans for accomplishing schoolwork; for vacationing; and for participating in school, social, and family activities cannot be carried out because of the onset of a crisis. If this happens repeatedly, particularly when much work and enthusiasm is invested in projects or events, the child understandably becomes discouraged from making long-range plans or undertaking activities that require preparatory work.

The delay in growth and sexual maturation that some children experience may be particularly disturbing during adolescence, when young people are preoccupied with body image and pubertal changes. This poses a problem for children who are striving to establish close same-sex relationships as well as relationships with the opposite sex. It is often a drawback to boys, who wish to engage in sports with children their own age.

Adolescents, knowing they have a serious disease, sometimes fear for the future. The impact of the disease may be particularly striking when a child learns of the death or very serious illness of another patient at the sickle cell center. Some children have heard of a definite lifespan for those having sickle cell anemia and harbor fears about this without telling others. A young college graduate reported that he had heard that persons with sickle cell anemia usually die before the age of 21. He said that he was very apprehensive during his twenty-first year, but when that year passed, he felt a sense of relief. Although this young man did not give up his goal of becoming a chemist, some young people do feel it is futile to make plans for the future, achieve in school, or even attend school regularly. When such attitudes are noticed in the classroom, the child's physician and family should be contacted so that counseling and appropriate education about sickle cell anemia can be given.

APPROACH TO THE CHILD WITH SICKLE CELL ANEMIA

Children with sickle cell anemia do not want to be singled out as being different from their classmates. Many patients, even those reaching adolescence, report that their friends do not know they have sickle cell anemia. Yet this is a serious illness that requires understanding from teachers and school nurses if these children are to get the most out of their schooling. Several things can be done to help without drawing unnecessary attention to the child or fostering the feeling that the disorder can be an excuse for poor academic performance.

Planning for Lost Time at School

Most important is for school personnel to formulate a plan well in advance for missed days and implement it at the first opportunity. Often, such plans are not made until well into the school year, after the child has already experienced several illnesses and lost enough school time to fall behind. When this situation is repeated year after year, the child is either retained, thus suffering the embarrassment of not moving forward with his or her own peers, or is passed from grade to grade without having acquired a true education. An hour or two spent early in the year can save hours of frustration for teachers, students, and parents later on if the child does experience illness.

At the beginning of the year, contact should be made with parents of children with sickle cell anemia and, when possible, with the child's physician or other sickle cell center personnel. Parents and teachers can decide together how work will be made up during the child's absence. Teachers should share as much information as possible about current and future classroom projects. This will enable parents to work with the child while the child is home and to encourage the child to succeed despite pain and illness. Encouragement by both parents and teacher is necessary to motivate the child to make every effort to keep up with the class. Also, such an approach will help parents to develop a rapport with educators, which will motivate them to see that work sent home is completed.

Parents, classmates, and young relatives should be used to transport work to the homebound student. Some teachers request that the parents supply them with a few stamped, addressed envelopes at the beginning of the school year so they can send material through the mail. It then arrives when the child begins to feel well enough to do some work at home.

It must be emphasized that the child with a painful crisis or infection generally feels too ill to work at home for the first few days. Much of makeup work must be done after the child returns to school, either through after-school tutoring sessions, during class with the help of peer tutors, or at home. Parents are the key to success in tutoring children with sickle cell anemia, since they must reinforce the necessity for making up work at home in the evenings. Specific hints on how to help the child are appreciated by parents who become frustrated in their efforts to tutor their children. Neighborhood tutoring centers, which offer programs in math, reading, and spelling, are usually incapable of offering specialized tutoring or assistance in special classroom assignments. Although teachers should recognize the child's illness as being uncomfortable and a good reason for staying home, they should not excuse extreme lateness in turning in makeup assignments, nor should makeup assignments be meaningless exercises. Children are usually aware of what work has real validity to their classroom situation and what is busywork, and they refuse to do the latter.

Although more absences can be expected in the child with sickle cell anemia than in other children, these absences should not be excused. When a child misses school for a day or two now and then, the reason should be sought. If the absence extends for a week or longer, a doctor's note should be requested. This may prompt a parent to seek medical treatment if this has not yet been done and will also alert the physician that the child may be staying home from school without really being ill. A child with a mild crisis or a cold can continue to go to school.

Career Guidance

Even though the lifespan of persons with sickle cell anemia may be shortened, there remain many years to be filled with meaningful and productive activity. Children with sickle cell anemia should be guided toward career choices in occupations that do not require a high degree of physical exertion. This leaves a broad range of occupations available, even for those who are not above average intellectually.

Guidance counselors should determine if there are programs available to help these students further their education. Community-based organizations sometimes encourage them by offering scholarship aid for post-high school education. Such organizations are usually known to area sickle cell centers. For the past five years, the Community Advisory Committee to the Sickle Cell Program at The Children's Hospital of Philadelphia has provided tuition support for young adults who desire to and are physically and intellectually able to pursue higher education. This group also encourages these students in developing skills necessary to form and work toward career goals. State vocational rehabilitation agencies provide services to eligible handicapped individuals leading to employment.

Concessions to the Inability to Concentrate Urine

Children with sickle cell anemia cannot concentrate their urine, and their kidneys do not act to conserve fluids when necessary, such as in hot weather. They always put out large amounts of urine, no matter what the condition may be. When fluids are also lost through other means, such as perspiration, diarrhea, or vomiting, dehydration results and a crisis may follow. For these reasons, these youngsters must be allowed to drink more frequently (see Table 1) and to use the lavatory more often than other classmates. During hot weather, they should be excused from strenuous outdoor activities, and younger children should be reminded to drink.

Table 1: Fluid Requirements for Children with Sickle Cell Anemia

Child's Weight	Daily Fluid Requirement
25 lb. (11 kg.)	Approx. 1½ to 1¾ qts. (1500-2000 ml.)
50 lb. (23 kg.)	Approx. 2 to 2½ qts. (2300-3000 ml.)
75 lb. (34 kg.)	Approx. 2¼ to 3 qts. (2600-3500 ml.)
100 lb. (45 kg.)	Approx 2½ to 3½ qts. (3000-4000 ml.)

It is inappropriate to assume that all children with sickle cell anemia will have all, or even most, of the problems mentioned here. Some will seem as healthy as normal children, while others will have a series of complications. It is also inappropriate to assume that if a child has a bad year, one with many illnesses, the same pattern will be repeated throughout the child's school career. Children must be treated as individuals. Each school year must be approached individually. Some patients miss a lot of school during one year, then little or none the next. Children should be motivated to strive to keep up with the class during periods of illness so they will have the skills to take advantage of educational opportunities when they get well.

Children should not be allowed to use sickle cell anemia as an excuse for all shortcomings. Teachers know that children can be extremely creative in avoiding things that they find unpleasant or difficult. When an excuse such as sickle cell anemia is available, to some children it is an opportunity too good to pass up. Be alert to developing tendencies to blame all failures and lack of participation on sickle cell anemia.

If a child insists he or she cannot participate in an activity that seems suitable from what is written here, request permission to call the child's doctor or request written verification from the doctor.

MEDICAL PROBLEMS THAT MAY OCCUR IN THE CLASSROOM

Painful Crisis

The most frequent medical problem that occurs in the classroom is the painful crisis. Even very severe crises are not life-threatening, although the pain can be excruciating. If a mild crisis occurs, and the child and the school nurse are knowledgeable about the proper procedures, such as taking acetaminophen, resting, and drinking extra fluids, it shouldn't be necessary to send the child home. Management in the school setting is often beneficial for the child's family as well as for the child. Parents often stress that they cannot afford to be called away from work for each mild crisis or low grade fever. Missing work when it is not absolutely necessary may put their jobs in jeopardy and prevent them from responding when a crisis is severe or a fever is very high. Parents should be informed about the child's illness, however, so that they can help determine the immediate needs of the child.

Stroke

One of the most serious complications that can occur in a classroom is a stroke. School personnel should be alert to both the onset of a stroke and the fact that the child may recently have had a stroke but not manifested symptoms noticed at home. If the child appears to lose balance, falls more than usual, has weakness in a limb or limbs on one side, limps, complains of a headache or visual disturbances, or exhibits changes in behavior or academic performance that cannot be explained by other reasons, the parent or physican should be called. A seizure in a child with no previous history of seizures may indicate a stroke.

Other Medical Problems

Since children with sickle cell anemia are very susceptible to infection, prompt investigation of fever (above 101°F) should be carried out. The signs of an aplastic or splenic sequestration crisis have been described (see Complications) and should be reported to parents and/or physicians. Rarely does a school-aged child with sickle cell anemia experience a splenic sequestration crisis, but if this occurs, it is a potentially life-threatening situation and medical help should be sought immediately.

FOSTERING CLASSMATES' UNDERSTANDING

A conscious effort should be made by the teacher whenever possible to highlight the positive characteristics of the child. This can be done by choosing the child for classroom jobs, assigning him or her parts in class plays, or encouraging him or her to participate in extracurricular activities in keeping with limitations. As every teacher knows, children respect competence in their peers. If the child can be viewed as competent in certain areas by classmates, he or she will feel more confident, have high self-esteem, and become more motivated to achieve in school.

Education about sickle cell anemia in general is important in fostering classmates' understanding. Although almost everyone is familiar with the term "sickle cell anemia," few have a true understanding of what causes the disease or of its effects. Among the common misconceptions are that a person "will die soon," that it is contagious, or that it reflects "having bad blood." Even very young children can understand a simplified explanation of sickle cell anemia trait. In upper grades, sickle cell anemia, along with other genetic diseases, can be covered in science or health classes. It should always be mentioned that inherited diseases occur in all ethnic groups, using Tay-Sachs disease in Jews and thalassemia in Mediterranean peoples as examples.

REFERENCES

1. E. Beutler, "The Sickle Cell Diseases and Related Disorders," in *Hematology,* 3d ed., ed. W. J. Williams, E. Beutler, A. J. Erslev, and M. A. Lichtman (New York: McGraw-Hill Book Co., 1983).
2. T. Asakura and R. S. Festa, "Hemoglobin Structure and Function," in *Hemoglobinopathies in Children,* ed. Elias Schwartz. (Littleton, MA: PSG Publishing Co., Inc., 1980).
3. N. L. Petrakis, "Sickle Cell Disease," *Lancet* (December 7, 1974): 1368.
4. Beutler, "The Sickle Cell Diseases."
5. D. Powars, B. Wilson, C. Imbus, C. Pegelow, and J. Allen, "The Natural History of Stroke in Sickle Cell Disease," *The American Journal of Medicine* 65 (1978): 461.
6. M. O. Russell, H. I. Goldberg, L. Reis, Sh. Friedman, et al. "Transfusion Therapy for Cerebrovascular Abnormalities in Sickle Cell Disease," *The Journal of Pediatrics* 88 (1976): 382.
7. M. O. Russell, H. I. Goldberg, A. Hodson, H. C. Kim, et al., "Effect of Transfusion Therapy on Arteriographic Abnormalities and on Recurrence of Stroke in Sickle Cell Disease," *Blood* 63 (1984): 162.
8. Powars, Wilson, Imbus, Pegelow, and Allen, "Stroke in Sickle Cell Disease," p. 461.
9. Russell, Goldberg, Hodson, Kim, et al., "Effect of Transfusion Therapy on Arteriographic Abnormalities and on Recurrence of Stroke in Sickle Cell Disease," p. 162.
10. C. S. Landefeld, M. Schambelan, S. L. Kaplan, and S. H. Embury, "Clomiphene-Responsive Hypogonadism in Sickle Cell Anemia," *Annals of Internal Medicine* 99 (1983): 480–83.
11. Russell, Goldberg, Hodson, Kim, et al., "Effect of Transfusion Therapy on Arteriographic Abnormalities and on Recurrence of Stroke in Sickle Cell Disease," p. 162.
12. D. Allesberry, J. Bonner, W. Jenkins, B. W. Parks, et al., "Assessment of Vocational Potential of Sickle Cell Anemics," Pennsylvania Bureau of Vocational Rehabilitation, Harrisburg, PA.
13. J. Greenberg, K. Ohene-Frempong, J. Halus, C. Way, and E. Schwartz, "Trial of Low Doses of Aspirin as Prophylaxis in Sickle Cell Disease," *The Journal of Pediatrics* 102 (1983): 781.
14. Allesberry, Bonner, Jenkins, Parks, et al., "Assessment of Vocational Potential of Sickle Cell Anemics."

RESOURCES

Suggested Reading

Bowman, J. E., and Goldwasser, E. *Sickle Cell Fundamentals*. Distributed as a public service by the National Sickle Cell Disease Program, National Heart, Lung and Blood Institute, National Institutes of Health, Building 31, Room 4A-27, NIH, Bethesda, MD 20014.

Directory of National, Federal, and Local Sickle Cell Disease Programs. U.S. Department of Health and Human Services, Public Health Service, National Institutes of Health. NIH Publication No. 81-714. Revised March 1981. Sickle Cell Disease Branch (EX-1), Building 31, Room 4A-27, NIH, Bethesda, MD 20014.

Earles, A. N. ''Symposium on Sickle Cell Disease,'' *Nursing Clinics of North America* (March 1983).

Help! A Guide to Sickle Cell Disease Programs and Services. United States, Bahamas, Puerto Rico, and the Virgin Islands. National Association for Sickle Cell Disease, Inc., 3460 Wilshire Blvd., Suite 1012, Los Angeles, CA 90010.

Sickle Cell Disease: Tell the Facts—Quell the Fables. Prepared in consultation with J. D. Desforges, P. Milner, D. L. Wethers, and C. F. Whitten. 1978. May be obtained from the National Association for Sickle Cell Disease, Inc., 3460 Wilshire Blvd., Suite 1012, Los Angeles, CA 90010.

Vaughn, W. M., and Cooke, C. E. ''Help for Children with Sickle Cell Disease.'' *The Journal of School Health* (September 1979).

Walker, J. E., ''What the School Health Team Should Know about Sickle Cell Anemia,'' *The Journal of School Health* (September 1982).

Useful Addresses

National Association for Sickle Cell Disease, Inc., 3460 Wilshire Blvd., Suite 1012, Los Angeles, CA 90010.

Sickle Cell Disease Branch (EX-1), National Heart, Lung and Blood Institute, National Institutes of Health, Building 31, Room 4A-27, NIH, Bethesda, MD 20014.

The Muscular Dystrophies

by Claire M. Chee, R.N. and
Roger J. Packer, M.D.

OVERVIEW

The muscular dystrophies are the most frequent cause of progressive muscle weakness in childhood. This group of diseases has varying patterns of inheritance, ages of onset, distributions of weakness, and rates of progression (Figures 1–3 and Table 1). The muscular dystrophies of childhood are Duchenne (pseudohypertrophic), Becker's, fascioscapulohumeral (FSH), myotonic, and limb-girdle muscular dystrophy. Although each type causes insidious muscle wasting, the manifestations, management, and outcome vary widely. It must be remembered that not all children with weakness have muscular dystrophy.

Figure 1. Duchenne Dystrophy

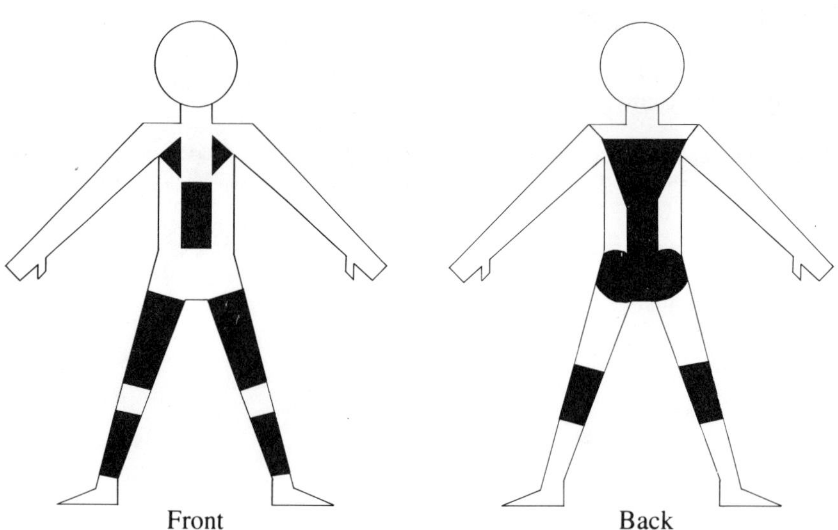

Figure 2. Limb-Girdle Dystrophy

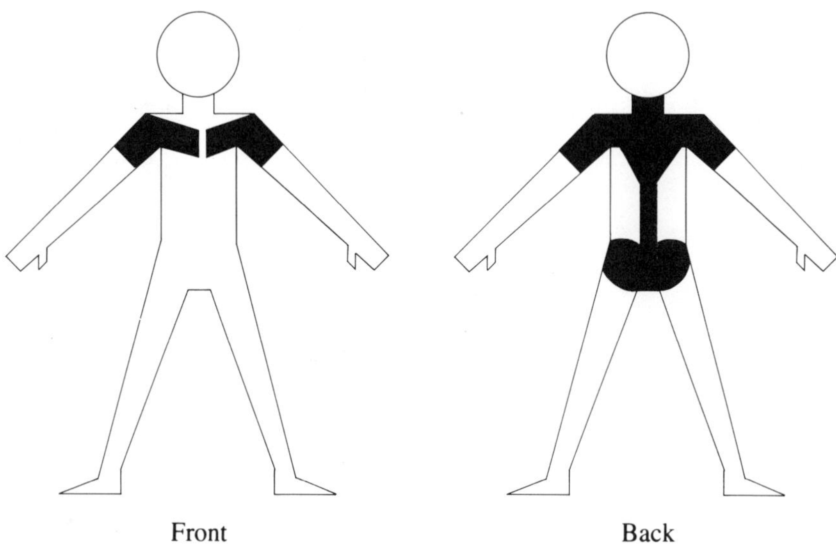

Figure 3. Fascioscapulohumeral Dystrophy

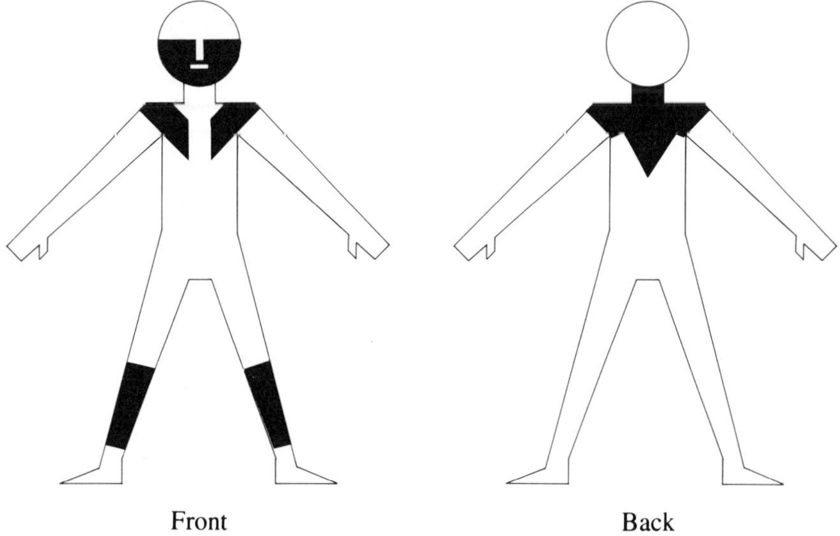

Table 1. Clinical Types of Muscular Dystrophy

	Duchenne	Becker's	Myotonic	Limb-girdle	Fascioscapulohumeral
Age of Onset	prior to 6 yrs	5–20 yrs	Childhood to fourth decade	Childhood to fourth decade	5–20 yrs
Inheritance	X-linked recessive	X-linked recessive	Autosomal dominant	Autosomal recessive	Autosomal dominant
Sex Incidence	Males only	Males only	Males and females equally affected	Males and females equally affected	Males and females equally affected
Muscle Groups Involved	Pelvic and shoulder-girdle muscles involved early; hands and feet later	Initially pelvic and upper legs with gradual involvement of shoulder-girdle and distal muscles	Distal extremities often affected before proximal muscles	Shoulder and pelvic girdles are initially involved. Proximal muscles are affected later	Largely confined to facial, pelvic, and pectoral girdle muscles
Prognosis	Death in adolescence	Variable: may survive to fourth decade	Progressive disability	Variable: occasional severe disability	Variable: occasional severe disability

Despite much research, the cause of muscular dystrophy is still unknown, and there is no treatment available to alter its course. However, effective treatment in the future is a real possibility, and the social, psychological, and educational needs of these youngsters must be met. It is essential for the family, school staff, and medical personnel to work together to help these children maintain the highest quality of life and cope with the increasing limitations imposed by their crippling disease.

SUBGROUPS

Duchenne (Pseudohypertrophic) Muscular Dystrophy

This is the most severe and, unfortunately, the most common type of muscular dystrophy among children. The incidence is approximately 1 to 3 per 10,000 live births.[1]

Genetics

Duchenne dystrophy is inherited as an X-linked recessive disease. A brief discussion of genetics is necessary for an understanding of the way the disease is inherited. Normally, everyone has 23 pairs of chromosomes—22 pairs of autosomal (nonsex) chromosomes and 1 pair of sex chromosomes. On these chromosomes are genes, which carry information about everything from eye color to blood groups. Each chromosome is like its partner in the pair except for the pair in males that determines sex in addition to carrying other genetic information. Males have one chromosome termed X and a shorter chromosome that is termed Y. Females have two X chromosomes.

At conception, the child receives a single set of chromosomes from the mother and a set from the father, making a total of 46 chromosomes. This naturally means that the genes are also passed onto the child, i.e., one gene to determine a trait such as blood group from the mother and another from the father. Genes can be either recessive or dominant. With a recessive gene, the information conveyed by that gene will be expressed only if the child inherits another similar recessive gene. In contrast, information from a single dominant gene will be expressed regardless of the information on the partner gene.

There is an exception to the rule that recessive genes are not expressed; the exception is when these genes are carried on the X chromosome and passed from a carrier (one who has the unexpressed defective gene) mother (XX) to a son (XY). Males do not have a second X chromosome to negate the information on the chromosome carrying the defect. If a carrier mother passes on the chromosome with the defect to a daughter, the daughter, being female, will have a second X chromosome with information to override that on the defective chromosome. She, like her mother, will only be a carrier. Girls can acquire X-linked recessive disorders only in the rare cases where the mother is a carrier and the father is affected with the disease.

Theoretically, women who are carriers of Duchenne muscular dystrophy have, with each pregnancy, a 50 percent chance of producing a carrier daughter or an affected son. There may be subtle laboratory evidence of the carrier state, such as a mild elevation of muscle enzymes in the blood. The frequency of a spontaneous mutation—when the disease arises in the child without the mother being a carrier—is estimated to be less than one-third of all cases.

Presentation

The illness initially affects the musculature of the trunk, shoulders, and legs. Late in the illness, the muscles of the feet and hands are affected. The bulging calf muscles of Duchenne dystrophy were first described in 1868 by Duchenne de Boulogne. This enlargement is not due to growth of muscle fibers but to the replacement of muscle with fatty tissue.

Parents generally seek medical attention when their child is three to five years old because of slow motor development or toe walking.[2] Though most children are relatively symptom-free until this time, in retrospect, parents do mention earlier concerns. The young child might have been considered clumsy because of frequent falls when learning to walk. When walking is accomplished, the gait itself seems normal, but when hurrying or running, a waddling gait is noticeable. The youngster may have to hesitate for balance when ascending stairs and cannot rise directly from the floor or a low chair. The child unconsciously shifts body weight a little to one side for balance and mastery of these movements. These events demonstrate a steady progression of muscle weakness and deterioration affecting the hips and legs.

Course

The year or two following diagnosis is referred to as the "golden age."[3] Developmental milestones are achieved, although the child may tire easily and have difficulty with some motor tasks, such as stair climbing. Usually after the age of seven or eight years, some functions become difficult. Walking becomes more difficult as the hip muscles weaken. The youngster will automatically tilt the head and shoulders backwards for balance. Eventually, a wåddling gait (mannered walk) develops because the child must swing the pelvis and upper body to ambulate. As the muscle deterioration continues, toe-walking becomes more evident. Though the rate of progression varies with each child, most youngsters experience difficulty in getting about within four years of diagnosis. As time goes on, falling becomes more frequent, and the child has difficulty getting up. Attempting to prevent falls, the child "locks" the knees when walking. The ability to climb stairs is soon lost. A progressive curvature of the spine develops as the muscles supporting the spine become more affected. Shoulder muscles appear strong, but neurological examination reveals that they are affected. Because of shoulder weakness, crutches cannot be used. These children are usually wheelchair-bound by the age of 12, but some are dependent upon a wheelchair as early as eight years of age. Parents often consider the need for a wheelchair as a sign of abrupt deterioration; actually, it is only the point in chronic degeneration of muscle that has made walking impossible.

In more than 90 percent of dystrophic youngsters, an electrocardiogram demonstrates heart muscle involvement which usually does not necessitate medical treatment. Infrequently, an individual will develop heart problems that require medication, but this generally arises in the late stage of the disease.

Death from pneumonia or heart failure usually occurs during the late teens or early adulthood. Both heart failure and lung disease are affected by the progressive curvature of the spine which occurs as the muscles around the spine weaken and the child spends most of the day wheelchair-bound.

Intellectual Deficits

A frequently overlooked problem in children with Duchenne is their intellectual deficits. Although some children may be extremely bright, mental retardation and learning disability are common in this disease. This intellectual impairment is unrelated to the severity of the disease and is not progressive. The reason for the association of intellectual difficulties with Duchenne muscular dystrophy is unknown.

Becker's Muscular Dystrophy

Becker's muscular dystrophy is often considered a variant of Duchenne muscular dystrophy. Although the clinical and laboratory findings are similar in these two diseases, Becker's dystrophy usually does not become evident before five years of age. Patients are often still ambulatory into early adult life, and death usually occurs in the third to fifth decades. Mental retardation is less frequent. The mode of inheritance is the same as that in Duchenne muscular dystrophy.[4]

Myotonic Dystrophy

Myotonic dystrophy causes deficits in many body systems. The disease gets its name from "myotonia," which means a decreased power to relax the muscles. Patients frequently complain of not being able to release an object once it is grasped, difficulty in performing tasks that require rapid movements, and cramp-like episodes. It should be stressed that myotonia may be present in other illnesses, and myotonia alone is not diagnostic of myotonic dystrophy.

Genetics

The pattern of inheritance is autosomal dominant, which means that the defect is on only a single chromosome of the 22 pairs of nonsex chromosomes and that the information on the defective chromosome overrides that on the normal chromosome. Unless a spontaneous mutation has occurred, the affected child will have one affected parent. Affected persons have a 50 percent chance with each pregnancy of having a child with the disease. Normal children of affected parents will have normal children. Myotonic dystrophy occurs in males and females with equal frequency.

Presentation and Course

Some patients with myotonic dystrophy are almost asymptomatic, while others are extremely weak and have multiple associated disabilities. This illness usually becomes apparent in adolescence, although some infants can be severely affected at birth. There is a characteristic facial appearance: the face seems elongated and droopy as a result of weakness and wasting of the facial muscles. Ptosis (eyelid dropping) is frequently present. Unlike the other dystrophies, weakness is most prominent in the distal muscles of arms and legs, especially the hands. This weakness may not be present until late in the disease. Also, the myotonia is more prominent later in the disease. Other associated difficulties include cardiac disease, cataracts, mental retardation, learning disabilities, early baldness, constipation, and hormonal difficulties, which may include diabetes. Although the weakness in myotonic dystrophy is irreversible, the symptoms can be treated. The outcome is extremely variable, and the tempo of the disease is unpredictable. Death may occur from cardiac or other associated complications.

Fascioscapulohumeral (FSH) Dystrophy

Genetics and Incidence

The pattern of inheritance is autosomal dominant (see Myotonic Dystrophy). The incidence is estimated to be between 3 to 10 cases per million.[5] This figure is probably erroneously low, as there are a large number of unrecogized cases.

Presentation and Course

Symptoms, which are often subtle, usually occur between the ages of 5 and 20 years. The face and shoulder muscles are the first to be involved. The weak facial muscles produce an inability to close the eyes tightly, wrinkle the forehead, puff out the cheeks, whistle, drink from a straw, or blow up a balloon. Many times, these symptoms are dismissed as idiosyncrasies rather than abnormalities. If the shoulder muscles are affected, the arms cannot be raised above the head. The muscles of the face, shoulders, and upper arms are frequently affected simultaneously. As FSH progresses, there can be weakness in the muscles of the thighs, wrists, and ankles and curvature of the spine. Generally, there is no clinically evident cardiac involvement, although heart conduction deficits causing arrythmias may occur.

Characteristically, progression is slow, with deterioration remaining at a standstill for years. Many individuals lead normal lives with very mild disabilities; however, others may become severely handicapped after several decades of illness. The progression of FSH dystrophy is quite variable within the same family.

A less benign infantile form of FSH dystrophy occurs rarely. Diagnosed during the first two years of life, this disease causes facial weakness, as well as weakness of the arms and legs. Persistent drooling is also a common early finding. This form progresses rapidly, and the child is usually confined to a wheelchair by the age of nine.

Limb-Girdle Dystrophy

Genetics

Limb-girdle dystrophy is a slowly progressive dystrophy, with an autosomal recessive pattern of inheritance.[6] As in all autosomal recessive disorders, both parents are carriers of the gene, but since they each also possess one unaffected gene, they are clinically unimpaired. With each pregnancy, there is a 50 percent chance that the child will be a carrier, a 25 percent chance of the child being affected, and a 25 percent possibility of the child being unaffected. Both males and females can have this type of dystrophy.

Presentation and Course

Symptoms of limb-girdle dystrophy usually appear during the second to fourth decades of life. Rarely, the disease may appear earlier and mimic Duchenne muscular dystrophy. Weakness is first noted in the hip and shoulder areas. Weakness of the neck and back muscles can cause low back pain. Even though the muscles of the legs, forearms, and hands can be affected with time, severe disabilities and contractures (stiffening and fixing of the muscles) are uncommon. Skeletal deformities are not frequently seen in this dystrophy. Cardiac and respiratory defects are also rare. Many people with limb-girdle dystrophy remain borderline ambulatory, although some prefer a wheelchair as an aid to mobilization and independence.

Other Muscular Dystrophies

Other rarer, progressive degenerative diseases of the muscles exist.[7] Distal muscular dystrophy, inherited as an autosomal dominant disease, results in slowly progressive weakness of the lower portions of the arms and legs in childhood with the trunk and upper arm and leg muscles being spared. Ocular muscular dystrophy, occurring in the first three decades of life, causes slowly progressive weakness of the muscles around the eyes. This may be accompanied by weakness of the face and limbs and is usually inherited as an autosomal recessive disease. Congenital muscular dystrophy, an autosomal recessive disease, may occur at birth, causing severe generalized weakness. Unlike the other dystrophies, there may be improvement with time.

DIAGNOSIS

The diagnosis of muscular dystrophy is established by family history, physical examination, and laboratory studies. The most common laboratory studies are measurement of muscle enzymes, electromyography, and muscle biopsy. As muscles degenerate, enzymes are released into the bloodstream that can be measured to document the presence and degree of muscle breakdown. In electromyography, a small needle called an electrode is placed in the muscle to assess the type of injury. In most cases, diagnosis is confirmed by muscle biopsy, which is the microscopic study of a small piece of muscle removed surgically from the patient.

TREATMENT

Specific medical treatment of the muscular dystrophies is not available. Until it is, the main goal is for the child to lead as normal a life as possible for as long as possible. Because muscular dystrophy is a progressive disorder with many medical complications, appropriate management requires an interdisciplinary approach that includes the inputs of neurologists, orthopedic surgeons, pediatricians, nurses, physical therapists, occupational therapists, nutritionists, and psychologists. The patient should be evaluated periodically; physical therapy, dietary instructions, bracing, and orthopedic surgery should be used to maintain ambulation and to avoid medical complications.

Physical therapy is an important aspect in the care of these youngsters. From the beginning, the therapist should fully evaluate the child and thereafter periodically assess the amount of weakness, imbalance, and contractures the child is experiencing. More important, the therapist can instruct the child on stretching exercises to delay or correct contractures and teach the child to get through the day using the least amount of energy.[8]

Swimming is an excellent from of physical therapy. Gentle stretching exercises are ideal in the pool. A qualified physical therapist should be available while the child is in the pool, since coughing sometimes develops and the child feels comforted by having an "expert" close at hand. Also, the therapist can monitor the swim program so that these children do not become fatigued. These youngsters are more buoyant than others in the water, so it is easy to exercise them in the pool, and time in the water can be unintentionally extended, causing exhaustion. For dystrophic children, it is recommended that the water temperature be between 86° and 88°F.

It is important to try to prevent obesity, as it may shorten the duration of ambulation, facilitate scoliosis (curvature of the spine), and contribute to respiratory problems. Decreased activity and depression potentiate weight gain.[9] Children with restricted opportunity for physical activity and those who suffer from boredom consume calories in excess of their needs. A diversified day will help reduce these youngsters' caloric intake. Good eating habits should be encouraged from the beginning. A balanced diet is recommended, with snacks such as fruit, celery, raisins, and carrots instead of cakes, soda, and chips.

Children with dystrophy are more susceptible to pneumonia as their strength declines.

Inactivity is detrimental. Immobilization tends to accelerate the rate of deterioration in strength, balance, and mental outlook. The best form of therapy is participation in as many activities as possible. This will provide the youngster with motivation and an interest in self and life.

SCHOOL LIFE

Preparation for School

A good school experience is essential for these children regardless of their degree of involvement. Many children with dystrophy have a shortened lifespan. Since much of their lives is spent at school, it is imperative that they have a healthy school experience—both educationally and socially. A positive school situation facilitates peer interaction and fosters a fulfilling life despite the physical handicaps. Admittedly, some problems are difficult for school staff to deal with. However, if the family, school, and hospital resources are unified, major obstacles may be overcome.[10]

Prior to the first day of school, a conference between a parent, the teacher, and a representative from the child's medical team will help clear up misconceptions and avoid misunderstandings. The teacher can be familiarized with the student's special needs, and parents can be alerted to the teacher's expectations for the child. School staff should know the natural history of the type of dystrophy the child has. This knowledge will prepare them to deal with day-to-day problems and guide them in setting realistic goals for the child in the classroom. School personnel should also know which symptoms require medical attention and which do not. Data base sheets and anecdotal records could be completed to facilitate ease of communication (see suggested format in Figures 4 and 5).

Figure 4. Anecdotal Record

NAME:____________________ DATE:____________________

TEACHER:__________________

Please give progress report. Stress difficulties as well as assets.

_____ Getting about and being mobile (in the classroom, halls, stairs, cafeteria, restroom, etc.)

_____ Ease with using special equipment (braces, writing devices, eating utensils)

_____ Classroom skills (writing skills, energy level, participation, need for adaptive equipment)

_____ Academic skills (in comparison with expectations, need for special evaluations or ancillary help, such as physical therapy, occupational therapy, speech therapy, psychological testing)

_____ Special notations: (include whether or not a conference is indicated)

Figure 5. Data Base for the Student with Muscular Dystrophy

NAME: ____________________ BIRTHDATE: ________________

PARENTS: __________________ HOME PHONE: ______________

ADDRESS: __________________ EMERGENCY#: ______________

__________________________ __________________________

(Relationship and Name)

Physician Name and Phone Number: __________________________

____

CHECK APPROPRIATE NEED:

WALKING ABILITY:

_____ Independent
_____ Uses furniture for support
_____ Wears braces
_____ Needs assistance
_____ Requires extra time
_____ Needs ''buddy'' system

Additional Information: ______________________________________

____

____

STEPS:

Going Up:
_____ Independent
_____ Uses railing
_____ Needs assistance
_____ Needs elevator

Coming Down:
_____ Independent
_____ Needs railing
_____ Requires assistance
_____ Needs elevator

Additional Information: ______________________________________

____

____

Figure 5. Data Base for the Student with Muscular Dystrophy (continued)

CHAIR:

Sitting Down:
_____ Independent
_____ Needs assistance

Getting Up:
_____ Independent
_____ Needs assistance

Additional Information: ____

____

____

WHEELCHAIR:
_____ Independent
_____ Needs assistance (explain: help on and off ramps, "buddy" system in halls, locking chair to make it immobile, etc.)

____

____

____

____

CAFETERIA:
_____ Independent
_____ Needs assistance (explain: needs help in carrying tray, cutting food, have special eating utensils)

____

____

____

____

TOILETTING:
_____ Independent
_____ Needs assistance (explain)

____

____

____

____

Figure 5. Data Base for the Student with Muscular Dystrophy (continued)

OUTER CLOTHING (Putting on and taking off):
_____ Independent
_____ Needs assistance (explain: needs extra time or help with buttons, etc.)

____

____

____

____

ANCILLARY HELP needed:
_____ Physical therapy
_____ Occupational therapy
_____ Speech therapy
_____ Explain frequency and type needed:

____

____

____

____

_____ ADDITIONAL INFORMATION (i.e. prescription sent to school, receiving therapy at home, etc.)

____

____

____

____

PERTINENT INFORMATION
_____ Information concerning the student (i.e. needs encouragement to participate, do NOT offer help unless requested, etc.)

____

____

____

____

____

____

____

Transportation and Accessibility

Because a dystrophic child has a limited energy supply, most of it should be saved for the actual school day. Attending a neighborhood school is beneficial, since long bus rides frequently fatigue these youngsters. Even children living close to school should be provided with bus transportation. Older students or the custodial staff can be taught to assist the child off and on the bus.

For the school to be accessible to these youngsters, architectural barriers should be assessed and shortcomings corrected. Hand railings, adequate-sized doorways, proper bathroom facilities, and ramps are necessary. For safety reasons, the slope of the ramp should be one inch per foot. The child's classrooms should be on the ground floor unless an elevator is provided.

Classroom Work

Some children with muscular dystrophy are intellectually slow, but others are not. Although patterns of learning disabilities have been reported in patients with dystrophy, overall there is no one "mold" these children can be fitted into. Some have reduced verbal scores; others have reduced performance abilities. This reduced ability is not a reflection of environmental deprivation but part of the disease process. Individualized programs are necessary, and formal psychological evaluation prior to the start of school is ideal. It is of utmost importance that the youngster be placed in the proper classroom setting.

Dystrophic children who display any difficulties with schoolwork are entitled to a full learning assessment. It is important to remember that although the muscles continue to deteriorate, the child's intellectual abilities are maintained.

Seating arrangement is an important issue, particularly if the youngster is confined to a wheelchair. The child must obviously see and have access to the chalkboard, wall charts, and maps. If the youngster is unable to keep up with note taking for neuromuscular reasons, the possibility of using a tape recorder or an adaptive writing device should be investigated. If these measures are carried out, most youngsters with dystrophy are able to keep up with classwork.

Occasionally, a child will miss school because of an upper respiratory infection, and they should be given work to make up. If the child will be absent from school for a prolonged period, temporary homebound tutoring is indicated. A long absence could be precipitated by severe pneumonia or orthopedic surgery. If surgery can be safely delayed, it is often performed during the summer.

Extracurricular and Social Activities

Children with dystrophy should be included in as many school functions as possible. While their classmates are enjoying sports, dancing, and aerobics, they are becoming more disabled. Unless they are included in social functions, they will become isolated from classmates. Participation in sports could come through scorekeeping and photography. For dances and class parties, they could be on planning and decorating committees. One means of involvement in school events could be through staffing ticket or refreshment stands.

When appropriate, participation in debates, art competitions, school newspaper, student council, glee club, or orchestra should be encouraged. In encouraging participation, stress the child's strengths and interests. To avoid frustration, focus the child's energies on creative activities rather than physical tasks.

Physical Activities

The child should participate in any activity that can be tolerated and is not harmful. Most youngsters with dystrophy find their own level of tolerance and adhere to it.

In the early stages of muscular dystrophy, the youngster can get around quite easily. During this time, standing, walking, running, bike riding, climbing stairs, baseball, and swimming are sources of functional physical therapy. As weakness progresses, a modified gym program should be devised. Because these children frequently have respiratory problems, this program should include breathing exercises that can be done through games.[11] Have the youngster sit at a table with two ping-pong balls and blow out gently with pursed lips to see how far he or she can make the balls travel. Making and blowing paper pinwheels can also be helpful. Encourage the youngster to breathe in deeply before blowing the pinwheel.

In schools with a physical therapist, the youngster should be seen on a regular basis during school hours. This is usually arranged by having the physician write a prescription and letter to the school. The hospital therapist could also enclose recommendations specific for that child. Since these children are unable to actively exercise all muscles appropriately, they depend on others to assist them. Passive range of motion exercises are useful in maintaining use of unaffected muscles. The school's physical therapist can also teach the classroom teacher how to assist the child in regular classroom activities. For example, the teacher could be instructed on how to maneuver a wheelchair and how to transfer a child from chair to chair.

Classroom Behavior

A dystrophic child should follow classroom rules and regulations unless the disease process indicates the need for special privileges. Unwarranted privileges tend to confuse these children, and they react by acting out. If a child with dystrophy is disruptive, he or she should be counseled as any other student would be.

Periodically these youngsters become overwhelmed by the progress of the disease. It is important that a teacher, counselor, or principal be available to listen to complaints without the child's feeling threatened. The youngster may not verbalize fears concerning his or her own health but, to cope with the disability, may just complain about the day in general. Having a good listener readily available is essential.

Art is another way for the child to unconsciously express thoughts, feelings, and attitudes about the world as he or she knows it. Teachers should not try to interpret this drawing unless they have been educated in this special field.[12]

Toiletting

Children with dystrophy generally do not have difficulties in bowel or bladder control. Difficulties arise when they are no longer able to get to the bathroom independently. Frequently, they are embarrassed to ask for help; therefore, most youngsters with dystrophy try to use the bathroom only when at home. To accomplish this goal, many will refuse to drink liquids in the early morning or during school. This problem may be avoided by assigning a bathroom "partner" to the child. A classmate, older student, or school nurse would be appropriate. If a child is incontinent of urine, this is usually attributable to the child's struggle to maintain a full bladder during school hours.

Early on, parents are encouraged to set up a bowel program for their child. Attempts are made to regulate the bowel to empty at basically the same time each day. Most youngsters prefer to use their own bathrooms immediately after breakfast or in the evening after dinner.

MEDICAL PROBLEMS THAT MAY OCCUR IN THE CLASSROOM

Difficulties in Ambulation

As the dystrophy progresses, the youngster develops a waddling gait and using the stairs becomes difficult. Ambulation should still be encouraged, but the child should be urged to hold onto railings and furniture for support. When muscle weakness progresses to the hips or legs, the youngster will need assistance in getting up from a chair. He or she can be safely guided to a standing position by grasping the waistband or belt and firmly lifting up. Once the child is standing, it is important to continue a firm hold until the child has balance. If the youngster needs help in getting up from the floor or a cot, it is best to begin by putting him or her in a sitting position. The sitting position can best be accomplished by supporting the child's neck with one hand and the back with the other. Once the child is sitting, continue lifting by firmly holding onto the belt or a sturdy waistband.[13]

In children with Duchenne dystrophy, falls may occur. Offer assistance only if the child isn't able to get up independently. If not, assist him or her to a standing position, then forget the incident. Dwelling on a fall frequently causes the child to develop a lack of self-confidence.

When the youngster cannot walk, a wheelchair that is customized to fit the child and to meet individual needs will be prescribed. A proper fitting wheelchair will provide skeletal support, help prevent spinal deformities, and, with a firm cushion, promote good posture. This chair will also make the child more independent, allowing participation in classroom activities, such as getting to the blackboard quickly or going on field trips. It must be emphasized, however, that the child who is able to walk with assistance or with braces should be encouraged to do so for as long as possible. Frequently, the wheelchair is introduced before it is absolutely necessary in order to improve the quality of the child's life and diminish the impact of the wheelchair as a sign of failure when walking becomes impossible. However, only when all attempts to maintain independent ambulation fail is wheelchair confinement necessary or advisable.

Orthopedic Equipment

If the youngster has any type of orthopedic "self-help" equipment, the teacher should know how to handle various situations that might arise from its use. If balanced arm supports are used, they may have to be adjusted if they are only needed periodically. Long leg braces help the child ambulate as well as to help prevent contractures. If the braces are equipped with a lock for standing, the teacher should be shown how to manipulate the lock. Frequently braces are made of a lightweight plastic securely fastened with Velcro straps (Figure 6). This type of brace is comfortable and helps prevent muscles from tiring.

Figure 6. Lightweight plastic braces with Velcro straps

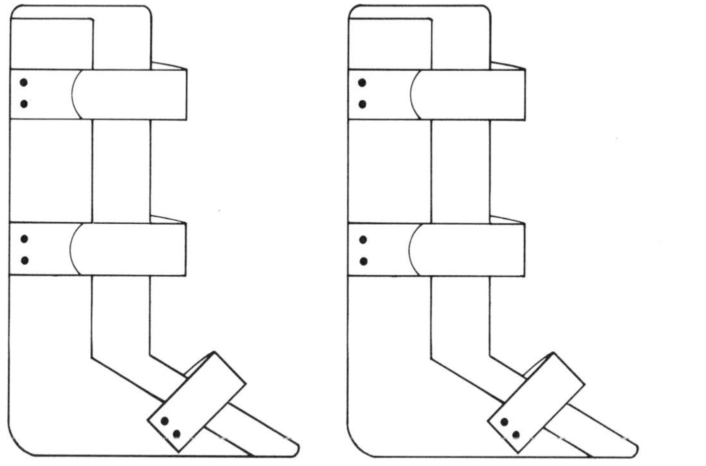

By Lisa Dieni, 1984

Heart Problems

Though heart problems are uncommon, if they do occur it is usually late in the disease process.[14] Youngsters experiencing respiratory insufficiency will become breathless while at rest and look sick. This is generally followed by confusion and restlessness with complaints of headache and eventually drowsiness. Medical help should be sought immediately.

Respiratory Infection

Respiratory infection is a constant threat to the dystrophic child.[15] Many times, coughing is ineffective in mobilizing secretions, as the respiratory and abdominal muscles may be unable to produce enough pressure. In some children, the gag reflex is also occasionally impaired. This increases the danger of aspiration and subsequent pneumonia. Youngsters experiencing these difficulties are usually able to maintain independently adequate respiratory function.

Leg Cramps

Leg cramps, especially in the calves, sometimes occur. Usually they are of short duration. Since we cannot prevent them, a sympathetic ear is beneficial.

To support the spine, braces, corsets, or jackets are sometimes worn. These restrain trunk movement, and until the child becomes accustomed to them, walking may be difficult.

APPROACH TO THE CHILD WITH DYSTROPHY

Without sufficient background knowledge, many teachers, initially, are leery of having these youngsters actively participate in class activities for fear of putting added stress on them. Actually, more stress emanates from being excluded. For these children to have a successful school experience, having the same commitments as their classmates is essential. Even children with the more disabling types of dystrophy should be motivated to learn; adequate treatment may become available in their lifetime, and they must be prepared for the future. Also, they should not be deprived of the feelings of accomplishment that come from meeting the challenges presented at school. Most youngsters with dystrophy are able to tolerate a full school day and should be encouraged to do so.

Many times these children are quiet and withdrawn for fear of being rejected. In these cases, special attention should be given to having them participate in class discussions and activities. If dystrophic children are to survive in the classroom, they cannot be ignored or "shelved."

Teachers should be alert for the need of ancillary help. Daily physical therapy, occupational therapy, speech therapy, or a particular classroom setting (e.g., learning disabled class) should be arranged when necessary. Difficulty in the classroom may not be apparent at home, so frequently, it is the teacher who recognizes the need for an adaptive piece of equipment. This information should be passed onto parents and the child's health care group. Difficulties such as writing could be alleviated by an arm support or writing device. A typewriter especially designed for the handicapped could enable long assignments to be completed independently. If a typewriter is used in the classroom, another student could be assigned to feed paper into the machine. Bookholders are helpful at school, and a book bag attached to a wheelchair also aids in independence.

Encourage independence at mealtimes. If the arms are weak, permitting the child to rest the elbows on the table will enable him or her to pivot the elbows in order to feed himself or herself. Later, to provide this continued independence, balanced arm supports could be attached to the wheelchair. The youngster's lunch tray should be monitored to see if the food must be cut into bite-sized pieces. A special straw that clips onto a cup might be indicated (see Figure 7).

Figure 7. Clip-on straw which enables the youngster to use the cup independently

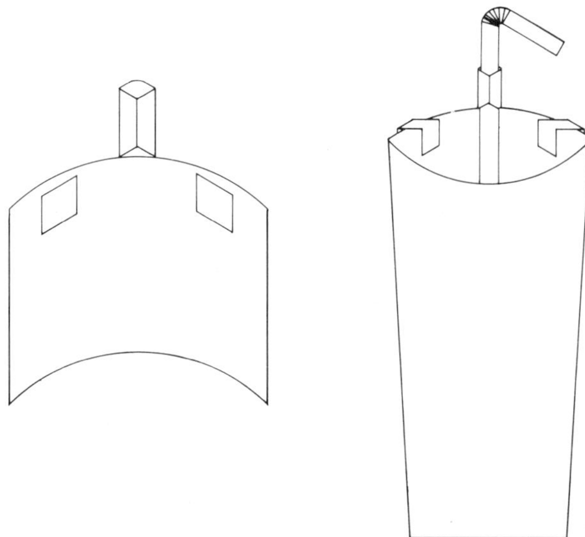

By Lisa Dieni, 1984

Vocational guidance should be offered early. The school counselor and/or state vocational rehabilitation center can be helpful in evaluating these youngsters by providing aptitude tests. Once their areas of interest are established, they can be directed toward appropriate job placement or college admission.

FOSTERING CLASSMATES' UNDERSTANDING

Many times, the teacher's attitude toward the youngster will determine peer acceptance—or rejection. It is vital that the teacher be informed about the dystrophy so he or she is comfortable having the child as a student and can convey this confidence to the other students. If the dystrophic child has any special needs, they should be discussed matter-of-factly with the class. This will allow the class to be aware of the child's needs as well as to relieve the class's curiosity. Such knowledge will foster an enthusiasm toward assisting the dystrophic child when the need is there. During health education classes, various handicaps and disorders should be discussed as part of the curriculum.

The help of peers is important in the daily life of the child with muscular dystrophy. Indeed, many could not make it without such assistance. Not only does such help provide physical assistance, but it also ensures a measure of companionship throughout the day. Many children without handicaps are shy around those who are disabled. Sometimes, it is only when a child feels useful that this shyness is overcome and the handicapped child is approached. The helping role can be assigned or voluntary, depending on the classroom situation. Following are a few suggestions as to how classmates may help: If the youngster's arm muscles are weak, a classmate can carry books or the lunchroom tray. A locker partner can be assigned to the dystrophic child. This would ensure help in getting objects from the top shelves which would otherwise be unreachable. Switching classrooms can be a problem if time is an issue, and permitting the child and a friend to leave two minutes earlier than dismissal time would facilitate promptness to the next class. A "hall monitor" partner would be very useful; having a partner would give the youngster a sense of security in knowing that help would be available, if needed. For children confined to a manual wheelchair and on a long outing, a peer could maneuver the chair periodically.

With proper knowledge, skills, and attitude, many potential school-related problems can be readily identified and successfully solved. A caring relationship will only strengthen the bonds between the family and the school.

REFERENCES

1. J. Bethlem, *Myopathies* (Philadelphia: J. B. Lippincott, 1977).
2. K. F. Swaiman and F. S. Wright, *The Practice of Pediatric Neurology* (St. Louis: C. V. Mosby, 1982).
3. J. C. Drennan, *Orthopaedic Management of Neuromuscular Disorders* (Philadelphia: J. B. Lippincott, 1983).
4. Swaiman and Wright, *The Practice of Pediatric Neurology*.
5. Ibid.
6. Ibid.
7. I. Flynn, K. Schwetz, and D. Williams, "Muscular Dystrophy: Comprehensive Nursing Care," *Nursing Clinics of North America* 14 (1979): 123–32.
8. I. M. Siegel, *The Clinical Management of Muscle Disease* (Philadelphia: J. B. Lippincott, 1977).
9. Flynn, Schwetz, and Williams, "Muscular Dystrophy: Comprehensive Nursing Care," pp. 123–32.
10. C. D. Hall and P. Porter, "School Intervention for the Neuromuscularly Handicapped Child," *The Journal of Pediatrics* 102 (1983): 210–14.
11. Siegel, *The Clinical Management of Muscle Disease*.
12. M. M. Pope-Gratten, C. N. Burnett, and C. V. Wolfe, "Human Figure Drawings by Children with Duchenne's Muscular Dystrophy," *Physical Therapy* 56 (1976): 168–76.
13. Swaiman and Wright, *The Practice of Pediatric Neurology*.
14. T. W. Farmer, *Pediatric Neurology,* 3d ed. (New York: Harper and Row, 1983).
15. J. M. Lavigne, "Respiratory Care of the Patients with Neuromuscular Disease," *Nursing Clinics of North America* 14 (1979): 133–43.

RESOURCES

Useful Addresses

Association for Children with Learning Disabilities, 5225 Grace St., Pittsburgh, PA 15236.

Closer Look, National Information Center for the Handicapped, Box 1492, Washington, DC 20036.

Muscular Dystrophy Association, 810 Seventh Ave., New York, NY 10019.

National Association for Retarded Children, 2909 Avenue E East, Arlington, TX 76011.

Orthopedic Problems

by Marilyn Boos, R.N., M.S., Roslyn M. Garlonsky, R.N., C., M.S.N., G. Dean MacEwen, M.D., C.M., and Nina Steg, M.D.

OVERVIEW

Orthopedic problems are those related to the skeletal system. In children these may be so slight that a child's comfort and physical capacities are minimally disturbed or so profound that a special school setting is needed. Also, within a specific disorder there can be a wide range of signs and symptoms. For example, scoliosis may require no treatment at all or may be severe enough to require surgery. Some children with myelomeningocele are so incapacitated from this birth defect that they must attend schools for the handicapped; others may receive their education in the ordinary classroom. This chapter will focus on disorders or manifestations of disorders that are severe enough to impinge on the child's life, if only temporarily, but that are not so disabling that the child is eligible for long-term specialized education. This information should provide the basis for addressing the needs of a child with orthopedic problems.

SCOLIOSIS

Scoliosis is a lateral curvature of the spine. In the normal spine, no curves are present when the spine is viewed from the back. The curvature may develop in any region of the spinal column.

The male-to-female ratio for mild curves is about even but is 1:8 in those patients with significant curves. In about 20 percent of cases, the cause can be identified. Such causes include congenital deformity, radiation, neurofibromatosis, and paralytic disorders. The remaining 80 percent have "idiopathic scoliosis," which means that the cause is unknown. Idiopathic scoliosis is most frequently diagnosed in preadolescent and adolescent children. Probably all significant curves, that is, those more than

20 degrees that may be expected to progress, begin in preadolescent youngsters. The disorder does have a genetic component, as evidenced by more than one child with scoliosis in the same family.

Signs

The signs associated with scoliosis are a prominent shoulder blade (usually the right), unlevel shoulders and hips, prominent breast, poor posture, and flattening of the flank area. With the youngster bent forward with arms dangling freely, and evenly, a rib hump may be seen. In looking for a curve, the youngster should be viewed from the back, front, and both sides while both erect and bending. A common observation in girls is that their clothes do not fit right and that hemlines are uneven. Not all of these signs are present in all youngsters with scoliosis.

While the signs of a significant scoliosis are clear-cut, early diagnosis at home is usually not made, for to properly assess the back, clothing must be removed. In the typical home, parents rarely see their children undressed, making it almost impossible to detect a problem with the back in its earliest stages.

Screening

The schools are in a unique position to screen large numbers of children for scoliosis. The importance of school screening cannot be overemphasized as the key to early detection. Since most curves become cosmetically obvious in the early teens, early detection in grade school would be beneficial. Schools in at least nine states are now required by law to periodically screen students for scoliosis.[1]

In families with a history of scoliosis, extra attention should be given to screening, for early diagnosis and treatment are preferred. Yearly pediatric examinations are important for early detection in these and all children. Also, a simple home screening test can be used in families at risk for having a youngster with scoliosis. Younger siblings of a child with scoliosis or the children of a parent with this disorder can then benefit by early diagnosis of the condition.*

---

*"A Simple Home Test for the Early Detection of Scoliosis" is available through the Scoliosis Association, One Penn Plaza, New York, NY 10001.

Treatment

The degree of curve is determined by measuring the "Cobb Angle" using x-ray films of the child's spine (Figure 1).

The kind of treatment will depend on the severity of the curvature and the age of the child. Mild curves of 15 to 20 degrees require only observation for signs of progression. It is generally agreed that curves over 50 degrees should be fused by a surgical procedure to prevent further progression. Without surgery, the curve may increase by adulthood and cause respiratory problems and sometimes pain. To prevent progression, curves between 20 and 45 degrees should be held in place by the use of an orthosis (brace). With these less severe curves, progression normally ceases after skeletal maturity.

Figure 1. Cobb Angle

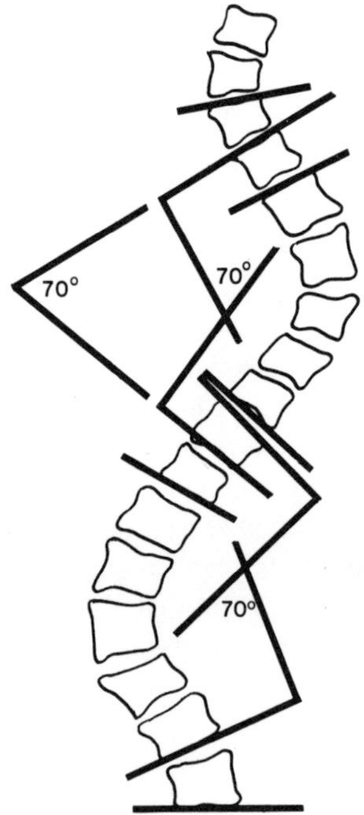

Method described by Cobb for measuring the degree of deformity in patients with curvature of the spine. The degree of curvature is measured as the angle of intersection between perpendicular lines drawn through the endplates of vertebrae at the upper and lower limits of the curve. (Redrawn from Ruge, D. and Wiltse, L. L. (Eds.): *Spinal Disorders: Diagnosis and Treatment*. Philadelphia, Lea & Febiger, 1977. p. 183.)

Bracing

Braces are applied to curves in the 20 and 45 degree range in the immature child to prevent progression while the spine continues to grow. Braces rarely decrease a curve.

When the youngster is placed in a brace, a period of adjustment will be required, since braces are applied snugly. For instance, a youngster's eating pattern may be altered—smaller meals more often—until adjustment occurs. Children wearing these braces are generally not restricted in physical activities and should participate in physical education classes to the limit of their abilities. After the initial adjustment, the youngster should have little trouble managing stairs, sitting at desks, or riding a school bus. It is advisable to require a statement from the physician listing activities that are prohibited due to treatment.

Students should be encouraged to return to their physician if the brace causes much physical discomfort. The brace may require a modification at the shop where it was fabricated, or the student may be asked to withstand the discomfort as part of the early treatment plan. At each brace change, minor skin irritations may occur. Abrasions and minor irritations are generally helped by rubbing alcohol, although this may dry the skin.

The child will be taught how to remove and reapply the brace by the physician or orthotist. It may be removed daily to check the skin, and bathing is permitted when the brace is off. When the child is skeletally mature, he or she will be weaned out of the brace gradually.

Surgery

The usual surgical procedure is a posterior spinal fusion with Harrington rod instrumentation. Bone taken from the iliac crest (hip bone) is placed along the vertebrae involved in the scoliotic curve. The bone graft will grow together with the vertebrae to form a solid mass of bone. This process is called "fusion."

Following surgery, the student is maintained in a device—either a cast or a brace or combination of the two—for several months. If a body cast is used after surgery, the patient's activities will be limited. If a brace is used, it may be removed long enough to take a shower, depending upon how solidly the bone has grafted.

When the student may return to school and participate in activities is decided by the physician through x-ray and clinical evaluations. Most often, patients return to school within a few weeks of surgery. A letter from the physician should be required delineating types of activities permitted. If the youngster cannot return to school within a few weeks, homebound instruction is necessary. This should be arranged early to minimize the interruption in the child's education.

Upon return to school, youngsters who have had surgery may sit at regular school desks. They can manage to walk to and from class. Most youngsters will be permitted to walk up and down stairs, although some physicians will prohibit this. Some youngsters may be permitted to use public transportation upon return to school. Others may have to be taken to school in an automobile.

When casts, which are thick, are applied high up under the arms, they will push the arms away from the sides, making it difficult or impossible for some patients to manage their own personal hygiene. The school nurse should try to keep abreast of such situations and keep the office open to the students.

A gradual return to activities can be expected. Full participation in sports and physical education classes is usually permitted one to two years after surgery. The range of permissable activities will be discussed by the physician at each check-up visit.

Psychosocial Concerns

In treatment programs using casts or braces, adolescents may be faced with peer criticism and be very conscious of looking different from peers. In a society in which being even slightly different implies inferiority, the adolescent in a brace may be painfully aware or his or her deformity.[2] Many adolescents complain that they cannot dress as their friends do or that the brace is visible no matter what they do. The adolescent fears rejection by peers and especially by members of the opposite sex. Some adolescents refuse to be seen in public, and some have refused to attend classes in any devices. Parents sometimes report that poor adaptation to bracing results in a lag in academic performance. Generally, a supportive family is the key to the success of the brace program. The adolescent needs encouragement, support, and praise for compliance with the program.

Parents often feel guilty that their child has developed scoliosis, especially if one of the parents has scoliosis. In contacts with parents, school staff should support and compliment them on their role in the adolescents' treatment.

Adolescents agree that contact with peers going through the same type of treatment is important to them in following a successful treatment program. Where possible, the schools are in a unique position to alert adolescents to other students going through treatment for scoliosis. Peer support is an invaluable asset to these students.

LEGG-CALVE-PERTHES CONDITION (LCP)

The medical definition of this condition is avascular necrosis of the femoral head (top of the thigh bone), which is death of bone cells in some or all of the femoral head due to a lack of blood supply. The exact cause of avascular necrosis has not been established. LCP goes through the predictable stages of avascular necrosis, in which the femoral head becomes soft, the dead bone cells are reabsorbed and are always replaced by new live bone cells. LCP is usually seen in boys (4 to 5 males to one female) between the ages of 4 and 12 years.[3]

Treatment of LCP is most critical in the initial stage when the femoral head softens and therefore lacks strength. The main concern is to maintain the round contour of the femoral head within the acetabulum in an effort to prevent hip problems and leg-length discrepancy. The acetabulum is the socket in which the femur is situated. Studies have shown that if the femoral head is maintained well inside the acetabulum, a rounded femoral head will develop. The best outcomes are in cases in which less than 50 percent of the femoral head is affected by the disease.

Diagnosis

A usually active child may begin to limp and tire easily. He or she may complain of hip discomfort, which the parents may brush off as overexertion. This may go on for several weeks before medical attention is sought. X-rays are important to the diagnosis of LCP. Also important are a complete history and clinical examination.

Treatment

The goals of treatment are to 1) obtain and maintain range of motion, which can become limited as a result of the bony changes in the hip and of pain and discomfort and 2) contain the femoral head in the acetabulum. Traction may be used to obtain wide abduction, or spreading apart of the legs, when the disease has limited movement to this position. Wide abduction positions the femoral head more centrally in the acetabulum. The greater the area of femoral head covered by the acetabulum, the more successful the treatment. Traction may be carried out at home or in the hospital.

Petrie casts are used to obtain abduction when traction is not successful or to maintain abduction. Petrie casts abduct the hips in a manner similar to traction. The advantage of Petrie casts is that the patient cannot remove them. These casts are applied with the patient awake, legs spread as far apart as possible without pain, and with hips internally rotated. Petrie casts cover both legs from the foot to groin and are cross-stabilized at the knee by a wooden support. The casts are changed periodically to check for range of motion and to regain motion in the knees. During cast treatment, weight-bearing with crutches is permitted. The child may go to school if transportation and special seating arrangements are provided.

Several different types of braces may be utilized to provide the abduction and range of motion required. For instance, the Atlanta brace has led to quite satisfactory performance at the Alfred I. duPont Institute. Braces may be removed for daily range of motion exercises.

Surgery

When changes in the hip have occurred that braces or casts cannot alter, surgery may be necessary to position the femoral head in the acetabulum. Sometimes treatment with braces has not been successful, or the patient has refused to use the brace. Surgical procedures include femoral osteotomy and pelvic osteotomy. Both are intended to provide better coverage of the femoral head in the hope that it will maintain a normal shape within the acetabulum. Femoral osteotomy properly angles the femoral head into the acetabulum; pelvic osteotomy is a procedure involving the acetabulum. After either surgical procedure, the youngster will usually be held in a cast for several weeks, and may be confined to bed for up to 8 to 10 weeks.

School Life

Braces and Petrie casts used in nonsurgical treatment do not prevent the child from going to school. Petrie casts, however, provide more of a challenge than do other types of casts as far as mobility in the school environment. Many schools just cannot accommodate students in this type of cast, thereby forcing the student to have homebound instruction. However, students in casts can maneuver about easily in wheelchairs from which side arms have been removed. The degree of abduction of the Petrie cast sometimes makes it impossible for the student to sit at a school desk. A wheelchair with a table makes school more accessible. Bathrooms that have been made wheelchair-accessible may be used by the student, but he or she will probably have to walk with crutches sideways through the door because the spread of the Petrie cast is usually wider than the conventional door. Transportation to and from school that can accommodate these casts is required.

If the child is in a brace, he or she can maneuver about the school, sit at a desk, and go up and down stairs without assistance. The Atlanta brace allows the child freedom of movement without assistance. While there may be restrictions in activity because of the degree of LCP present, the child in a brace usually can participate in most activities. Activity levels for the child should be established in writing by the physician.

Some children at this age, especially those from six to eight years old, thrive from the extra attention, and parents may at times overindulge them. Parents sometimes feel guilty that the child has the condition and feel that somehow they could have prevented it.

The child who has had surgery will be out of school for several weeks and will require homebound instruction. Because of special positioning in bed, either on the back, abdomen, or positioned to the side and supported with pillows, it is difficult to do a large amount of written work. Overhead tilt tables are helpful to the child doing written work.

OSGOOD-SCHLATTER CONDITION

Osgood-Schlatter condition is a painful swelling around the tibial tubercle and patellar tendon, located on the front of the leg just below the knee. The patient will exhibit extreme tenderness in that area and will resist flexing the knee because of the discomfort. While the exact cause of the condition is not known, physical trauma is frequently associated with it. Osgood-Schlatter condition usually occurs in active children between the ages of 10 and 15. Prognosis is good, since the symptoms are almost always relieved by restricting activities such as running and bicycle riding.

The adolescent often experiences difficulty in complying with a treatment regimen that restricts activities. Redirecting the energies of an adolescent toward activities that are suitable may be a difficult task. The adolescent should be encouraged to participate in as many activities as the treatment regimen will allow.

SLIPPED CAPITAL FEMORAL EPIPHYSIS (SCFE)

The capital epiphysis is located at the head of the femur, and SCFE is a downward and backward displacement of the femoral head on the neck of the femur. The cause of slippage is unknown. This condition is found more frequently in males than females (male-female ratio 2-5:1).[4] It usually occurs during the rapid growth period of adolescence and is most often seen between the ages of 10 and 17. The youngsters who are more apt to have it are those who are obese or those who are tall, slender, and growing rapidly.

Symptoms

The onset of SCFE is usually gradual, with early symptoms being fatigue after walking or standing. The patient may walk with a slight limp and will complain of referred pain in the hip or knee. As the SCFE progresses, the patient will experience intense pain in the hip. In the rare case of an acute or sudden onset of SCFE, an episode of physical trauma may be associated with a significant impairment of a previously functional hip joint.

Diagnosis

Since an early symptom of SCFE is referred pain to the knee or groin, a hip problem may not be suspected. X-rays of the hip are necessary to determine the diagnosis.

Treatment

SCFE is a condition that requires prompt treatment to prevent further slippage and to maintain union between the neck of the femur and the epiphysis.

Complete bed rest with no weightbearing is recommended immediately upon diagnosis. Traction may be used to relieve the pain of muscle spasm. A surgical pinning of the epiphysis is usually performed, or the growth plate may be closed surgically. In severe cases of SCFE, more extensive surgery may be necessary.

When there has been surgical pinning for less severe cases, limb movement in bed is encouraged when the wound has healed. Crutch-walking without weightbearing is permitted when painless, adequate range of motion is achieved. Weightbearing may be permitted within six to eight weeks.

Cases in which the slip is more complete require more extensive surgery. The patient may be placed in a cast postoperatively and confined to bed for several weeks. Gradual return to walking is permitted several months after surgery.

Prognosis is dependent on the severity of the slip, with good results expected in mild cases. In those individuals with severe slippage, there is often a residual deformity despite treatment.

Psychosocial Aspects

At a stage of development when participation in peer-related activities is so important, the adolescent with SCFE may not be able to participate because of hospitalization, long-term casting, bed rest, or residual hip problems. Body image may be affected negatively in the adolescent who associates physical problems with being less attractive.

The student should be approached positively, and emphasis should be placed on those activities in which the adolescent can participate. Every school offers many such activities, and these students should be guided toward them, even though their interests were previously in more active pursuits.

SPINA BIFIDA

The most common congenital condition resulting in spinal dysfunction is myelomeningocele, or spina bifida cystica. Accidents account for most acquired spinal dysfunctions in older children, while tumors and/or radiation therapy are most often responsible for spinal dysfunction in younger children. This section will focus on spina bifida and will center around those children with this condition who are able to receive their education in a regular classroom setting. Much of this information will be applicable to children with either congenital or acquired spinal dysfunction.

Incidence and Cause

Spina bifida is the general term used to describe any incomplete development of the spinal column or spinal cord. It is the most common birth defect in the U.S. after congenital heart defects. While it can affect anyone, there is a higher incidence among those of Irish or English descent. Figures for the incidence of spina bifida vary depending upon what source is used. For instance, the March of Dimes states that the chances of a woman having a baby with spina bifida is one in 2,000[5], while the Spina Bifida Association quotes a figure of three out of 1,000.[6] The cause is not known, but it is thought to result from a combination of environmental and genetic factors. There is no straightforward pattern of inheritance, as there is in such diseases as sickle cell anemia and hemophilia, but it has been shown that parents of one child with spina bifida have a one in 40 chance of having a second child with this birth defect.[7]

Development of Spinal Malformation

In the human fetus, the nervous system begins to develop two weeks after conception. The neural plate, which will later become the spinal cord, first appears as a proliferation of cells. During the third to fifth week of embryonic development, the neural plate invaginates to form the neural groove and then closes forming the neural tube. Any malformations of the neural tube will have occurred within the first three to five weeks of development. While this incomplete closure can occur anywhere along the spinal column, it most commonly occurs from the mid- to lower back. A meningocele is a form of spina bifida in which there is incomplete closure of the spine with outpocketing of the meninges, which are the membranes that cover the spinal cord. The spinal cord is not involved. Few, if any, symptoms are seen with this condition. Shortly after birth, the defect is corrected surgically primarily to reduce the chance of an infection. Because of the closeness of the spinal cord, the roots of some nerves may be affected. Bowel and bladder function may be disrupted to a limited extent in these patients.

More serious is the myelomeningocele (or spina bifida cystica). This birth defect involves nonclosure of the spinal column with an associated outpocketing of the meninges and the spinal cord. Theoretically, all function below the level of the lesion is affected, but for reasons not yet clear, the effect on motor ability may differ from that on the sensory level. It is this form of spina bifida that will be discussed in the remainder of this section.

Manifestations of Myelomeningocele and Their Management

The child with a myelomeningocele usually manifests orthopedic problems such as club feet, contractures of the hips, knees, ankles, and/or foot, and scoliosis. These are a result of decreased innervation to the muscles. Problems vary from child to child, depending upon where the lesion is located on the back and the degree to which the nervous system has been damaged. These problems are, in general, treated as they are in any child with damage to the nervous system. Pain perception is decreased as a result of decreased innervation, and additional attention is paid to a child's healing and circulation postsurgery.

In the newborn with myelomeningocele, it is important to prevent infection. Within the first day or two of life, surgery is done to cover the membranes and spinal cord with muscle and skin from the surrounding tissues. This surgery does not restore nerve function lost as a result of the defect, nor can subsequent surgery restore this function.

Shortly after this surgery, many infants will develop hydrocephalus, a rapid accumulation of cerebrospinal fluid in the cavities within the brain. In severe cases this can cause a great deal of intercranial pressure. Brain damage will result unless the pressure is relieved. To accomplish this, a shunt, which is a flexible tube designed to drain cerebrospinal fluid, is inserted into a ventricle in the brain through a small opening in the skull and then placed underneath the skin leading from the head to another part of the body. The shunt that is used most often in children is a V-P (ventriculo-peritoneal) shunt, which has tubing that ends in the peritoneal (abdominal) cavity. Extra lengths of tubing are placed in the peritoneal cavity to allow for the growth of the child.

The myelomeningocele is a fixed lesion, which means that the disability or dysfunction resulting from it does not ordinarily change. However, as the child grows and develops, different areas of dysfunction become more apparent. For example, bowel and urinary incontinence, not a problem in infancy, does become a problem in a school-aged child.

School Life

Because a child has spina bifida or has been shunted for hydrocephalus does not indicate that the child will have a learning disability. If any difficulties are perceived, testing and, if necessary, special class placement and remedial services should be provided.

Neurogenic Bowel

Most children with myelomeningocle have some degree of neurogenic bowel, that is, decreased or absent innervation to the areas responsible for bowel control. The child will usually become constipated and/or have uncontrolled bowel movements. For this reason, some school-aged children with spina bifida must wear diapers or protective pants. These are sometimes difficult to adjust, so a young child may need a little assistance in getting redressed after visiting the bathroom.

By placing these children on a fairly rigid bowel program, through the use of oral laxatives, suppositories, enemas, and/or timing so that the child can be taught to completely empty the bowels at about the same time every day, it is possible to achieve some kind of control. Theoretically, there will then be no stool in the lower bowel to cause an accident. Getting a child onto a regulated bowel program is probably one of the most difficult things that the families with a spina bifida child have to deal with. It can take weeks or months before a workable program is achieved. The child must be an integral part of this program and must show interest if it is to work. The bowel program must be individualized for each patient, with medications being adjusted until a combination is found that works best for that child. Once the family achieves the best system for their child, the program tends to increase the child's self-image and the ability to join in various social activities without the constant concern of soiling.

While establishing this program, the child will be going to school. School personnel should be aware that this is a trying time for both the child and family. The timing of the daily bowel evacuation is usually after dinner, so school personnel would not ordinarily be involved with that aspect of the program. However, accidents may still occur, and the child should be helped to deal with these physically and emotionally. Also, school personnel may be required to provide a means whereby the child can take medications at school.

Neurogenic Bladder

It is common to see decreased or absent innervation to the bladder and bladder sphincters, the ring-like bands of muscle that constrict the opening from the bladder. This is manifested in a number of ways. Incontinence of urine may be because of an inability of the child to hold, or store, urine. The sphincter may be flaccid, so that there is a constant dribble from the urethra. Also, the sphincter may be spastic and keep the bladder from emptying completely. Urinary incontinence is then caused by overflow urine when the bladder fills to capacity. Vesicoureteral reflux may develop whereby the urine backs up into the ureters. In severe cases it can back up into the kidneys.

The child with a neurogenic bladder is prone to urinary tract infections because the bladder retains urine. Sometimes these urinary tract infections do not produce symptoms and can only be discovered through a positive urine culture. It is vital that the urinary status of these children be closely followed by a physician.

Clean Intermittent Catheterization

Children with myelomeningocele may be put on a clean intermittent catheterization program. This is the timed emptying of the bladder by means of inserting a clean catheter into the bladder by way of the urethra. Clean intermittent catheterization is usually done three or four times a day, and the schedule varies with the preference of the physician and the child's condition. This procedure involves no special equipment aside from the catheter itself. The catheters may be metal tubes for females or plastic tubes of varying lengths and sizes for either males or females. The hands are washed with soap and water. No gloves are used. The clean catheter, which is also washed with soap and rinsed well with water, is lubricated with a water soluble lubricant and inserted into the urethra. The bladder is allowed to empty, and the catheter is removed when the urine stops flowing. The catheter is washed with soap and water and reused. Provision should be made for the child's supplies, and a private area should be provided for the procedure. This should be worked out among the child, school personnel, and parents.

Children may be placed on the program for one of two reasons. For the child who has reflux, clean intermittent catheterization will assure an emptying of the bladder, with the main goal of preserving the upper urinary tract and decreasing the chances of urinary tract infections. The kidneys can be damaged by reflux and continuous infections. These children may or may not be dry between catheterizations. A second group of children, usually older, are started on clean intermittent catheterization to achieve increased dryness for social reasons. In addition, medication may help increase dryness.

Every attempt is made to have the child do self-catheterization as early as possible. The child's interest in self-catheterization is the best indicator of when to start this. However, there may be times when the child will have to be catheterized by someone else. The person doing the catheterization does not have to be a nurse. Nearly anyone can be taught the procedure.

A child on a clean intermittent catheterization program should also be taking medication to prevent urinary tract infections. If these medications have to be taken at school, some provision should be made for this.

Possibility of Shunt Failure

The child should be watched for signs of shunt failure, which are the same for a child with myelomeningocele as those in a child shunted for hydrocephalus for other reasons. These signs are projectile vomiting, headaches, "sunset" eyes, bulging scalp veins, personality changes, and seizures. A decrease in academic performance may also signify a sluggish or failing shunt. When such changes are noticed, the parents should be notified so that a neurosurgeon may be consulted to determine if problems with the shunt are indeed the cause of such changes. Sometimes changes in personality and/or academic progress have nothing to do with the shunt and are caused by the child's developmental stage or reasons that precipitate the same problem in children who do not have shunts. There is no easy way to differentiate these without consulting a neurosurgeon or a physician with expertise in dealing with patients who are shunted for hydrocephalus.

Ambulation and the Use of Orthopedic Appliances

Children with myelomeningocele vary in their abilities to ambulate. They may walk without using any orthopedic appliances (orthoses), or they may be able to get around only in wheelchairs. Several kinds of orthoses may be used. Molded ankle foot orthoses are splint-like devices made of polypropylene from a mold of the child's foot. These help keep the child's foot, or feet, in alignment. When more support is needed for ambulation, long metal and leather leg braces are used with a walker or crutches to aid balance and mobility. A pelvic band may or may not be used, depending upon the child's trunk control.

Upon reaching adolescence, these children may be more inclined to use a wheelchair. This does not indicate a deterioration of the child's condition. As the child grows, it becomes more difficult to walk with full braces because of increased weight of the braces and the child. The adolescent may find it easier to keep up with peers at school using a wheelchair and may elect to use braces at home or for walking short distances.

Children with spina bifida may develop scoliotic curves early. A stabilizing device, usually an orthoplast jacket, is used until surgery becomes necessary (see Scoliosis). In addition, they may develop lordosis, a concave curve of the spine, or kyphosis, a convex curvature of the spine. Specialized equipment may be needed for these problems, and surgery may be considered, depending upon the degree of the curve and how much it interferes with the child's day-to-day functioning.

Closely associated with the child's orthopedic status is skin integrity. Close attention must be paid to proper fit and function of orthotic devices, shoes, and even diapers. All of these may come in contact with skin areas of decreased or absent sensation and must be checked often for redness or skin breakdown.

Early Maturation

Children with myelomeningocele tend to attain puberty and mature earlier than their more able-bodied counterparts. The reason for this is not known. This has implications in the school situation, as it is possible that they may be undergoing developmental changes prior to their peers. Although guidance is offered to parents by the physician or nurse concerning this early maturation, school personnel are not always aware of this. The child's classmates may react positively or negatively to the early maturing child. Support from a teacher or other adult friend can be of great help and comfort.

Summary

Many of the effects of myelomeningocele make these children different from their peers. These differences can be a basis for growth in the affected child and his or her classmates. The subject of disabilities can be introduced as a general topic, paving the way for greater sensitivity and understanding. If the child is secure enough in his or her self-image, he or she may be asked to present a paper or talk about what it is like to have this problem. Classmates and teachers are often surprised to find out that the concerns of a child with myelomeningocele are the same as those of any child at a given developmental stage. In interacting with a person with a myelomeningocele, it is more positive to think of him or her as an individual first and as a person having a handicap second.

CONCLUSION

A complete review of orthopedic problems in children is beyond the scope of this chapter. However, much of the information regarding the school life of children who must have casts or braces and who experience symptoms and limitations similar to those described here should be helpful in dealing with children in similar situations regardless of the cause. At a time of life when physical activity is normally at a high level, those children may not be able to be as active as peers, either temporarily or permanently. It is most important for school staff to include them in as many activities as possible and to provide stimulating alternatives when physical activity must be limited.

REFERENCES

1. D. M. Berwick, "Scoliosis Screening," *Pediatrics in Review* 5 (1984): 238.
2. S. W. Nathan, "Body Image of Scoliotic Female Adolescents Before and After Surgery," *Maternal Child Nursing Journal* 6 (1977): 139.
3. S. Chung, "Diseases of the Developing Hip Joint," *Pediatric Clinics of North America* 24 (1977): 857.
4. Chung, "Diseases of the Developing Hip Joint," p. 857.
5. "Spina Bifida," *Public Health Education Information Sheet* (White Plains, NY: March of Dimes Birth Defect Foundation).
6. "Spina Bifida," Chicago, IL: Spina Bifida Association of America.
7. "Spina Bifida," *Public Health Education Information Sheet*.

RESOURCES

Suggested Reading

Ayrault, Evelyn West. *Growing Up Handicapped: A Guide for Parents and Professionals to Helping the Exceptional Child*. New York: Seabury Press, 1977.

Cowell, H. R.; Hall, J.; and MacEwen, G. D. "Genetic Aspects of Idiopathic Scoliosis. *Clinical Orthopedics and Related Research* 86 (1972): 121.

Foster, B. K., and Bowen, J. R. "Perthes-Disease: Returning Children to Sports." *The Physician and Sportsmedicine* 10 (1982): 69.

Griffin, P. P. "Legg-Calve-Perthes Disease: Treatment and Prognosis." *Orthopedia Clinics of North America* 11 (1980): 127.

Johnson, J. E.; Kirchhoff, K. T.; and Endress, M. P. "Altering Children's Distress Behavior during Orthopedic Cast Removal." *Nursing Research* 24 (1975): 404.

MacEwen, G. D. "Treatment of Legg-Calve-Perthes Disease." *Instructional Course Lectures* 30 (1981): 75.

Myers, Gary J., ed. *A Guide for Helping the Child with Spina Bifida*. Springfield, IL: Charles C. Thomas, 1981.

Tibbits, C. W. "Adolescent Idiopathic Scoliosis." *Nurse Practitioner* (March–April 1980).

Turek, S. *Orthopaedics*. Philadelphia, PA: J. B. Lippincott, 1984.

Wynne-Davies, R. "Familial (Idiopathic) Scoliosis." *The Journal of Bone and Joint Surgery* 50B (1968): 24.

Pamphlets are available from the Spina Bifida Association offering general information on spina bifida and specific information for teachers, teenagers, and adults.

Useful Addresses

March of Dimes Birth Defect Foundation, 1275 Mamaroneck Ave., White Plains, NY 10605. (Local chapters are listed in the telephone directory.)

Scoliosis Association, One Penn Plaza, New York, NY 10001.

Spina Bifida Association of America, National Headquarters, 343 South Dearborn St., Chicago, IL 60604. (Local chapters are listed in the telephone directory.)

Spina Bifida Foundation, 18 Harker Ave., Berlin, NJ 08009.

Index

Compiled by Linda Webster